The New Campus Anti-Rape Movement

The New Campus Anti-Rape Movement

Internet Activism and Social Justice

Caroline Heldman
Alissa R. Ackerman
Ian Breckenridge-Jackson

LEXINGTON BOOKS
Lanham • Boulder • New York • London

Published by Lexington Books
An imprint of The Rowman & Littlefield Publishing Group, Inc.
4501 Forbes Boulevard, Suite 200, Lanham, Maryland 20706
www.rowman.com

Unit A, Whitacre Mews, 26-34 Stannary Street, London SE11 4AB

British Library Cataloguing in Publication Information Available

Library of Congress Cataloging-in-Publication Data Available

LCCN 2018937620 | ISBN 978-1-4985-5401-5 (cloth : alk. paper) | ISBN 978-1-4985-5403-9 (pbk. : alk. paper) | ISBN 978-1-4985-5402-2 (ebook)

∞™ The paper used in this publication meets the minimum requirements of American National Standard for Information Sciences Permanence of Paper for Printed Library Materials, ANSI/NISO Z39.48-1992.

Printed in the United States of America

To Lili Bernard.

To Cantor Leah Elstein.

To Kathryn Breckenridge.

Contents

List of Figures

Acknowledgments

This book is the culmination of decades of scholarship and activism on the subject of sexual violence. We are thankful to many people who have guided us along our respective paths. Alissa Ackerman is indebted to Michelle Seyler, whose courage, bravery, and heart are an inspiration to everyone who knows her. Ian Breckenridge-Jackson is thankful to Kathryn Breckenridge for planting the seeds of a feminist consciousness and to Karen Pyke, Chris Chase-Dunn, Katja Guenther, and Ellen Reese for shaping his understanding of social injustices. Caroline Heldman is grateful to the faculty members, students, and other survivor activists with whom she has worked on this issue, but especially Danielle Dirks, Kamilah Willingham, Mary Christianakis, Richard Mora, Nalsey Tinberg, Audrey Logan, and Carly Mee. She also thanks Baillee Brown and Rebecca Cooper for their superior research assistance on this project.

Introduction

One-in-five women and six percent of men will face sexual assault or rape during their time in college.[1] This high rate of sexual violence on campus is a national crisis, one that has inspired half a century of activism. Campus sexual violence was first documented in an academic study in 1957.[2] Activism around this issue came to life in the early 1970s. The first national public debate on the issue occurred in the late 1980s. The first national law to address campus rape, the Clery Act, was passed in 1990. The first backlash against campus anti-rape activism took place in the early 1990s. The Department of Education officially classified sexual violence as a Title IX (equitable learning environment) issue in 2001 and issued guidance to schools about addressing this issue in 2011.[3] A new peak of activism emerged in 2013—the new Campus Anti-Rape Movement (CARM).

After more than five decades of activism on this issue, the new CARM effectively put the issue of campus rape on the national policy agenda. In 2014, President Barack Obama credited "an inspiring wave of student-led activism" for catapulting campus rape into public consciousness, and according to longtime anti-sexual violence activist S. Daniel Carter, today's activism is "unlike anything I've ever seen." The purpose of this book is to examine the origins, context, and significance of the new CARM.

The new CARM is a social movement that has been able to accomplish what five decades of activism could not. Analyzing this movement sheds light on the policy considerations and politics of campus rape, and it also advances our knowledge of social movements, social media, and sexual violence policy. Our book is the first academic project to analyze the new CARM through a social movement lens, and the first to situate it within the long history of anti-sexual violence in the United States. This is also the first book to examine the role of new laws and social media in facilitating the

CARM and its success. We approach this topic using a mixed methods approach involving case study methodology, participant observation, interviews with early architects of the new CARM, an examination of key events in the new CARM, anonymous testimonials from stakeholders, and application of legal and social movement theory to unpack the meaning of the movement.

The primary questions of this book are: What is the history and current status of sexual violence on college campuses? What previous activism has taken place on college campuses and in the United States more broadly around issues of sexual violence, and how is the new CARM different?

When did the new CARM emerge, how, and why? How did new laws and shifting interpretations of existing laws facilitate the new CARM? How has the legal landscape shifted as a result of new CARM activism? What role did social media and online organizing play in the emergence and success of the new CARM? How have social media changed the way social movements operate in the United States? Did social media improve the effectiveness of campus anti-rape work? What rape prevention programs have colleges and universities instituted to date? What are best practices for reducing rates of sexual violence on campus? What lies ahead for the new CARM? What does the new political environment mean for the movement going forward? We engage these questions in seven dense chapters that are organized in loose chronological order.

Chapter 1 presents an overview of sexual violence on college campuses. We provide the latest statistics on types and prevalence of sexual violence, and research on how it affects survivors. This chapter includes narratives to illustrate the variety and veracity of this form of violence. Readers will learn who experiences sexual assault and rape, which students perpetrate these crimes, what factors increase the likelihood of victimization, and where these crimes typically occur. Special attention is paid to the intersectional experiences of survivors of color, queer survivors, and male survivors. This chapter also details institutional factors that increase the likelihood of sexual violence on campus.

In Chapter 2, we provide an original analysis of the four peaks of anti-sexual violence activism in the United States that preceded the new CARM. The purpose of this overview is to furnish a context for contemporary activism. We begin with the first peak of anti-sexual violence activism that occurred during Reconstruction with white vigilantes' use of rape as a weapon of social control over black women. We then examine organized anti-rape efforts in the years leading up to the Civil Rights Movement. Native American and black women led the first two peaks of activism, but their labor has mostly been erased in modern accounts of sexual violence work. The third peak of anti-sexual violence activism coincided with the Women's Movement in the 1960s and 1970s—the first time white women were heavily involved in reform efforts. Activism on college campuses around this issue first happened during this period. The fourth peak came about in the mid-1980s with the release of data showing that one-in-four college women experienced sexual assault. This peak was the first time that national attention was paid to high rates of sexual violence occurring on college campuses. Chapter 2 illustrates how the CARM is but the newest episode in a 140 year struggle against gendered violence in America.

In Chapter 3, we describe the rise of the new CARM with a detailed timeline of events and the major players that catapulted this issue onto the national policy agenda. We describe legal efforts in the 1990s and early 2000s to apply Title IX to campus rape, and student use of Title IX complaints throughout the 2000s to get the Department of Education to pay attention to campus rape. We spotlight key activists whose work led up to the new CARM, those who launched the movement in 2013, and activists that have carried the momentum forward since its launch. This chapter also describes the tools of the movement—federal complaints, group lawsuits, and social media campaigns. We conclude with a look at whose voices are heard in the movement, and whose voices are not heard. Readers will get a front row seat to the ups and downs of the early days of the movement as well as a good sense of how it differs from previous activism around this issue.

Chapter 4 describes the shifting legal landscape that brought about the new CARM. We examine national legislation pertaining to campus sexual violence, starting with the Title IX education amendments (1972) that mandate that schools provide a gender-equitable learning environment; the Clery Act (1990) that requires school to report crime on campus (including sexual violence); the Sexual Assault Victims Bill of Rights (1992) that directs schools to provide basic support to rape survivors; the Dear Colleague Letter (2011) that officially extends Title IX to sexual assault cases; and The Campus Sexual Violence Elimination Act (SaVE) act (2013) that requires schools enact programs to prevent sexual violence. Taken together, these laws constitute the strongest legal patchwork of campus anti-rape laws to date in the United States. Chapter 4 also provides basic information on the campus adjudication process, the process for filing federal complaints, and a discussion of why law enforcement is not a viable replacement for campus procedures. Readers will gain a solid understanding of campus procedures, the laws that govern them, and how they have been used by the new CARM.

Chapter 5 analyzes the role of shifting technologies—social media and new online networking devices. We argue that social media use mostly accounts for the unparalleled success of the new CARM. Our analysis here is situated within a burgeoning literature on new networked social movements to better understand how online networking has changed the face of contemporary social movements. New networked movements are decentralized, leaderless campaigns that derive great effectiveness from their ability to control the message and respond to backlash rhetoric. We find that new CARM activists used social media to connect behind the scenes, to publicly promote survivor stories, and to control the framing of the campus sexual violence issue. Social media was an effective medium for attracting the mainstream media coverage that was so vital for the new CARM's success.

Chapter 6 describes the history of campus rape prevention programs and analyzes best practices for preventing sexual violence on campus as laid out by existing research. We begin with a nuanced definition of prevention and describe the conditions under which prevention can actually work. We then describe the major campus rape prevention programs that schools have developed or adopted over the years. The underlying paradigm of campus rape programs has shifted over time, starting with programs of the 1970s that focused on stranger rape and self-defense, programs developed in the 1990s that focused on acquaintance rape, and contemporary programs that emphasize bystander training (empowering witnesses to intervene when they see a situation that could lead to sexual violence). We describe college and university programs aimed at raising awareness, preventing sexual violence, and supporting survivors. Then we evaluate the most popular prevention programs that are currently being used in high school and college settings today. Academic and evaluation research on this topic is scant, so we set out a research agenda that includes directives for how to best operationalize success and measure impact. We conclude this chapter with recommendations for reducing sexual assault perpetration on campus.

Chapter 7 tackles the question of what lies ahead for the new CARM. Will this decentralized, leaderless movement achieve its ultimate goal of reducing rates of sexual violence on college campuses, or will political opposition and institutional prerogatives stand in its way? In this chapter, we lay out the biggest challenges for the movement moving forward: a new political climate that threatens to stall or even reverse legislative gains; a renewed backlash against the movement, emboldened by the new political environment; campus administrators who are more reluctant to make significant reform given perverse economic incentives and the new political climate; and internal struggles and compassion fatigue that have slowed the CARM's momentum. We end the book on the positive note that the new CARM being one of the most successful social movements of the last decade, and the reforms it has produced will not easily disappear. It started a wave that crested with the #MeToo Movement that swept the nation in 2017. #MeToo crashed through Hollywood, news media, the ballet world, the music industry, and many other sectors as women (and some men) publicly outed prominent sexual harassers and rapists. The new CARM inspired a national conversation that in turn inspired a generation of young feminists who will fight for gender justice well beyond issues of sexual violence on campus.

NOTES

1. David Cantor, Bonnie Fisher, Susan Chibnall, Reanne Townsend, Hyunshik Lee, Carol Bruce, and Gail Thomas, "Report on the AAU campus climate survey on sexual assault and sexual misconduct," *Association of American Universities* 21 (2015).

2. Clifford Kirkpatrick and Eugene Kanin, "Male sex aggression on a university campus," *American Sociological Review* 22, no. 1 (1957): 52–58.

3. For a thorough accounting of Dear Colleague Letters of 2001 and 2011, see Catherine Kaukinen, Michelle Miller, and Rachael A. Powers, *Addressing Violence Against Women on Campus* (Philadelphia, Temple University Press, 2017).

"I Said Nothing"

Sexual Violence on Campus

"You're being paranoid. You're gay and he knows it. Stop assuming the worst in people." This is what Shelley repeatedly told herself when her law school clinic partner made advances at her, mentioning while driving home from a client's house that their law school partners had been talking at a local bar about how "hot" she was. It made her squirm, but she laughed it off and stared out the window as the darkness and the trees sped by. She realized that if he decided to pull over and assault her, no one would hear her screaming. Changing the subject to their law school clinic work, Shelley repeated, *"You're being paranoid. You're gay and he knows it. Stop assuming the worst in people."*

It was the last day of classes of the second semester of law school when Shelley's law school partner raped her. He raped her for two and a half hours in her own apartment—in her own bed. Shelley recounts:

> I like to tell myself it lasted this long because I put up a good fight. I tried to push him out of my bed with my legs, reasoning that they were the strongest part of me. I reminded him countless times that I was gay and nothing was going to happen. He said he would leave, he said he would call a cab soon. When he continued to assault me, I again told him I was gay. I felt like I was begging, but I didn't care.

Shelley continued with her classes, one of which her rapist was a student in. Whenever she saw him in class or on campus her heart would inevitably skip a beat, though she refused to acknowledge why. Shelley convinced herself that she had just made a mistake that night that didn't truly fit her identity.

She was a lesbian, and she had sex with a man. *Even though she didn't want to.*

This false narrative finally broke open when Shelley was facing the prospect of final exams. She finally told a friend what really happened—that she had been raped and had not told anyone. A few weeks later, Shelley would find herself meeting face-to-face with the dean, detailing what had happened. She didn't expect much, but the dean did do the best she could to help Shelley navigate what was, in her words, "less of a system and more a reaction to a crisis."

Shelley was told she had options, none of which felt viable. She could testify before the academic standards committee and tell them her side of the story while he had a chance to tell his own. She could write to the board of bar examiners and tell them that she didn't believe he was fit to practice law. Or, she could do nothing. She searched for middle ground—an option that kept her safe while also enabling her to tell her story.

For Shelley, the fear won. She says:

> I was too afraid of him to officially report the rape to the school. He had already raped me once—what would he do if he knew I filed a report? This fear took hold of my heart and festered in me like a disease. It followed me everywhere I went. This was not an "option" I could opt into.

It has been just over five years since Shelley was raped. Pieces of the rape still haunt her and she believes there will always be pieces that do. As with many other survivors, she finds peace for a while and then allows her mind to re-explore already known terrain. For example, in the aftermath of the rape, Shelley finally realized that what happened to her was a hate crime. She couldn't prove it, to herself or anyone else, but she knew that he likely attacked her because of her sexual orientation. She believed he felt emasculated by the fact that she was not interested in him sexually and she knew that he believed that being gay could be corrected if a person has intercourse with the "right" person of the opposite sex.

Was he trying to cure her?

When Shelley thinks about the night she was raped, she can't help but wonder what was going through her rapist's mind. She imagines the hate festering in him and it makes her feel even more violated and exposed. She believes that she wasn't only attacked because she was a woman, but also because of who she loves—two central pieces of her identity that shattered into pieces when she finally admitted what had happened to her. She has learned that she does not need to carry his burden of hatred. She says, "that is his demon, not mine." Still, the fear that he ignited in her in the aftermath of her rape has left her feeling exposed, preferring, at times, to cower in a corner rather than stand up and fight.

In this chapter we present statistics on sexual violence on college campuses. We discuss what is currently known about campus rape and sexual assault, including what we know about where and how sexual violence occurs, who perpetrates it, and who they perpetrate violence against. Readers will learn about where sexual violence happens and how universities handle reports. We pay particular attention to the experiences and voices of survivors of color, queer survivors, and male survivors. We begin with a discussion about what the literature tells us about the nature, context, and scope of campus sexual violence. Each section of the chapter offers a description about what is currently known about the given topic and what we miss when we approach campus sexual violence from a white, heterosexual, cis-gender perspective. (Cis-gender refers to a person whose gender, as expressed through their personal appearance, corresponds with their sex assigned at birth.) The chapter ends with a discussion about institutional factors that increase the likelihood that sexual violence occurs on campus.

STUDIES OF SEXUAL VIOLENCE

Shelley's story is an important reminder that survivors do not fit into any one specific category. Sexual violence is intersectional, and many survivors do not fit the stereotypical narrative created and perpetuated by the media. Most media accounts of survivors of campus sexual violence focus almost exclusively on white, heterosexual, cis-gender females. The experiences of survivors of color, LGBTQIA+ and male survivors are not only ignored, but these survivors are more likely to be discredited, ostracized, and disbelieved than survivors who fit the ideal victim. (LGBTQIA+ refers to lesbian, gay, bisexual, transgender, queer or questioning, intersex, asexual or allies. The "+" refers to other gender/sex non-conforming identities that are not included in the acronym.) In Shelley's case, one can see how she created a false narrative, disbelieving herself.

There is a movement within the field of criminology to "queer" the field.[1] Citing historical evidence and current practice, advocates of queering this discourse argue that too often LGBTQIA+ individuals in general, and intersectional queer people are victimized while simultaneously being labeled as criminal and deviant. The same sentiment is obvious when we examine both current and historical acts of violence committed against people of color. Within the field of study pertaining to sexual violence, both within the general population and on college campuses specifically, very little attention has been given to these groups of survivors.

While it is difficult for most survivors to come forward to report their victimization, intersectionality creates additional barriers to disclosure. According to the 2014 *National Crime Victimization Survey* (NCVS), approximately 34% of rapes are reported to law enforcement.[2] Fewer survivors report campus sexual violence; in fact, current estimates place the percentage of female students who report their victimizations at about 20%.[3] The number of reports of sexual violence against queer, gay, and gender-nonconforming students is even lower.

The first published studies on campus sexual violence were conducted in the 1950s by sociologist Eugene Kanin and colleagues.[4] Over 55% of the 291 female participants in his first study reported that they had experienced some form of "erotic aggressiveness."[5] Almost 21% of respondents reported that someone used force to attempt sexual intercourse and 6.2% reported aggressive and/or forceful attempts at sex using "menacing threats or coercive infliction of physical pain."[6] The 162 respondents who reported some form of sexual victimization acknowledged 1,022 experiences with sexual aggression. Kanin et al. noted that between 20 and 25% of college women experienced forceful attempts for sex.[7] It is important to note that these researchers went to great lengths to avoid using any criminal term, like "rape," choosing to classify these incidences as displeasing behaviors.

In 1985, psychologist Mary Koss and colleagues administered The Sexual Experiences Survey (SES) to university students in the Midwest. Thirteen percent of the women in the study (n=2,016) reported that they had experienced rape and 4.6% of the men in the study (n=1,846) reported that they had committed an act that met the legal definition of rape.[8] Findings from previous studies on college men found higher rates of self-reported sexual aggression ranging between 15 and 26%.[9] By 1987, researchers broadened the scope of studies from the local to the national. Koss and her colleagues administered the first methodologically rigorous survey to over six thousand (n=6,159) women and men at 32 institutions of higher education.[10] Findings from this nationally representative sample showed that 53.7% of college women experienced some unwanted sexual act, with 15.4% and 12.1% experiencing a completed or attempted rape, respectively. Just over 25% of the male respondents in the survey reported their involvement in the perpetration of an unwanted sex act.

Studies on sexual victimization became more frequent in the late 1990s and early 2000s. In 2000, Fisher, Cullen, and Turner produced a report on the National College Women Sexual Victimization (NCWSV) study, through grants awarded by the National Institute of Justice (NIJ) and the Bureau of Justice Statistics (BJS).[11] The study included a randomly selected national sample of 4,446 women who were attending college in the fall of 1996. Just under 3% (n=123) reported that they had experienced a completed (n=74) or attempted (n=49) rape. The authors cautioned that this number reflects only seven months of a calendar year. If the full calendar year had been taken into account, the data suggest that about 5% of college women experience rape. A study by Christopher Krebs and his colleagues found that 20% of undergraduate women experience a completed sexual assault since entering college.[12] The study also found that just over 6% or about 1 in 16 men will be sexually assaulted while in college. It has been sixty years since Eugene Kanin's original work, and although some variation in the prevalence and incidence of sexual violence on campus exists between studies, estimates of sexual violence perpetrated against college females has remained consistently high.

A report by the Bureau of Justice Statistics which focused on rape and sexual assault among college-age females over an eighteen year period was published in 2014.[13] In general, the report paralleled what researchers already knew—college-age women have higher rates of rape and sexual assault than women and girls in other age brackets. However, despite previous research that hypothesized women enrolled in colleges and universities would have higher rates of sexual assault, the 2014 report suggests otherwise.[14] According to the BJS report, the rate of rape and sexual assault for non-students was nearly 20 percent higher than for college-enrolled women. While enrolled females were less likely to be victimized than those who were not enrolled, the opposite is the case for males. College-age male students were 78% more likely to be victimized than non-students.[15] In some ways, the two groups have similarities in their experiences of rape and sexual assault. About 80% of survivors in this age group knew their perpetrators, and in most instances the perpetrator did not use a weapon during the assault. However, there are distinct differences that may shed light on why the report concludes that students reported a lower rate of sexual victimization. Students were more likely to experience victimization while engaging in leisure activities, they were far less likely to report their experiences, and they were less likely to view their experience as important enough to report.[16] Below, you will read the story of Jillian, a college professor, survivor, and activist who was raped at an off-campus club when she was in college. Her experience and her lack of reporting it to her university speak to the facts you've just read above. Her assault took place during leisure activities, she did not report it, and she didn't think it was important enough to report. Jillian's experience is a lot like other rapes and sexual assaults on college campuses or with college students, in that very few formally report to law enforcement. In fact, fewer than 5% of attempted and completed rapes on college campuses are reported to law enforcement.[17]

A caveat to these studies is that they did not take sexual orientation into account. This is troublesome, given that research shows that gay, lesbian, and bisexual individuals have equal or higher risk of sexual victimization.[18] There has been little research on victimization about gay and bisexual college students, but one recent study found that gay and bisexual college men have reported rates of sexual assault that are similar to heterosexual women.[19] Bisexual women had the highest rates of sexual assault with approximately 2 in 5 experiencing victimization while in college.

Just as there has been little research on sexual violence among LGBTQIA+ individuals, very little attention has been given to students from other marginalized and minority communities. There is some evidence to suggest that racial and ethnic minority students are more likely to experience sexual violence and that the type of sexual violence they experience differs from white survivors.[20] More research on the ways that race and ethnicity impact sexual victimization among college students is necessary. This is particularly important when addressing intersectionality and risk.

Jillian's Story—Polyvictimization and Sexual Assault

The night I was raped at an off campus club I just froze. I was just shy of 19 and had a long list of experiences with sexual violence in my past. I had been dancing with a young man when I began to feel dizzy after drinking the alcoholic beverage I watched him buy for me. I checked in with my friends and then stumbled to the bathroom to wash my face with cold water. As I went to close the door, the young man pushed through it and locked it behind him. I knew exactly what was going to happen and the only thought that went through my head was "you've got to be kidding me . . . again?" Then I just submitted to the rape. I knew from previous assaults that fighting back would end badly for me.

The next afternoon I woke up in my dorm room with a pounding headache and no recollection of how I made it back home. The drive from the club was less than a mile—I think I was brought back in the back seat of a friend's car. I remember the color of his blue button down shirt and the sweat stains on it. I remember the dress I was wearing. I remember the taste of the drink he bought me. I remember the color of the tile in the bathroom that I stared at as he raped me. Mostly, I remember the thoughts going through my head about how it made perfect sense that this kept happening to me, like "rape victim" was tattooed on my face.

Toward the end of the academic year, I was told that my scholarship was being rescinded because my performance, both athletically and academically, was sub-par. I didn't have the fight left in me to say or do anything. It was a small school—I assumed that the adults around me could see my struggles and that they just chose to turn a blind eye.

For several reasons, I never outwardly disclosed the rape. First and foremost, several of my friends were there that night. Several questioned my demeanor. Several knew I was headed for the bathroom to wash my face because I felt "off." None of us ever spoke of that night again. No one brought it up to me. Nobody asked me what had happened. It was as if everyone knew and it was the "unspoken thing." This rape was also the last of a string of assaults that began when I was a child. Given my history, this was relatively insignificant in my teenage mind. It was just what was expected of me. So I said nothing.

It took me almost two decades to recognize that none of this was my fault. I always just assumed that there was something about me that alerted perpetrators that I was an easy target. I now understand that the shame is not mine and that I am not to blame for the acts of others. I now understand that when you've experienced multiple types of trauma, including but not limited to child sexual abuse, that your ability to perceive danger or to trust your instinct can be severely compromised.

I am now an activist, scholar, and professor. I have students who disclose acts of rape and sexual assault to me all the time. I have been told by administration that campus sexual violence does not fall within the faculty purview, that it is an administrative issue. I have been told that I am a mandated reporter and that I should urge my students to report their experiences. I hold safe spaces for my students and will never back away from doing so. I think about what it would have meant for me to have one faculty member I could trust when I was an undergraduate student; one faculty member who checked in to make sure I was okay; one professor who noticed that I showed up to 8am courses still drunk from the night before. I can't say that I am glad I have had these experiences, but I am grateful for the person I've become because of them. If my experiences make it bearable for a student to disclose and to feel safe, I'd experience it all over again.

CAMPUS CLIMATE SURVEYS

The New Campus Anti-Rape Movement (CARM), which you will read about at length in Chapter 3, started to gather steam in 2011. It was in this year that the U.S. Department of Education finally and formally recognized that sexual violence on campus was a Title IX issue. As the new CARM grew, so did the realization that sexual violence on campus remains a serious issue. This realization is particularly meaningful because despite sixty years of research, it was not until the success of the new CARM that public discourse around this epidemic grew. One outcome of this shift was the creation of the White House Task Force to Protect Students from Sexual Assault.[21] The first report of this task force outlined four action steps and recommendations to protect students. The first action step was to create and conduct campus climate surveys to identify the extent of the problem.

Two large scale climate surveys were conceived. The first was created when the Association of American Universities (AAU) contracted with Westat, a research corporation based in Maryland, to create one of the first campus climate surveys on campus sexual assault.[22] (It is worth noting that faculty activists were critical of the AAU survey because it was only administered to its members in order to get "ahead of federal regulations," and it did not include questions about perpetration of sexual violence on campus.[23] The second large climate survey was the Campus Climate Survey Validation Study (CCSVS) conducted in partnership with the Bureau of Justice Statistics.[24] Both offer additional and up-to-date data on sexual violence on college campuses, but neither are without limitations or critics.

The AAU survey included 150,072 students across 26 colleges and universities. It was one of the first surveys to estimate rates of sexual violence against transgender, genderqueer, and gender-nonconforming students. The inclusion of these variables is key, because research has shown that this population experiences higher rates of sexual victimization than cis-gender individuals.[25] Just under 12% of survey participants (11.7%) across the 26 universities experienced "nonconsensual penetration or sexual touching by force or incapacitation since enrolling" in college.[26] Trans and gender-nonconforming undergraduate students had the highest rates of this type of sexual victimization at 12.4%, followed by undergraduate females at 10.8%. Freshmen were at higher risk and this risk declined steadily as years in school increased. Overall, transgender and gender-nonconforming students have the highest rates of all forms of sexual victimization at 21%.[27]

The total experience with nonconsensual sexual contact includes penetration or sexual touching by force or incapacitation, as well as through coercion and the absence of affirmative consent, and the survey found that 21.2% of seniors had been victimized since entering college. Again the prevalence is higher for females and trans and gender-nonconforming students with rates of 33.1% and 39.1%, respectively. In the 2014–2015 academic year, 11% of undergraduates experienced nonconsensual sexual contact, with 6.9% of female and 9.0% of trans and gender-nonconforming students experiencing an act involving penetration. Across the board, male students have the lowest reported rates of sexual victimization while in college.

Though the findings of the AAU study were taken by many to be groundbreaking, the survey was flawed from the first step. At a cost of 2.5 million dollars, the survey was created without content experts, and early on many of these experts expressed concern about this lack of inclusion. Additionally, the survey does not include a nationally representative sample as previous studies had. Seventy-five universities were invited to participate in the AAU survey, but only 27 did so. The response rate from those universities was 19.3%. Finally, and most likely the biggest criticism of the AAU survey, is that in order to achieve the 1 in 4 statistic, all forms of unwanted sexual contact were included. They were not included in previous studies, which makes it difficult to tease out rape.

In response to the White House Task Force the Office of Violence Against Women (OVW) funded the BJS to take on the task of designing and implementing a climate survey. The BJS, in partnership with the non-profit research firm RTI International, developed the CCSVS and the final pilot test report was published in January of 2016.[28] Twenty-four schools were invited to participate in the study and 9 agreed. Nonetheless, during the 2014–2015 academic year, 5.6% of students across these 9 institutions reported a completed "sexual battery" and 4.1% reported a completed rape. These rates varied across the participating institutions with some institutions having significantly lower rates of victimization than others. Similar to previous studies, the CCSVS found that younger students and those identifying as non-hetersosexual were at higher risk of experiencing sexual victimization. It is important to remember that the CCSVS was a pilot test of a survey that could be used by institutions or individual researchers after validation. Therefore, the findings from this study are not representative of all students in the United States.

A Free Open Access Option

By 2014 a record number of colleges and universities were under federal investigation for their handling of reports of sexual assault. The panic over campus sexual assault continued to escalate and many individuals and organizations sought to profit from this fear. According to Dr. Jennifer Freyd in an interview with *The Huffington Post*, colleges and universities would rather spend large sums of money for an outside product to address the issue than to work with their own faculty to combat the problem.[29] An entire "anti-rape," for-profit industry grew with products ranging from a nail polish that allegedly detects "rape drugs" to smartphone apps.[30] Academics and activists alike were concerned that people may be more concerned with profit over actually ending the rape crisis at hand.

A group of administrators and researchers from across the United States came together to create a free, online campus climate survey that universities could access. This survey, the Administrator Research Campus Climate Collaborate Survey (ARC3), is considered the gold standard for measuring sexual violence on campus. The group that created it was comprised of nearly two dozen of the leading academic researchers on the subject, including Mary Koss and Jennifer Freyd. Campus sexual assault and sex crimes experts who were not consulted on either the AAU or CCSVS surveys participated in crafting the ARC3, making its creation a true grassroots effort on the part of faculty in the new CARM. In September 2015 the ARC3 survey was released. Since its release, over fifty schools have administered ARC3 and over 300 colleges and universities have requested access to it.

Having nationally representative studies on sexual victimization on campuses and having campus specific data helps researchers, policy makers, and campus administrators ascertain the extent of the problem at hand. What we have learned since Kanin's work in the 1950s is that not much has changed. Approximately 1 in 4 to 1 in 5 female students will experience unwanted sexual contact during college and few will report it. LGBTQIA+ people have even higher rates of victimization than college females and college-enrolled males have significantly higher rates of victimization than non-enrolled men of the same age group. Still, prevalence rates vary across institutions. Having campus specific survey data helps individual institutions combat sexual violence in ways that are unique to the campus culture.

Campuses can choose from one of several previously created climate surveys, including the three discussed in this chapter, or they can create their own campus specific surveys. Choosing the right survey depends on what answers are being sought and all currently available surveys have limitations. Some of these limitations, including low response rates, lack of focus on underrepresented populations, and lack of representativeness, can be overcome. What cannot be addressed by victimization surveys and has yet to be confronted are nationally representative surveys measuring rates of perpetration. The ARC3 holds the possibility of providing more comprehensive data on who perpetrates these sexual crimes on campus and how often they do so.

Finally, Koss and her colleagues recently noted that sexual violence can and should be addressed by studying the characteristics of those who perpetrate sexual violence.[31] According to both the Centers for Disease Control (CDC) and a review published by the National Sexual Violence Resource Center (NSVRC), prevention efforts must include combating perpetration and surveys should measure the characteristics of perpetration accordingly.[32] Nonetheless, there are some available data on who perpetrates sexual violence on campus and this knowledge should inform campus policy.

WHO PERPETRATES SEXUAL VIOLENCE ON CAMPUS?

Over the last three decades, research has consistently shown that the commission of campus sexual violence is more nuanced and varied than the public claim that only fraternity members or athletes commit these crimes. The groundwork for research on the perpetration of campus sexual violence began in the 1950s with Kanin's work, but the field truly gained prominence several decades later with the work of Koss and her colleagues.[33] Despite what scholars have learned from research—that multiple factors are associated with committing campus sexual assault—it is not surprising that the dominant narrative has not changed. Beginning in the late 1980s articles began appearing in public, non-academic venues that bolstered the claim that certain men affiliated with these organizations were more likely to commit sexual assault.[34] In the ensuing years this focus has continued. Stories about young women being assaulted by well-known athletes or members of popular fraternities abound. The dominant narrative certainly has some merit, but to fully understand campus sexual violence we must broaden our understanding of the individual, situational, and cultural variables at play. In this section we evaluate the role of fraternities, athletics, and "other" variables in the commission of campus sexual violence.

Fraternities and Athletics

In 1984, University of Virginia freshman Liz Securro was drugged and gang-raped at a party at the Phi Kappa Psi fraternity house.[35] In 2011, after receiving an apology letter from one of her attackers, William Beebe, Securro published a memoir about her experience. It was one of the first public and personal accounts of such a horrifying crime and a survivor's quest for justice. Beebe was ultimately convicted and served five months behind bars while the two other alleged attackers were never charged. It was twenty-one years earlier, however, that Peggy Sanday published her groundbreaking book on fraternity gang-rape.[36] Sanday's research offers insight as to why certain fraternities are more prone to rape. She is quick to point out that not all fraternities are rape prone and that not all fraternity members will commit rape. This finding is important to note because research on fraternities and sexual assault has been mixed. In fact, in one publication Sanday noted that it should not be surprising that the results of research on this topic are mixed, unless one "assumes that fraternities are culturally homogenous."[37]

Some early studies on the topic found a positive association between fraternity membership and both individual and group sexual aggression.[38] These studies were limited by small sample sizes, generalizability, and other methodological concerns and some scholars were quick to point out that a positive association is not the same as causality. Studies that accounted for some of the methodological flaws described above found that it was actually heavy drinking that was more strongly associated with sexual aggression than was fraternity affiliation.[39] These findings were replicated in a follow-up study at a large Midwestern university.[40] Still, the narrative endures. One potential explanation for this enduring narrative is that most of the research on campus sexual aggression has focused on identifying men who admit to sexual violence and has practically ignored the social context that promulgates rape.[41]

The argument that we must take a cultural and contextual approach to understanding campus sexual violence is a compelling one. While much of

the research on campus sexual violence has been viewed through psychological and criminological lenses, a sociological approach has been largely ab-
sent in the academic literature. Viewed through this lens, sociologist Pamela
Yancey Martin argues that fraternities and athletics provide the context and
environment for rape and sexual assault to occur. In short, "fraternities and
intercollegiate athletic programs actively encourage the kinds of masculinity
that make their involvement in sexual assaults of women more probable."[42]

It should come as no surprise that participation in intercollegiate athletics
may impact both attitudes supportive of and behaviors akin to sexual aggression. It is typically stories about well-known, top performing athletes who
are accused of rape that become headline news. Take for example the case of
Jameis Winston, quarterback for the nationally ranked Florida State University football team. Erica Kinsman reported to the Tallahassee Police Department that she has been raped, but at the time she did not know the perpetrator's name. Only later was Winston's name linked to the offense and despite
a mishandling of evidence in the case, his DNA was a positive match to the
evidence available in the case. Similar to other cases around the United
States, Winston was never formally charged criminally or by the university.
Kinsman's credibility was questioned and Winston went on to become a
Heisman Trophy recipient and a first round draft pick for the Tampa Bay
Buccaneers. In December 2016, a civil suit filed by Kinsman and countersuit
filed by Winston were both settled out of court with undisclosed terms. In
January 2016, Florida State University settled the Title IX lawsuit filed by
Kinsman against the institution by agreeing to pay Kinsman $950,000 and to
make a commitment to campus rape prevention programs over the next five
years.

Jon Krakauer painstakingly documents rape and its aftermath, including
the path to justice for several rape survivors at the University of Montana.[43]
Their perpetrators? Members of the university's football team. In an eerily
similar fashion, the survivors whose stories were documented in *Missoula*
faced the same types of victim blaming and questions regarding their credibility as Erica Kinsman and countless other campus sexual assault survivors.
These instances, though anecdotal in nature, come as no surprise to those
who study the link between intercollegiate athletics and sexual violence. For
example, studies from the last two decades have found that male student-
athletes are more likely to endorse rape-supportive attitudes and rape
myths.[44] In a 2007 meta-analysis of 29 studies on rape-supportive attitudes
among athletes and fraternity members, it was determined that membership
in either group increased attitudes supportive of sexual aggression and hyper-
masculinity.[45]

Studies have also found that intercollegiate athletes are more likely to be
represented in statistics on perpetration of sexual violence.[46] In one study of
NCAA Division 1 universities, male college-athletes composed 3% of the

student population, but 19% of reported sexual assaults.[47] Only a handful of studies have focused on intercollegiate athletics and sexual assault and we could find only one study that shifted focus to recreational college athletes.[48] Here, the authors found that while there were differences in sexually aggressive attitudes and sexually coercive practices between athletes and non-athletes, these differences did not hold when comparing intercollegiate-athletes and recreational athletes. Intercollegiate and recreational athletes did not differ on measures of self-reported sexual coercion. In sum, the research on fraternity membership and participation in college athletics suggests that the social, cultural, and environmental contexts of *some* organizations are linked with rape-supportive attitudes and sexual violence. Membership in these organizations certainly cannot explain all forms of sexual violence on campus. In fact, researchers recognize that perpetration of sexual violence has multiple determinants. Still, more research on the link between college athletics, fraternity membership, and sexual violence is needed.

Other Variables of Violence

In the previous section we discussed the link between fraternity membership, college athletics, and sexual violence. While it is important to understand the culture and context of hyper-masculine endeavors and violence against women, it is crucial that we not lose sight of the fact that there are other variables that influence one's propensity to commit rape. Even if 19% of reported sexual assaults on a university campus are committed by athletes, 81% are not. What accounts for these assaults? The following section outlines what we know about the less well-known predictors of campus sexual violence. For starters, sexual violence committed on college campuses is, in many ways, similar to sexual violence in the general population.

While anyone can be sexually violated, research shows that it is predominantly men who perpetrate acts of sexual violence.[49] This has led early writers to suggest that sexual violence was a tool used by men to keep all women in fear.[50] In reality, the perpetration of sexual violence is determined by multiple variables that tend to work in combination with one another.[51] In general, men who perpetrate sexual violence tend to exhibit higher levels of hostility toward women, acceptance of rape myths, peers who condone violence toward women, lower levels of empathy, and higher levels of drinking.[52] These men are also more likely to have frequent and casual sexual encounters and are more likely to be victims of child abuse.[53]

Malamuth and colleagues proposed two specific paths to committing sexual assault.[54] The first, hostile attitudes toward women, suggests that men who hold hostile attitudes use sexual aggression to maintain power and control over women. The second path, sexual promiscuity-impersonal sex, is typically defined as engaging in sex such that having multiple partners and encounters is prioritized over intimacy. Malamuth posits that these two pathways reinforce one another; that is, when one endorses both hostile attitudes toward women *and* promiscuous, non-intimacy based sexual encounters, they are most likely to perpetrate rape and sexual assault. Indeed, Wheeler and colleagues found that high scores on both significantly increased risk for sexual violence.[55] Still, other research finds that hostile attitudes toward women are more likely to result in perpetration than impersonal or promiscuous sex. One study found that a group of males with high scores on hostile masculinity compared to other groups of men with lower scores on this measure were significantly more likely to behave in sexually aggressive ways.[56] Though study participants who rated high on impersonal sex measures had higher rates of sexual aggression than the "no risk" men, it was not a statistically significant finding. When researchers compared men who committed multiple sexual assaults with non-assaulters, those with multiple assaults exhibited significantly higher scores on measures of hostility, as well as drinking during sexual situations, multiple sexual partners, and delinquency in adolescence.[57]

Some scholars have claimed that this hostility measure is actually quite similar to the characteristics of narcissism.[58] One group of researchers even suggested a narcissistic reactance theory of rape and sexual coercion, suggesting that it was a risk factor because of the sense of entitlement that is often associated with narcissism.[59] A recent study of college sexual assault perpetrators found that perpetrators scored higher on measures of narcissism, as measured by several scales. Interestingly, one of the measures suggested that it is only maladaptive features of narcissism that are linked to sexual violence. A separate measure, the *Hypersensitive Narcissism Scale* (HSNS), only correlated with sexual assault perpetration via alcohol or drugs.[60]

The link between alcohol consumption and sexual violence is also important to explore. While research suggests that such a link exists, it appears to be a complicated connection. In more than 50% of sexual assaults alcohol consumption is present for the perpetrator, the survivor, or both, but the role alcohol plays in the commission of the assault is not always clear.[61] For instance, using the SES, Koss found that the severity of sexual aggression was correlated with increased use of alcohol.[62] Parkhill and Abbey found that men who report using alcohol during sexual situations are also more likely to report using sexually aggressive tactics.[63] The most recent study to date found that college men who drank excessively at parties and bars were most likely to commit sexual assault.[64] Conversely, Abbey and her colleagues found that the relationship between men's alcohol consumption and sexual assault perpetration was actually a curvilinear relationship.[65] This means that the more alcohol consumed by the potential perpetrator the more likely they are to commit a sexual assault, but only to a point. After a certain amount of alcohol both the type and severity of perpetration declined.

Others have attempted to ascertain the role of alcohol use in predicting different types of strategies for sexual aggression among college men. For instance, Tyler and colleagues found that the more alcohol a perpetrator used and the more often he was intoxicated predicted whether or not he used alcohol as a strategy to have sex.[66] Conversely, Fischer found that increased alcohol consumption was more likely to result in college men lying to obtain sex.[67] Maria Testa, in a review of the literature on the association between alcohol use and sexual aggressions, notes that the link between the two is a modest one.[68] She cites two studies to support this claim. The first example provided is a study by Koss and Gaines that found a link between alcohol and sexual aggression that was weakened when other potential variables were controlled.[69] Testa, like Koss and Gaines, hypothesizes that alcohol is linked to perpetration, but that another variable complicates the association. The second example was a study that found that alcohol strongly predicted certain types of perpetrators, but not others.[70] Testa points out that there are multiple bodies of literature on alcohol consumption and sexual violence, each looking at different roles it plays. All of this literature suggests that alcohol plays some role, but she conveys the importance of integrating the various types of studies.[71] Testa offers an integrative model that may help to explain alcohol consumption in general, though with specific explanatory power for campus sexual violence. This integrative model incorporates much of what has been outlined throughout this chapter.

INSTITUTIONAL FACTORS AND SEXUAL VIOLENCE

Most of the research on sexual violence on college campuses has focused on the micro and meso (group or organization) level individual and social factors that might be associated with the problem. Very little attention has been given to the role that institutional factors play in the commission of sexual violence. Nonetheless, the few studies that have been conducted show that there are institutional factors that influence sexual violence.[72] Additionally, there are scholars who have taken a unique approach to explaining how institutions exacerbate the problem. Here, they assess whether (and how) institutional failure exacerbates trauma symptoms in survivors who have already experienced sexual victimization.[73]

As noted, only a few studies have analyzed links between institutional factors and sexual violence. A study by sociologist John Sloan in the early 1990s found that campus location, cost, acceptance rate, size of Greek life, and security staff to student ratio were possibly linked to the prevalence of rape on campus.[74] A more recent study confirmed and furthered some of Sloan's findings. Mohler-Kuo and colleagues found that campus location, including region of the United States, and heavy drinking rates on campus were related to rates of experiencing rape while intoxicated.[75] Importantly, a study using Routine Activities Theory to explain both individual and institutional level factors and sexual violence found that no institutional factors were related to rates of sexual assault.[76] The most recent study on institutional factors and reported rape prevalence found that the number of students living on campus, the school's alcohol policy, and NCAA athletic division affiliation were all associated with rape prevalence.[77]

The number of students living on campus is an important institutional variable because the vast majority of assaults occur in traditional college campus living spaces. One study found that approximately 60%, 30%, and 10% of completed campus rapes occur in the victim's on-campus residence, other on-campus living spaces, and fraternities, respectively.[78] A more recent study found that 81% of rapes reported to medical professionals occurred in dorm rooms.[79]

Institutional factors, such as percentage of students living on campus, are noteworthy, but institutional actions or inactions play a role in how survivors heal. As Sanday pointed out over twenty years ago, not all fraternities and not all campuses are rape prone.[80] There are cultural and environmental factors that impact rates of sexual violence. Culture and environment have as much to do with individuals as they do with administration and campus level values.

One area of research focus that is deserving of attention is how or whether the actions or inaction of a college or university exacerbate the effects of trauma, increase secondary trauma, and potentially increase the risk of additional victimization. Drawing on the work of Rebecca Campbell, Jennifer Freyd, and Carly Smith developed a framework that seeks to explain the impact of institutional betrayal among survivors.[81] Campbell articulates that survivors put their trust in law enforcement, medical personnel, and mental health counselors when they disclose their trauma. When that trust is betrayed it increases the amount of trauma, resulting in secondary victimization. Institutional betrayal results in increased feelings of blame, depression, and anxiety and the vast majority of survivors who experience secondary victimization state they are less likely to seek further help.[82] At the end of this section, you will read about Jayne's experience being raped by her boyfriend. Jayne told her martial arts instructor and the Dean about the rape. She was betrayed by both of them. The trauma of rape is very real and Jayne openly discusses how it impacted her life. The trauma of institutional betrayal only added to that trauma for her and for countless other survivors. Indeed, institutional betrayal from colleges and universities results in similar outcomes, including anxiety, sexual dysfunction, and dissociation.[83] Survivors of campus sexual violence from all across the United States have noted the deep sense of betrayal experienced by their campuses. The perception that one's university will not protect them decreases the likelihood that a survivor will speak up after victimization. This is especially true if the survivor felt that before the assault the institution could have done something to protect them.

Jayne's Experience—Sexual Violence at a Community College

I was raped by my 29-year-old boyfriend when I was 17. We were both community college students. I met him in a martial arts class, and we hit it off. We dated for a while, but I didn't want to have sex because I was waiting for marriage. One night, I asked if he could come and get me because my brother had beaten me up. He took me to his house and raped me. In the morning, he served me breakfast and told me that no one would believe me because it was "he said, she said." He was right.

I told our mutual martial arts instructor that he had raped me, but the sensei did nothing. Years later, the instructor would be fired for sexually assaulting a student on a class trip. I told the dean of students, but he laughed it off and told me my rapist boyfriend was a "good guy." He told me we just needed to work through our relationship problems like adults. For years, I thought my rape was just a misunderstanding because I was so much younger than my rapist.

After my rape, I became depressed, dropped out of martial arts, put on 30 pounds in a matter of months, and wanted to kill myself. I had suicidal thoughts for a decade. Once I realized that, regardless of what the college dean told me, it was not my fault, I began to heal. Today, I name my rapist at public events and in social media, and I worry about all the other women he's raped because he wasn't stopped back in college.

CONCLUSION

In many ways campus sexual violence resembles sexual violence within everyday communities, but given the nature of college life, there are also distinct differences. Overall, what we know is that sexual violence is primarily perpetrated by men and that the vast majority of survivors are women. Little attention has been given to the incidence and prevalence of sexual violence among marginalized communities, though some research suggests that racial and ethnic minorities, as well as LGBTQIA+ people are at higher risk of victimization. We have come to understand that college athletics and Greek life play a role in sexual violence on campus, as does campus drinking culture; however, we have also learned that those factors alone cannot explain all campus sexual violence. Indeed, the vast majority of sexual assaults do not happen in these spaces—most occur in the on-campus residence of the survivor.

Sexual violence is determined by multiple factors, both individual and institutional in nature. An integrative model that addresses both sets of factors is necessary to best explain why campus sexual violence occurs. Considerably more research that focuses on the intersectional lives of both survivors and perpetrators is necessary. Similarly, additional research on campus culture and institutional action/inaction should be conducted. Finally, a broader and more in-depth understanding of perpetration is necessary if we seek prevention programs that actually prevent this type of victimization from ever occurring in the first place.

NOTES

1. Joey Mogul, Andrea Ritchie, and Kay Whitlock, *Queer (In)Justice: The Criminalization of LGBT People in the United States* (Boston: Beacon Press, 2012).

2. Department of Justice, Office of Justice Programs, Bureau of Justice Statistics, "National Crime Victimization Survey," 2010–2014 (2015).

3. Department of Justice, Office of Justice Programs, Bureau of Justice Statistics, "Rape and Sexual Victimization Among College-Aged Females," 1995–2013 (2014).

4. Clifford Kirkpatrick and Eugene Kanin, "Male sex aggression on a university campus," *American Sociological Review* 22, no. 1 (1957): 52–58.

5. Kirkpatrick, Clifford, and Eugene Kanin.

6. Kirkpatrick, Clifford, and Eugene Kanin.

7. Eugene J. Kanin, "Male aggression in dating-courtship relations," *American Journal of Sociology* 63, no. 2 (1957): 197–204.

8. Mary P. Koss, "The hidden rape victim: Personality, attitudinal, and situational characteristics," *Psychology of Women Quarterly* 9, no. 2 (1985): 193–212; Mary P. Koss, Kenneth E. Leonard, Dana A. Beezley, and Cheryl J. Oros, "Nonstranger sexual aggression: A discriminant analysis of the psychological characteristics of undetected offenders," *Sex Roles* 12, no. 9–10 (1985): 981–992; Mary P. Koss, and Cheryl J. Oros, "Sexual Experiences Survey: a research instrument investigating sexual aggression and victimization," *Journal of Consulting and Clinical Psychology* 50, no. 3 (1982): 455.

9. Karen Rapaport, and Barry R. Burkhart, "Personality and attitudinal characteristics of sexually coercive college males," *Journal of Abnormal Psychology* 93, no. 2 (1984): 216–221.

10. Mary P. Koss, Christine A. Gidycz, and Nadine Wisniewski, "The scope of rape: incidence and prevalence of sexual aggression and victimization in a national sample of higher education students," *Journal of Consulting and Clinical Psychology* 55, no. 2 (1987): 162.

11. Bonnie S. Fisher, Francis T. Cullen, and Michael G. Turner, "The Sexual Victimization of College Women. Research Report." (2000).

12. Christopher P. Krebs, Christine H. Lindquist, Tara D. Warner, Bonnie S. Fisher, and Sandra L. Martin, "The campus sexual assault (CSA) study: Final report," Washington, DC: National Institute of Justice, US Department of Justice (2007); Christopher P. Krebs, Christine H. Lindquist, Tara D. Warner, Bonnie S. Fisher, and Sandra L. Martin, "College women's experiences with physically forced, alcohol- or other drug-enabled, and drug-facilitated sexual assault before and since entering college," *Journal of American College Health* 57, no. 6 (2009): 639–649.

13. Sofi Sinozich and Lynn Langton, "Rape and sexual assault victimization among college-age females, 1995–2013," Report NCJ248471. Washington, DC: US Department of Justice. Bureau of Justice Statistics (2014).

14. Bonnie S. Fisher, John J. Sloan, Francis T. Cullen, and Chunmeng Lu, "Crime in the ivory tower: The level and sources of student victimization," *Criminology* 36, no. 3 (1998): 671–710.

15. Sinozich & Langton.

16. Sinozich & Langton.

17. Fisher, Cullen, & Turner (2000).

18. L. Kann, E. O. Olsen, T. McManus, S. Kinchen, D. Chyen, W. A. Harris, and H. Wechsler, "Centers for Disease Control and Prevention (CDC) Sexual identity, sex of sexual contacts, and health-risk behaviors among students in grades 9–12—youth risk behavior surveillance, selected sites, United States, 2001–2009," *Morbidity and Mortality Weekly Report.* Surveillance Summaries (Washington, DC: 2002) 60, no. 7 (2011): 1–133; Mikel L. Walters, Jieru Chen, and Matthew J. Breiding, "The National Intimate Partner and Sexual Violence Survey (NISVS): 2010 findings on victimization by sexual orientation," Atlanta, GA: National Center for Injury Prevention and Control, Centers for Disease Control and Prevention 648, no. 73 (2013): 6.

19. Jessie Ford and José G. Soto-Marquez, "Sexual assault victimization among straight, gay/lesbian, and bisexual college students," *Violence and Gender* 3, no. 2 (2016): 107–115.

20. Christopher P. Krebs, Christine H. Lindquist, Tara D. Warner, Bonnie S. Fisher, and Sandra L. Martin, "The differential risk factors of physically forced and alcohol- or other drug-enabled sexual assault among university women," *Violence and Victims* 24, no. 3 (2009): 302–321; Alan M. Gross, Andrea Winslett, Miguel Roberts, and Carol L. Gohm, "An examination of sexual violence against college women," *Violence Against Women* 12, no. 3 (2006): 288–300.

21. White House Task Force, *Not Alone: The First Report of the White House Task Force to Protect Students from Sexual Assault,* 2014. Accessed December 3, 2016. https://www.whitehouse.gov/sites/default/files/docs/report_0.pdf.

22. David Cantor, Bonnie Fisher, Susan Chibnall, Reanne Townsend, Hyunshik Lee, Carol Bruce, and Gail Thomas, "Report on the AAU campus climate survey on sexual assault and sexual misconduct," *Association of American Universities* 21 (2015).

23. Tyler Kingkade, "A supergroup of academics is trying to stop people who profit from campus rape," *Huffington Post.* Accessed December 3, 2016. http://www.huffingtonpost.com/entry/professor-group-fighting-campus-rape_us_55e5120de4b0aec9f35459d9.

24. Christopher Krebs, Christine Lindquist, Marcus Berzofsky, Bonnie Shook-Sa, Kimberly Peterson, Michael Planty, Lynn Langton, and Jessica Stroop, "Campus climate survey validation study final technical report," *Bureau of Justice Statistics Research and Development Series* (2016): 1–193.

25. Cantor, et al.

26. Krebs, C., et al.

27. Cantor, D., et al.

28. Krebs, C., et al.

29. Tyler Kingkade, "A supergroup of academics is trying to stop people who profit from campus rape," *Huffington Post.* Accessed December 3, 2016 from http://www.huffingtonpost.com/entry/professor-group-fighting-campus-rape_us_55e5120de4b0aec9f35459d9.

30. Tara Cupp-Ressler, "Profit and peril in the anti-rape industry," Thinkprogress.org. Accessed December 3, 2016. https://thinkprogress.org/profit-and-peril-in-the-anti-rape-industry-e497c017b0ec#.g3cfe8xyo.

31. Koss, Cook, & White.

32. Centers for Disease Control and Prevention, "The social-ecological model: A framework for prevention," *Injury center: Violence prevention* (2009); Sarah DeGue, Linda Anne Valle, Melissa K. Holt, Greta M. Massetti, Jennifer L. Matjasko, and Andra Teten Tharp. "A systematic review of primary prevention strategies for sexual violence perpetration," *Aggression and Violent Behavior* 19, no. 4 (2014): 346–362.

33. Kanin

34. Gerald Eskenazi, "Athletic aggression and sexual assault," *The New York Times*, p. A27. (June 3, 1990); M. Hirschorn, "Behavior of students in fraternities worsens on many campuses as membership soars," *Chronicle of Higher Education*, pp. A34-A36. (March 16, 1988).

35. Liz Securro, *Crash Into Me*, (Bloomsbury USA, 2011).

36. Peggy Reeves Sanday, *Fraternity Gang Rape: Sex, Brotherhood, and Privilege on Campus*, (NYU Press, 2007).

37. Peggy Reeves Sanday, "Rape-prone versus rape-free campus cultures," *Violence Against Women* 2, no. 2 (1996): 191–208.

38. J. Ehrhart and B. Sandler, *Campus gang rape: Party Games*. Unpublished manuscript, Association of American Colleges, Project on the Status and Education of Women, Washington, DC, 1985 (as cited in M. Koss & Gaines, J. [1993], The prediction of sexual aggression by alcohol use, athletic participation, and fraternity affiliation, *Journal of Interpersonal Violence*, 8, 94–108); Joy Garrett-Gooding and Richard Senter, "Attitudes and acts of sexual aggression on a university campus," *Sociological Inquiry* 57, no. 4 (1987): 348–371; C. Maloy, J. Sheril, C. Bausell, D. Siegle, and C. Raymond. (n.d.) Unpublished manuscript, Towson State University Center for the Study and Prevention of Campus Violence, Towson, MD (as cited in Koss, M. & Gaines, J. [1993]).

39. Koss & Gaines.

40. Martin D. Schwartz and Carol A. Nogrady, "Fraternity membership, rape myths, and sexual aggression on a college campus," *Violence Against Women* 2, no. 2 (1996): 148–162.

41. Patricia Yancey Martin, "The rape prone culture of academic contexts fraternities and athletics," *Gender & Society* 30, no. 1 (2016): 30–43.

42. Martin, pg. 32.

43. Jon Krakauer, *Missoula: Rape and the justice system in a college town*, (Anchor, 2016).

44. Scot B. Boeringer, "Influences of fraternity membership, athletics, and male living arrangements on sexual aggression," *Violence Against Women* 2, no. 2 (1996): 134–147; Scot B. Boeringer, "Associations of rape-supportive attitudes with fraternal and athletic participation," *Violence Against Women* 5, no. 1 (1999): 81–90; Robin G. Sawyer, Estina E. Thompson, and Anne Marie Chicorelli, "Rape myth acceptance among intercollegiate student athletes: A preliminary examination," *American Journal of Health Studies* 18, no. 1 (2002): 19.

45. Sarah K. Murnen and Marla H. Kohlman, "Athletic participation, fraternity membership, and sexual aggression among college men: A meta-analytic review," *Sex Roles* 57, no. 1-2 (2007): 145–157.

46. Koss & Gaines; Todd W. Crosset, James Ptacek, Mark A. McDonald, and Jeffrey R. Benedict, "Male student-athletes and violence against women: A survey of campus judicial affairs offices," *Violence Against Women* 2, no. 2 (1996): 163–179.

47. Todd W. Crosset, Jeffrey R. Benedict, and Mark A. McDonald, "Male student-athletes reported for sexual assault: A survey of campus police departments and judicial affairs offices," *Journal of Sport & Social Issues* 19, no. 2 (1995): 126–140.

48. Belinda-Rose Young, Sarah L. Desmarais, Julie A. Baldwin, and Rasheeta Chandler, "Sexual coercion practices among undergraduate male recreational athletes, intercollegiate athletes, and non-athletes," *Violence Against Women* (2016): 1077801216651339.

49. Michele C. Black, Kathleen C. Basile, Matthew J. Breiding, and George W. Ryan, "Prevalence of sexual violence against women in 23 states and two US territories, BRFSS 2005," *Violence Against Women* 20, no. 5 (2014): 485–499.

50. Susan Brownmiller, *Against Our Will*. (New York: Simon and Schuster, 1975).

51. Antonia Abbey, "Lessons learned and unanswered questions about sexual assault perpetration," *Journal of Interpersonal Violence* 20, no. 1 (2005): 39–42.

52. Martie P. Thompson, Kevin M. Swartout, and Mary P. Koss, "Trajectories and predictors of sexually aggressive behaviors during emerging adulthood," *Psychology of Violence* 3, no. 3 (2013): 247.

53. Antonia Abbey, Tina Zawacki, Philip O. Buck, A. Monique Clinton, and Pam McAuslan, "Sexual assault and alcohol consumption: What do we know about their relationship and what types of research are still needed?," *Aggression and violent behavior* 9, no. 3 (2004): 271–303.

54. Neil M. Malamuth, Robert J. Sockloskie, Mary P. Koss, and Jeffrey S. Tanaka, "Characteristics of aggressors against women: Testing a model using a national sample of college students," *Journal of Consulting and Clinical Psychology* 59, no. 5 (1991): 670; Neil M. Malamuth, Daniel Linz, Christopher L. Heavey, Gordon Barnes, and Michele Acker, "Using the confluence model of sexual aggression to predict men's conflict with women: a 10-year follow-up study," *Journal of Personality and Social Psychology* 69, no. 2 (1995): 353.

55. Jennifer G. Wheeler, William H. George, and Barbara J. Dahl, "Sexually aggressive college males: Empathy as a moderator in the "Confluence Model" of sexual aggression," *Personality and Individual Differences* 33, no. 5 (2002): 759–775.

56. Patricia Logan Greene and Kelly Cue Davis, "Latent profiles of risk among a community sample of men: Implications for sexual aggression," *Journal of Interpersonal Violence* 26, no. 7 (2011): 1463–1477.

57. Antonia Abbey and Pam McAuslan, "A longitudinal examination of male college students' perpetration of sexual assault," *Journal of Consulting and Clinical Psychology* 72, no. 5 (2004): 747.

58. Neil M. Malamuth and Nancy Wilmsen Thornhill, "Hostile masculinity, sexual aggression, and gender-biased domineeringness in conversations," *Aggressive Behavior* 20, no. 3 (1994): 185–193; Emily R. Mouilso and Karen S. Calhoun, "Narcissism, psychopathy and five-factor model in sexual assault perpetration," *Personality and Mental Health* 6, no. 3 (2012): 228–241.

59. Roy F. Baumeister, Kathleen R. Catanese, and Harry M. Wallace, "Conquest by force: A narcissistic reactance theory of rape and sexual coercion," *Review of General Psychology* 6, no. 1 (2002): 92.

60. Emily R. Mouilso and Karen S. Calhoun, "Personality and perpetration: narcissism among college sexual assault perpetrators," *Violence Against Women* 22, no. 10 (2016): 1228–1242.

61. Antonia et al. (2004).

62. Mary P. Koss, "Hidden rape: Incidence, prevalence, and descriptive characteristics of sexual aggression and victimization in a national sample of college students," *Sexual Assault* 2 (1988): 3–25.

63. Michele R. Parkhill and Antonia Abbey, "Does alcohol contribute to the confluence model of sexual assault perpetration?," *Journal of Social and Clinical Psychology* 27, no. 6 (2008): 529–554.

64. Maria Testa and Michael J. Cleveland, "Does alcohol contribute to college men's sexual assault perpetration? Between- and within-person effects over five semesters," *Journal of Studies on Alcohol and Drugs* 78, no. 1 (2016): 5–13.

65. A. Abbey, A. Monique Clinton-Sherrod, Pam McAuslan, Tina Zawacki, and Philip O. Buck, "The relationship between the quantity of alcohol consumed and the severity of sexual assaults committed by college men," *Journal of Interpersonal Violence* 18, no. 7 (2003): 813–833.

66. Kimberly A. Tyler, Danny R. Hoyt, and Les B. Whitbeck, "Coercive sexual strategies," *Violence and Victims* 13, no. 1 (1998): 47.

67. Gloria J. Fischer, "Deceptive, verbally coercive college males: Attitudinal predictors and lies told," *Archives of Sexual Behavior* 25, no. 5 (1996): 527–533.

68. Maria Testa, "The impact of men's alcohol consumption on perpetration of sexual aggression," *Clinical Psychology Review* 22, no. 8 (2002): 1239–1263.

69. Koss & Gaines (1993).

70. Grant T. Harris and N. Zoe Hilton, "Theoretical note: Interpreting moderate effects in interpersonal violence," *Journal of Interpersonal Violence* 16, no. 10 (2001): 1094–1098.

71. Testa, (2002).

72. Amy I. Cass, "Routine activities and sexual assault: An analysis of individual- and school-level factors," *Violence and victims* 22, no. 3 (2007): 350–366; Rebecca L. Stotzer and Danielle MacCartney, "The role of institutional factors on on-campus reported rape prevalence," *Journal of interpersonal violence* 31, no. 16 (2016): 2687–2707.

73. Carly Parnitzke Smith and Jennifer J. Freyd, "Institutional betrayal," *American Psychologist* 69, no. 6 (2014): 575; Carly Parnitzke Smith and Jennifer J. Freyd. "Dangerous

safe havens: Institutional betrayal exacerbates sexual trauma," *Journal of Traumatic Stress* 26, no. 1 (2013): 119–124.

74. John J. Sloan, "Campus crime and campus communities: An analysis of crimes known to campus police and security," *Journal of Security Administration* 15, no. 2 (1992): 31–47.

75. M. Mohler-Kuo, G.W. Dowdall, M.P Koss, and Wechsler, H., "Correlates of rape while intoxicated in a national sample of college women." *Journal of Studies on Alcohol,* 65(1), (2004): 37–45.

76. Cass (2007).

77. R.L. Stotzer and D. MacCartney, "The role of institutional factors on on-campus reported rape prevalence," *Journal of Interpersonal Violence,* 31(16), (2016): 2687–2707.

78. Fisher, et al. (2000).

79. B. Peters, *Analysis of college campus rape and sexual assault reports, 2000-2011: Using medical provider data to describe the nature and context of college campus rape and sexual assault reports in Massachusetts.* Boston, Executive Office of Public Safety and Security, 2012.

80. Sanday (1990; 1996).

81. Rebecca Campbell, "Rape survivors' experiences with the legal and medical systems do rape victim advocates make a difference?," *Violence Against women* 12, no. 1 (2006): 30–45; Rebecca Campbell, "The psychological impact of rape victims," *American Psychologist* 63, no. 8 (2008): 702.

82. Rebecca Campbell, "The neurobiology of sexual assault," *National Institute of Justice* (2012).

83. Smith & Freyd (2013).

Chapter Two

Women of Color Leading the Way

A History of Anti-Sexual Violence Activism

Recy Taylor was kidnapped on her way home from Rock Hill Holiness Church in a small Alabama town in 1944.[1] Taylor, a 24-year-old mother, was walking with a friend and her friend's teenage son when U.S. Army Private Herbert Lovett drove up in a green Chevrolet with six other men and forced her into the car at gunpoint.[2] Lovett drove her down the road to a copse of trees where the six men took turns raping her. Lovett demanded that Taylor "act just like you do with your husband or I'll cut your damn throat."[3] They left Taylor for dead and drove off, but Taylor did not die. She immediately reported the rape to local police, and one witness to the incident identified the owner of the car. Law enforcement soon identified all seven of the men involved in the rape, and even though the men admitted to the rape, two grand juries failed to indict, and no charges were ever filed against Taylor's attackers. Taylor's case drew the ire of local black community members and caught the attention of the National Association for the Advancement of Colored People (NAACP). The NAACP sent a staff member to investigate the case by the name of Rosa Parks. While Taylor would have to wait 67 years for justice in the form of an apology from the state of Alabama,[4] her case was one of the first national campaigns for black justice that were instrumental in the formation of the Civil Rights Movement in the 1960s. Black women like Taylor would face sexual violence at the hands of white men who faced virtually no consequences from the Reconstruction era through the 1960s.

The United States has experienced five peaks of heightened activism against sexual violence: (1) during the Reconstruction era (1880s), (2) leading up to the Civil Rights Movement (1940s), (3) during the second wave of the Women's Movement (1960s and 1970s), (4) the late 1980s, and (5) the new Campus Anti-Rape Movement (CARM) (2011–today). In this chapter, we examine the first four peaks of activism in order to better understand the historical context leading up to the emergence of the new CARM. This chapter illuminates the long history of anti-rape activism in America, and also demonstrates the leadership and historical erasure of Native American and black women in organized efforts against sexual violence.

We begin this chapter with a look at the first organized anti-sexual violence efforts after the Civil War to raise awareness of rape as a tool of social control against black women. The second section examines the peak of activism leading up to the Civil Rights Movement, while the third section focuses on work during the Women's Movement. The fourth section centers on the national debate about rape that took place in the late 1980s and early 1990s. We pay particular attention to the backlash that essentially silenced public discussion during this peak.

RECONSTRUCTION ERA PEAK

Gillian Greensite writes that "The history of the rape crisis movement in the United States is also a history of the struggle of African American women against racism and sexism."[5] The early peaks of anti-rape activism were led by women of color. The first peak of heightened activism around this issue emerged during Reconstruction, the era immediately following the Civil War that was waged from 1861 to 1865. Reconstruction was a tumultuous period of rebuilding and healing the wounds of the war that split the nation in two. The existing racial hierarchy, codified into law with slavery, came apart with abolition, and white vigilantes responded to the shifting social order by using lynching and rape as tools to maintain the second class position of black Americans, and to maintain a racially segregated society.

The rape of black women was commonplace well before the Civil War, so the use of this tool to maintain the racial order post-abolition was simply an extension of a previous pattern of domestic terrorism against black women's bodies. On plantations and farms, enslaved black women were at the mercy of white men since the rape of slaves was legal, expected, and common. Many masters also used rape as a tool to improve their economic prospects by producing more slaves to work the land.[6] Furthermore, some slaves— "fancy maids"—were explicitly bought and sold for sexual service. "Fancy maids" endured thousands of rapes over the course of their lifetime.[7] Evidence of the routine rape of black women over a century ago is apparent in the United States today. An estimated three-fourths of black people in the United States today are descendents of at least one white ancestor—often from rape,[8] including former First Lady Michelle Obama.[9]

Rape was also common during the Civil War. President Lincoln issued an explicit legal prohibition against soldiers engaging in rape during the Civil War.[10] Nonetheless, women of all races were raped across the south, and black women were especially vulnerable to this crime.[11] Rape during war carries symbolic importance as an individual act of gendered power within a larger context of battle.[12] In the American Civil War, rape was used as a strategic tool to insult the masculinity of Southern men in an effort to demoralize them. Crystal Feimster writes that "Just as the rape of white women implied that Southern men were unable to protect their mothers, wives and daughters, the rape of slave women told whites they could no longer protect their property."[13] Feimster located 450 court martial cases from the Civil War that related to sexual crimes, but she is quick to point out that cases of sexual violence were vastly underreported during this time. The historical record is scant, but from what we know, rape was widely used as a weapon of war in the Civil War.

As noted above, the routine rape of black women accelerated during Reconstruction, especially in the South where vigilantism was incorporated as informal law enforcement to maintain the crumbling racial hierarchy. With slavery now outlawed, many white men reestablished racial control over black men through lynching and black women through rape.[14] The era from 1865 to 1877 was a particularly violent period when the Ku Klux Klan and other terror organizations raped black women and burned black homes and churches with regularity in response to the changing social order.[15] The Klan existed to keep black Americans in a lower social position through intimidation, rape, and murder. Between 1882 and 1946, approximately 5,000 African Americans (mostly men) were lynched, and a high number of women were raped to maintain white social control over blacks.[16] For the most part, law enforcement authorities turned a blind eye to vigilante violence targeting recently freed slaves.

The first peak of organized anti-rape efforts emerged in the Reconstruction era. The first daring action came from a group of black women who testified before Congress about a white mob that perpetrated gang rapes during the Memphis Riot in 1866.[17] These riots were the result of class conflicts between poor whites and a group of black soldiers. They were started by a heated exchange between a white police officer and a black ex-soldier. Over 50 black residents tried to stop the ex-soldier's arrest, and people on both sides opened fire. The violence quickly spread to black neighborhoods where white law enforcement officers and vigilantes attacked and destroyed churches and homes. White missionaries and teachers working in black neighborhoods were also targeted for violence. The riots lasted for three days during which white people injured over 100 black people, killing 46, and raping at least five black women.[18]

One rape survivor, 17-year-old Lucy Smith testified that seven white men, including two police officers, demanded dinner before raping her and elderly, crippled friend, Frances Smith.[19] Smith and Smith both testified before Congress about the sexual violence they endured. They were joined by several other women who also testified to the routine rapes during the Memphis Riot. Congress did not take any action in response to the Memphis Riot rapes, injuries, or murders. Not a single arrest was made and none of the perpetrators were punished. Nonetheless, this case raised public awareness of the use of rape as a tool for social control of black women, and it inspired the formation of the first national organization to address sexual violence in the United States.

In the early 1870s, Ida B. Wells-Barnett worked with a network of activists, including Julia Cooper and Fannie Barrier Williams, to keep sexual violence on the public agenda.[20] In the 1890s, Wells-Barnett formed black Women's Clubs to address women's suffrage, education, sanitation, and other "women's issues." These clubs also tackled lynching and sexual violence—the first organized anti-violence efforts in the United States Wells-Barnett also published *A Red Record*, a pamphlet about the terrifying details of lynching and rape that was critical of how few people cared about the rape of black women, and how often false rape charges were lobbied against black men to justify their lynching.[21]

Around the same time black women were first organizing against sexual violence, Sarah Winnemucca of the Northern Paiute Tribe was waging a one-woman war against the commonplace rape of Native women by white men. According to historian Rose Stremlau, the rape of Native women was part of the conquest of the American West.[22] Colonial domination was achieved through state-sanctioned, systematic violence against Native tribes and sexual violence directed at Native women. In *Sexual Violence and American Indian Genocide*, Andrea Smith documents that, beyond sexual violation, early colonizers would sometimes cut off the genitals of native women, an act stemming from the idea that Native women's genitals are "dirty" and contaminated by sexual sin.[23] Records of the percentage of Native women who experienced sexual violence do not exist, but based on accounts from Winnemucca and other writers of the time, rape on reservations was common.

Winnemucca documented this widespread sexual violence in her 1883 biography, the first book published in English by a Native woman. Historian Jennifer Bailey notes that this book was more a political critique of the use of sexual violence to further colonialism than an account of Winnemuca's personal life.[24] She spent much of her adult life travelling the country to raise awareness of the use of rape as a tool to suppress Native people, giving talks, promoting her book, and speaking with the press. Winnemucca also lobbied military leaders, the Interior Department, and President Hayes to provide state protection against sexual violence on reservations. On occasion, her bloodying of would-be rapists made the press pages. When Winnemucca passed away, the front page of the *New York Times* read "Princess Winnemucca Dead: The Most Remarkable Woman among the Piutes of Nevada.[25] Although her activism was met with skepticism and resistance by lawmakers, Winnemucca put the rape of Native women on the public agenda.

The historical record is scant on statistics of sexual violence in the first century of our republic, but legal records and biographical accounts indicate that black and Native American women faced higher rates of sexual violence than white women given the dynamics of slavery and genocide that amplified the patriarchal dynamics of the day. In other words, gender-based oppression was compounded by racial oppression for women of color in an intersectional way that increased their risk of rape. It is no surprise, then, that black and Native women led the first organized efforts against sexual violence in the United States. It is also no surprise that their activism is mostly missing from history books given that the political efforts of women of color are often overlooked and erased in academic studies.[26]

PRE–CIVIL RIGHTS MOVEMENT PEAK

Black women also led efforts in the second peak of anti-sexual violence activism in the United States. A decade before activist Rosa Parks refused to sit at the back of a city bus in 1955, an action that launched the Civil Rights Movement, she was leading an organized campaign against sexual violence.[27] In her capacity as secretary of the Montgomery, Alabama, branch of the NAACP, Parks investigated the rampant sexual violence perpetrated by white men against black women in the workplace, public spaces, and private places. Galvanized by the egregious injustice in Recy Taylor's case, Parks formed the Committee for Equal Justice to fight against the everyday sexual violence experienced by black women.[28] The *Chicago Defender* described the organization as "the strongest campaign for equal justice to be seen in a decade."[29] For the next decade, Parks led this national coalition that raised awareness of the issue and provided support for girls and women who spoke out about their experiences. In the retelling of history, Parks is known for her work against racial injustice, but her work as an anti-sexual violence pioneer is rarely noted.

In the decade leading up to the Civil Rights Movement, anti-rape activists ran dozens of high-profile campaigns that once again put sexual violence on the national agenda. They organized on behalf of Gertrude Perkins, a woman who was raped by two police officers in Montgomery in 1949. A school teacher, Perkins was waiting for the bus after work when the officers forced her into the squad car, drove her to a secluded area, and raped her. They dropped her back off at the same bus stop and threatened her life if she were to tell anyone what happened. Two white lawyers took up Perkins' case, but the Montgomery police refused to release the names of the officers that were on patrol that night. After months of death threats and the burning of a Ku Klux Klan cross in front of one of the lawyer's homes, Perkins withdrew her case. Even though Perkins' perpetrators went unpunished, her case drew concern from black communities and some white activists across the nation.

Anti-rape campaigns were able to obtain justice (of a kind) for some victims. In 1951, 15-year-old Flossie Hardman was raped by her white boss, Sam Green. Hardman worked under Green at a local grocery store and relied on him for transportation to and from work. One evening on a drive home from work, Green pulled over to the side of the road and forced himself on Hardman. An all-white jury found Green "not guilty" after five minutes of deliberation, so the black community pushed back with a boycott of Green's store. The store was located in a black neighborhood, and without a customer base, it went out of business within a few months. This campaign "established the boycott as a powerful weapon for justice and sent a message to whites that African Americans would not allow white men to disrespect, abuse, and violate black women's bodies with impunity."[30]

According to McGuire, the late 1950s were a turning point for taking sexual violence against black women seriously. Activism and media brought increased attention to the issue that "led to trials and even convictions" of white perpetrators.[31] For example, the four perpetrators in the case of Betty Jean Owens received life sentences for kidnapping and raping her in 1959. They kidnapped Owens, a student at Florida A&M University, at gunpoint after a school dance with the intent of having an "all night party."[32] The sentence the four perpetrators received was not as harsh as the typical sentence meted out for black men (death by the electric chair), but it was severe enough to shatter the impunity with which white men had been raping black women.

McGuire notes that early anti-rape efforts were pivotal in launching the Civil Rights Movement in the 1960s because they laid the strategic and organizing groundwork.[33] For example, the campaign mounted in Recy Taylor's defense would later be called the Montgomery Improvement Association, the vehicle for organizing the Montgomery bus boycott. The frequent, ritualistic rape of black women for the purpose of economic and social intimidation instigated the second peak of anti-sexual violence in the United States that enabled the more significant and sustained movement for civil rights in America. However, as with the first peak of anti-sexual violence activism, the contributions of women of color are rarely acknowledged in history lessons or academic studies of activism on this issue.

WOMEN'S MOVEMENT PEAK

The third peak of increased activism against sexual violence coincided with the second wave of the Women's Movement in the 1970s. During this peak, sexual violence was redefined as a common experience for women of all races, which made it a higher priority for white Americans. Popular sources for feminist events tend to misidentify the Women's Movement as the start of activism against sexual violence in the United States, but this rewriting of history erases nearly a century of anti-sexual violence work initiated and led by women of color.[34] For example, in 1975, Susan Brownmiller published her influential book *Against Our Will* in which she reframed rape as a societally sanctioned practice rather than an act carried out by mentally ill men:

> That *some* men rape provides a sufficient threat to keep all women in a constant state of intimidation, forever conscious of the knowledge that the biological tool must be held in awe, for it may turn to weapon with sudden swiftness born of harmful intent. . . . Rather than society's aberrants or "spoilers of purity," men who commit rape have served in effect as front-line masculine shock troops, terrorist guerrillas in the longest sustained battle the world has ever known.[35]

Brownmiller's argument about the systemic role of rape in maintaining the social order was considered revolutionary by many white feminists at the time, but black and Native anti-rape activists had arrived at this conclusion a century earlier. Furthermore, women of color had articulated the use of this tool in a more sophisticated intersectional way that accounted for its use for maintaining both racial and gender hierarchy. White women's involvement in anti-rape work brought new attention and urgency to a longstanding problem that black and Native women had been working on for nearly 100 years.

This peak garnered support from more women than previous peaks, likely because white women were now leading the charge, and their voices and victimhood matter more in a society marked by racial bias. This was the first peak in which rape became part of the broader national discussion taking place about gender justice. Anti-rape activism in the 1970s was distinct from previous peaks in its use of consciousness raising groups and speak-outs that sprang up across the country.[36] The first speak-out event was organized by the New York Radical Feminists in 1971, followed by a conference on sexual violence later that year.[37] These speak-outs were the first time survivors publicly shared their experiences in organized forums, and media coverage of these events amplified the messages of the speak-outs well beyond just the crowd in attendance. Consciousness-raising groups were more private, but they served the vital function of conveying sexual violence as a common experience for women across social and racial identities. As well-known radical feminist Andrea Dworkin points out, this peak of activism "changed the moral algebra of rape" by persuading the justice system and a sizable number of Americans that "anyone who rapes is a rapist and belongs in jail," regardless of their race or social position in society.[38]

This third peak marked the first time major resources were allocated to address sexual violence in the form of institutions, programs, and legislation. The first rape crisis centers opened their doors in Berkeley and Washington, D.C. in 1972 to provide legal and medical services for survivors. The D.C. Rape Crisis Center played a pivotal role in establishing similar organizations in other cities with their pamphlet, *How to Start a Rape Crisis Center*. This pamphlet was a template for do-it-yourself grassroots activists, and within a decade, a network of rape crisis centers (RCCs) were established in major cities throughout the United States.[39] Early RCCs were mostly funded by donations and staffed by volunteers, and were firmly anti-establishment and feminist in their approach to service provision. RCCs also organized political events and protests to raise awareness of the extent of sexual violence in the United States.

Dozens of anti-sexual violence programs and organizations were also formed during this time. In 1974, Feminist Alliance Against Rape (FAAR) was established to bring anti-rape activists under one umbrella organization in response to new interest in the subject from politicians and government agencies.[40] The National Organization for Women (NOW) was the first national feminist group in this peak to make an organized effort to reduce sexual violence. They led legislative reforms in every state, and within a decade, they had revolutionized the way Americans think about and respond to sexual violence under the law. Within a decade, NOW in collaboration with other anti-rape organizations successfully lobbied for laws making it illegal to rape one's spouse, passed rape shield laws that prevent consideration of the survivor's previous sexual behavior, and extended the definition of rape to include incapacitation. Anti-rape activists also implemented better enforcement of rape laws and they vastly expanded governmental support for rape prevention.[41] The sustained efforts of anti-rape activists culminated in the passage of the Violence Against Women Act (VAWA) in 1994, the first national law requiring law enforcement to treat gendered violence as a crime rather than a private family matter.[42] The law mostly focused public attention and policy on domestic violence, but it did include programs and funding aimed specifically at addressing sexual violence.

VAWA was championed by Senator Joe Biden (D-DE) and initially passed with broad bi-partisan support. It was swiftly passed in a climate of heightened national concern about domestic violence after famed football player O. J. Simpson was charged with the murder of his ex-wife, Nicole Brown Simpson, and her friend, Ron Goldman.[43] VAWA was reauthorized in 2000 and 2005 with little partisan rancor. It was reauthorized in 2013, but over stiff opposition from congressional Republicans over extended protections for Native American, gay, lesbian, immigrant, and transgendered victims.[44] Government interventions for violence against women, including sexual violence, have become a partisan issue in the current political landscape.

Emergence of Campus Activism

The earliest documented activism around sexual violence prevention on campus occurred during the third peak of anti-sexual violence work (that coincided with the Women's Movement in the 1970s). Sexual violence has been a problem on college campuses since many institutions of higher education first opened their doors to women in the United States in the 1950s. According to the National Center for Education Statistics, women constituted 37.9% of college students in 1960, which rose to 48.5% by 1970.[45] Women became the majority of undergraduate college students (51.8%) by 1980, and have remained so since that time.[46]

In the 1970s, campus activists collaborated with community rape crisis centers to provide advocacy, support services, and self-defense workshops. Jodi Gold and Susan Villari provide the best account of activism during this time in their book *Just Sex: Students Rewrite the Rules of Sex, Violence, Equality, and Activism*.[47] They report that students effectively lobbied for the first campus-based rape crisis center at the University of Maryland in 1972.[48] In 1973, women at the University of Pennsylvania staged a four day sit-in in response to several gang rapes and abductions on campus, and administrators met their demands to tighten campus security and create a women's studies program and a rape crisis center.[49] Then, in 1976, student and faculty advocates worked with administrators to implement campus-wide prevention programs for the University of California system, a program that is still in place today.[50]

1980–1990s PEAK

The fourth peak of anti-sexual violence activism in the United States was the first to focus on rape on campus, although its reach went beyond the walls of academia because it raised awareness of the epidemic of sexual violence and rape culture in the United States. Psychologist Mary Koss, now the best-known researcher on sexual violence, was just starting her academic career in 1982 when she published "Date Rape: A Campus Epidemic" in *Ms. Magazine*. This study was the first large-scale examinations of sexual violence, and it put the issue on the feminist agenda. This ambitious study used college students because Koss was interested in this group from her work with them in a clinical setting, but her findings suggest that sexual assault was an issue beyond academic institutions. Koss and her colleagues followed up with two additional studies in 1985 and 1987, the latter of which spurred a national debate on sexual violence.

Prior to Koss' research that produced the fourth peak, most Americans thought of rape as an act perpetrated by strangers, but Koss' 1987 study—a three-year study of over 7,000 students—showed that assault/rape was mostly committed by acquaintances and friends. A year later, in 1988, Robin Warshaw published *I Never Called It Rape* a book with over 150 personal stories that verified Koss' statistical findings and extended the problem beyond college campuses.[51] This influential book focused on confirming the existence of "acquaintance rape" and "date rape," mapping its prevalence, analyzing the role of societal institutions and beliefs in normalizing this crime, and examining why this crime remains hidden for the most part. Warshaw reported that only 27% of women who experienced rape as defined by federal and state laws defined it themselves as rape, meaning that the crime was so misunderstood that many victims were unaware that what happened to them was unlawful.[52] Using Koss' data, Warshaw also reported that 84% of survivors knew their perpetrator, and 57% of rapes took place during dates.[53] Koss and Warshaw's work made "acquaintance rape" and "date rape" part of the national dialogue in the late 1980s and into the 1990s.

"Date rape" and "acquaintance rape" were intensely debated in news magazines and talk shows. Popular magazines and talk shows featured survivor stories and experts to debate the issue. Larry King interviewed students whose institutions had failed to adjudicate their rapes, and popular talk show host Phil Donahue interviewed student survivor activists. Sexual violence was hotly debated in the halls of academia and around water coolers. Survivor activists made rape part of the national discourse. During this peak, Dworkin noted that "when women my age (now in their fifties and sixties) were trying to figure out what rape was and what rape was not, there was no community in which stories of rape had any cogency."[54] Public awareness and the sharing of survivor stories firmly established sexual violence as a common problem for women.

More Campus Activism

Student activism on college campuses heated up during this time peak. In 1990, a group of survivor activists at Brown University scrawled the names of men they believe were sexual predators on bathroom walls and stalls to warn other students. The first poster wrote, "Beware of _____, he doesn't take no for an answer." The list quickly populated to over thirty names. Janitors would remove the names, only to see them quickly reappear. The posters of the list remained anonymous, but their actions pressured administrators to publicly discuss the issue. Survivor activists used public forums and meetings to raise awareness of the university's inadequate response to

Figure 2.1.   Mary Koss, Psychologist and Pioneering Sexual Violence Research-er. *Mary Koss*

sexual violence. During one public forum, John Robinson, the dean of student life, said "Your outrage at the administration is justified."[55] Brown's anonymous lists of campus rapists put this small Ivy League school in the national news and inspired copy cat actions at colleges and universities across the nation. Popular talk shows at the time debated the legality and ethics of rapist lists.

The fourth peak of anti-rape efforts on college campuses was led by a diverse coalition of student and faculty survivor activists. Jodi Gold and Susan Villari edited a volume with the most comprehensive account of activism in the 1980s and 1990s titled *Just Sex: Students Rewrite the Rules on Sex, Violence, Equality, and Activism* that highlights the diversity of movement participants, voices, and approaches. Gold, a former student of Villari, writes that her mentor

> made critical observations about the student movement against sexual violence. She was impressed by the number of men in the student anti-sexual violence movement, the unlikely coalitions, and the changing sexual climate on campus. Not everyone agrees with a single method or ideology, but everyone deplores violence. At Penn it was commonplace to see religious group members, gay and lesbian student leaders, and football players join together with more "traditional" feminists to fight sexual violence.[56]

This assorted coalition of students, sexual health educators, and other faculty brought programs and events to campuses that are still in place today. As one student leader noted, "We were the experts in this new movement, and our professors became colleagues who worked with us to find solutions. Through our tears and our laughter, we created a national dialogue on sex, violence, and activism."[57] A new organization was formed to coordinate the movement called Speak Out: The North American Student Coalition Against Sexual Violence. A local anti-sexual violence STAAR conference became a large conference encompassing North America that would later become fifteen different conferences on the subject across the United States and Canada.[58]

The Antioch Rules

In 1991, the feminist group Womyn of Antioch lobbied for a sexual assault policy at Antioch College that turned notions of consent on their head. This policy was revolutionary in that it required that "consent must be obtained each and every time there is sexual activity," and more notably, "each new level of sexual activity requires consent."[59] Antioch, a small liberal arts college located in Yellow Springs, Ohio, embraced these rules, but the reaction off campus was not as warm.

In 1993, the Antioch Rules became part of the national conversation when *Saturday Night Live* made light of the policy in a comedy sketch called "Is It

Date Rape?" It featured Shannen Doherty, a star of the hit show *Beverly Hills 90210*, playing an uptight feminist contestant on a game show against a goofy fraternity brother played by comedian Chris Farley. The game show host posed hypothetical situations and asked whether they constitute rape. Doherty's character responds "yes" to increasingly ridiculous scenarios inaccurately applying almost verbatim quotes from the Antioch Rules. The takeaway from the *Saturday Night Live* bit was that uptight feminists lose to even goofy frat boys when it comes to drawing sexual boundaries.

The backlash against sexual violence activism was well under way when the *Saturday Night Live* sketch aired, and national conversation about the Antioch Rules was framed as campus activists trying to legislate romance rather than a movement to legislate against sexual violence. Karen Hall, the director of Antioch's sexual offense prevention program, stated that "We are not trying to reduce the romance, passion, or spontaneity of sex; we are trying to reduce the spontaneity of rape."[60]

The Backlash

The national dialogue around sexual violence was spurred by Koss' research and high-profile cases of sexual harassment and rape. In 1991, law professor Anita Hill and three other women reported that Supreme Court nominee Clarence Thomas had sexually harassed them as co-workers, but he was appointed to the highest court nonetheless. That same year, William Kennedy-Smith, the nephew of President John F. Kennedy, was acquitted of raping a woman after a judge excluded the testimony of three women with similar experiences. In 1992, heavyweight boxer Mike Tyson was found guilty of raping Desiree Washington.

Public attention and national dialogue about rape inspired a "tremendous backlash" with critiques that rape was not as widespread as reported, and that "date rape" and "acquaintance rape" did not constitute *real* rape. Men's rights organizations and journalists in mainstream media publications led the backlash charged with commentary reflecting three primary rape myths: that rape is rare, that "date rape" is not "real rape" because it does not involve a stranger rape using force, and that women lie about being raped. This last point was premised on the idea that "date rape" was mostly young women regretting a decision to engage in consensual sex.[61] The actions of men's rights organizations and how quickly members of the public bought into these myths speaks to the presence of "rape culture." Rape culture describes a society in which rape is common and normalized by societal attitudes and practices. In the United States, rape is tacitly condoned through denial of the rape epidemic, denial of the harms of rape, not considering rape a "real" crime, victim-blaming, trivializing rape, and the normalization of female sexual objectification and rape eroticization in pop culture.

One important component of the backlash against activism in the fourth peak was a national best-selling book, *The Morning After: Fear, Feminism, and Sex*. Penned by Katie Roiphe, an undergraduate English major with no social science training, this book was accepted as a legitimate counter to Koss' scientific data on sexual violence.[62] Roiphe dismissed Koss' finding that one-in-four college students experience sexual violence during college with anecdotal data that few of Roiphe's friends had experienced this during their college years. She wrote that "If I were really standing in the middle of an epidemic, a crisis, if 25 percent of my female friends were being raped, wouldn't I know it?"[63] Roiphe also echoed the backlash arguments from men's right organizations that women are partially to blame for "date rape" because it often involves drugs and alcohol.[64] Roiphe also painted anti-rape activists as hysterical and unattractive, and her points resonated with many Americans who already held these myths about feminists from the right-wing backlash against the Women's Movement that took place in the early 1980s.[65] Roiphe was aided in her backlash efforts by Neil Gilbert, a social welfare professor at Berkeley, and philosopher Christina Hoff Summers, both of whom dismissed the prevalence of sexual violence and accused Koss and others of engaging in advocacy research. Ad hominem critiques of feminists in the backlash against the fourth peak looked remarkably similar to the language used to discredit feminists a decade before.

Today, we recognize these backlash arguments—that rape is rare or that only real rape involves a stranger using force—as rape myths, but during the fourth peak, this victim-blaming rhetoric effectively dampened public outrage and action around the issue.[66] By the mid-1990s, the national conversation about rape of any kind had mostly dissipated. Nonetheless, activists during this peak effectively reframed rape as not only stranger rape involving force. This peak of activism permanently altered the ways rape is understood—as inevitable, as perpetrated by strangers, and as only reportable if physical injuries result. Society saw rape in a new light that feminists of the Women's Movement did not conceive possible. According to Dworkin, young survivor activists during this peak shut down rape as "taken for granted as normal, natural, inevitable, and 'But did he hurt you?' will be an unspeakable insult."[67] This shift in cultural acceptance of rape was a crucial foundation for the next peak of anti-rape activism—the new CARM that broke the surface in 2013.

CONCLUSION

In this chapter, we briefly described the first four peaks of anti-sexual violence activism in the United States. During the Reconstruction era, black women led the first organized efforts to address routine sexual violence that was perpetrated by white men against black women as a form of social control. Around this time, Sarah Winnemucca was writing and travelling to raise awareness of an epidemic of sexual violence committed by mostly white men against Native American women. Little national attention was paid to sexual violence at this time, probably because it was an act that was mostly perpetrated against women of color who held lower social value than white women.

The second peak of anti-rape activism in the United States occurred in the 1940s and 1950s when activists organized against the routine rape of black women in the South. Prominent leaders in the anti-rape movement would go on to be leaders in the Civil Rights Movement. Historian Danielle McGuire persuasively argues that organized efforts against sexual violence established the organizations and networks that made the Civil Rights Movement possible. As with the first peak, sexual violence did not receive much national public attention, probably due to the fact that the victims were black women.

The third peak of anti-sexual violence activism in the United States corresponded with the second wave of the Women's Movement in the 1960s. During this peak, rape crisis centers were created and activists passed national legislation to address violence against women. This was the first peak to involve white women in sizeable numbers, and the first to bring sustained national attention to the issue. Anti-sexual violence activism began nearly a century before the third peak of activism around this issue, but popular accounts of this work often erase the history of previous efforts because they were smaller moments of activism led by women of color.

The fourth peak of anti-rape activism came about in the 1980s with the publication of three large-scale studies of sexual violence conducted by Mary Koss. These studies revealed that sexual violence is common and mostly perpetrated by people known to the victim. This new peak was met with a fierce backlash from critics who argued that "date rape" was not real rape unless it involved physical force. The rape myth ideas behind the backlash painted "date rape" as women feeling regret after consensual sexual encounters. Backlash rhetoric and misinformation blurred the national conversation, and the "date rape" debate disappeared as quickly as it appeared with millions of Americans concluding that the sexual violence epidemic was overblown.

The new Campus Anti-Rape Movement comes on the recent heels of a push by academics, students, feminists, and advocates that ended in the early 1990s. It is a peculiar fact that each new generation of anti-sexual violence activists believe that they are the first to tackle the issue when activists have been addressing it for nearly 140 years in the United States. For example, one CARM activist in the popular 2015 documentary *The Hunting Ground* comments that she was hearing from survivors on campuses across the country, but "no one had connected the dots."[68] Of course these dots had been connected many decades prior, and activists had been blowing the whistle on rape both on and off campus for over a century.

The fifth peak of anti-rape activism, the new CARM, is distinct from previous peaks in many ways. It is a multi-generational, multi-racial coalitional peak that is pushing for shifts in how rape is perceived through social media messaging. We explore this contemporary peak in the next chapter.

NOTES

1. Danielle L. McGuire, "It Was Like All of Us Had Been Raped: Sexual Violence, Community Mobilization, and the African American Freedom Struggle," *The Journal of American History* 91 (2004): 906–931.

2. Cynthia Gordy, "Recy Taylor: A Symbol of Jim Crow's Forgotten Horror," *The Root*, 2011. http://www.theroot.com/articles/culture/2011/02/recy_taylor_a_symbol_of_jim_crows_forgotten_horror.html.

3. Danielle L. McGuire, *At the Dark End of the Street: Black Women, Rape, and Resistance—a New History of the Civil Rights Movement from Rosa Parks to the Rise of Black Power,* (New York: Random House, 2011).

4. Benjamin Greenberg, "Alabama Senate Apologizes to Recy Taylor for 1944 Rape Case," *Colorlines*, April 22, 2011. Accessed March 23, 2017. http://www.colorlines.com/articles/alabama-senate-apologizes-recy-taylor-1944-rape-case.

5. Gillian Greensite, "History of the Rape Crisis Movement," *California Coalition Against Sexual Assault,* November 1, 2009. Accessed January 25, 2014. http://www.calcasa.org/2009/11/history-of-the-rape-crisis-movement.

6. Jeffrey J. Pokorak, "Rape as Badge of Slavery: The Legal History of, and Remedies for, Prosecutorial Race-of-Victim Charging Disparities," *Nevada Law Journal* 7 (2006): 1–53.

7. Edward E. Baptiste, "'Cuffy,' 'Fancy Maids,' and 'One-Eyed Men': Rape, Commodification, and the Domestic Slave Trade in the United States," *The American Historical Review* 106 (2001): 1619–1650.

8. Joe R. Feagin, *Racist America: Roots, Current Realities, and Future Reparations* (New York: Routledge, 2001).

9. Joe Feagin, "The Rape of Black Women by White Men: Systemic Racism Again," *Racism Review*, October 11 2009. Accessed March 23, 2017. http://www.racismreview.com/blog/2009/10/11/the-rape-of-black-women-by-white-men-systemic-racism-again/.

10. Kim Murphy, *I Had Rather Die: Rape in the Civil War* (New York: Coachlight Press, 2014).

11. Crystal N. Feimster, *Southern Horrors: Women and the Politics of Rape and Lynching* (Cambridge: Harvard University Press, 2011).

12. Jonathan Gottschall, "Explaining Wartime Rape," *Journal of Sex Research* 41 (2004): 129–136.

13. Crystal N. Feimster, "Rape and Justice in the Civil War," *The New York Times.* April 25, 2013. Accessed February 11, 2015. http://opinionator.blogs.nytimes.com/2013/04/25/rape-and-justice-in-the-civil-war/?_php=true&_type=blogs&_r=0.

14. Jacquelyn Dowd Hall, "The Mind That Burns in Each Body: Women, Rape, and Racial Violence," in *Desire: The Politics of Sexuality*, edited by Ann Snitow, Christine Stansell, and Sharon Thompson, 339–360. London: Virago, 1983.

15. Greensite (2014).

16. Dowd Hall, 340.

17. Gerda Lerner, *Black Women in White America: A Documentary History* (New York: Vintage, 1992).

18. James Gilbert Ryan, "The Memphis Riots of 1866: Terror in a Black Community During Reconstruction," *The Journal of Negro History* 62 (1977): 243–257.

19. Hannah Rosen, *Terror in the Heart of Freedom: Citizenship, Sexual Violence, and the Meaning of Race in the Postemancipation South* (Chapel Hill: University of North Carolina Press, 2009).

20. McGuire (2011).

21. Estelle B. Freedman, *Redefining Rape* (Boston: Harvard University Press, 2013).

22. Rose Stremlau, "Rape Narratives on the Northern Paiute Frontier: Sarah Winnemucca, Sexual Sovereignty, and Economic Autonomy, 1844–1891," In *Portraits of Women in the American West*, ed. Dee Garceau, 37–60 (New York: Routledge, 2005).

23. Andrea Smith, *Sexual Violence and American Indian Genocide* (New York: McGraw Hill, 1999: 274).

24. Jennifer Bailey, "Voicing Oppositional Conformity: Sarah Winnemucca and the Politics of Rape, Colonialism, and "Citizenship": 1870–1890" (PhD Diss., 2012).

25. Bailey.

26. Joy James, *Resisting State Violence: Radicalism, Gender, and Race in U.S. Culture* (Minneapolis, University of Minnesota Press, 1996).

27. McGuire (2011).

28. Cynthia Gordy, "Recy Taylor: A Symbol of Jim Crow's Forgotten Horror," *The Root*, February 9, 2011. Accessed Janary 25, 2013. http://www.theroot.com/articles/culture/2011/02/recy_taylor_a_symbol_of_jim_crows_forgotten_horror.html.

29. McGuire (2011): xvii.

30. McGuire (2011): 58.

31. McGuire (2011): 130.

32. Quoted in McGuire (2011): 130.

33. McGuire (2011).

34. Wikipedia and other online resources inaccurately place the beginning of anti-rape efforts in the United States in the 1970s.

35. Susan Brownmiller, *Against Our Will: Men, Women, and Rape* (New York: Simon and Schuster, 1975) 208–209.

36. Nancy A. Matthews, *Confronting Rape: The Feminist Anti-Rape Movement and the State* (New York: Routledge, 1994).

37. Nancy A. Matthews, *Confronting Rape: The Feminist Anti-Rape Movement and the State* (London: Routledge, 1994).

38. Quoted in Jodi Gold and Susan Villari, *Just Sex: Students Rewrite the Rules on Sex, Violence, Equality, and Activism* (New York: Rowman & Littlefield, 1999), p. xii.

39. Greensite, "History of the Rape Crisis Movement."

40. The Feminist Alliance Against Rape, "Initial Invitation Letter (Untitled)." July 30, 1974, accessed on April 12, 2015, http://www.faar-aegis.org/Intro_74/intro_74.html.

41. Matthews, *Confronting Rape.*

42. Joan Zorza, *Violence Against Women, Volume III*. Civic Research Institute, 2006, accessed on March 8, 2016, http://www.civicresearchinstitute.com/toc/VAWA_VOL3_frontmatter.pdf.

43. Charisse Jones, "Nicole Simpson, in Death, Lifting Domestic Violence to the Forefront as National Issue," *New York Times*, October 13, 1995. Accessed December 20, 2017, http://www.nytimes.com/1995/10/13/us/nicole-simpson-death-lifting-domestic-violence-forefront-national-issue.html?pagewanted=all.

44. Ashley Parker, "House Renews Violence Against Women Measure," *The New York Times*, February 28, 2013. Accessed on June 11, 2015, http://www.nytimes.com/2013/03/01/us/politics/congress-passes-reauthorization-of-violence-against-women-act.html?pagewanted=all.

45. National Center for Education Statistics, "Digest of Education Statistics," accessed April 15, 2017, https://nces.ed.gov/programs/digest/d99/d99t187.asp.

46. Ibid.

47. Jodi Gold and Susan Villari, *Just Sex: Students Rewrite the Rules on Sex, Violence, Equality, and Activism* (New York: Rowman & Littlefield, 1999).

48. Ibid.

49. Ibid.

50. Ibid.

51. Robin Warshaw, *I Never Called It Rape* (New York: Harper Collins, 1994).

52. Warshaw (1994): 57.

53. Warshaw (1994): 11.

54. Quoted in Gold and Villari (1999): xii.

55. As quoted in William Celis, "Date Rape and a List at Brown." *New York Times*, November 18, 1990. Accessed April 15, 2017, http://www.nytimes.com/1990/11/18/us/date-rape-and-a-list-at-brown.html.

56. Gold and Villari (1999): xx.

57. Gold and Villari (1999): xxi.

58. Gold and Villari (1999): p. xxi.

59. *New York Times*, "'Ask First' at Antioch," October 11, 1993. Accessed April 30, 2017, http://www.nytimes.com/1993/10/11/opinion/ask-first-at-antioch.html.

60. Quoted in Nicolaus Mills, "How Antioch College Got Rape Right 20 Years Ago," *The Daily Beast*, December 10, 2014, accessed April 30, 2017, http://www.thedailybeast.com/articles/2014/12/10/how-antioch-solved-campus-sexual-offenses-two-decades-ago.

61. Alexandra Neame, "Revisiting America's 'Date Rape' Controversy," *Family Matters* 68 (2004): 55.

62. Katie Roiphe, *The Morning After: Fear, Feminism, and Sex* (New York: Back Bay Books, 1994).

63. Roiphe, (1994): p.54.

64. Roiphe, (1994).

65. Neame, (2004).

66. Ibid.

67. Gold and Villari, (1999): xvi.

68. This comment was made by Annie Clark in *The Hunting Ground* (The Weinstein Company).

Chapter Three

"Silence Has the Rusty Taste of Shame"

The New Campus Anti-Rape Movement

In 1990, students at Brown University wrote the names of alleged rapists on stalls and walls in women's bathrooms on campus to warn others. In 2017, rapist lists again appeared on bathroom stalls at Brown University,[1] but this time, students at the school were not alone in using this approach to raise awareness of campus sexual violence. Students at Columbia University listed the names of students who had been found responsible for sexual misconduct but were allowed to remain or return to campus. Over the period of about a week, university officials quickly scrubbed the lists every time they were put up, so students distributed flyers that named students who have been found responsible for sexual misconduct.[2] Later that year, students at the University of Chicago circulated the Hyde Park List of male students known for having perpetrated rape or sexual assault.[3] This list was initially posted to the online blog site Tumblr by a person who remained anonymous, but it was quickly removed after it received widespread media attention. Students then posted paper copies of the rapist list around campus with the most serious offenders as "red," while others received an orange designation.

Following list actions at Brown University, Columbia University, and the University of Chicago, students on campuses across the country have re-created rapist lists in their own ways, using printed flyers, chalking on the campus quad, and in online forums such as Facebook and Tumblr. The aim of rapist list vigilante activism—students warning the community about perpetrators when the institution does not do enough to keep the campus safe—is the same today as it was when feminists at Brown University first took a

41

marker to the bathroom walls and stalls nearly three decades ago. But rapist list activism is more common today, and it has a wider reach given the use of social media to spread the word and the new CARM.

Activists have been organized in the fight against sexual violence in the United States for the past 150 years. Activists have been organized on college campuses for the past 50 years, but what is happening now is different. According to longtime sexual violence activist S. Daniel Carter, "It's unlike anything I've ever seen."[4] This new wave of activism is characterized by the use of new tools (e.g., federal complaints, lawsuits, group and social media), the networked nature of the movement, and intense media coverage of and public interest in the issue. This new campus anti-rape movement has been more successful than previous efforts since, for the first time in our nation's history, campus sexual assault/rape became a national policy priority. In January of 2014, President Obama credited "an inspiring wave of student-led activism" for putting the issue on the agenda.[5]

This chapter follows the rise of the new CARM with a detailed timeline of events and the major players that catapulted this issue onto the national policy agenda. It describes legal efforts in the 1990s and early 2000s to get Title IX applied to campus rape, and student use of Title IX complaints throughout the 2000s to get the Department of Education to pay attention to the issue. We spotlight key activists whose work led up to the new CARM, those who launched the movement in 2013, and activists that have carried the momentum forward since 2013. This chapter also describes the tools of the movement—federal complaints, group lawsuits, and social media campaigns. We conclude with a look at whose voices are heard in the movement, and why this matters.

THE NEW CARM TIMELINE

The story of the new anti-rape movement on campus is the story of survivor activists networking in new ways that were not possible in previous peaks of activism around this issue. It is also the story of using social media and other online networking tools to share personal experiences that were previously hidden. Activists strategically used a wave of Title IX complaints coupled with social media shaming to garner press attention that then sparked a national dialogue about the issue. In this section, we outline the key moments and people that propelled the new CARM. We place the start of the movement proper in 2013 when a flurry of federal complaints attracted mainstream media coverage and widespread public attention. But first, we start with a crucial case in 1980 that established the argument that campus sexual harassment/violence violates federal law.

The Yale Case (1980)

Feminist legal scholar Catharine MacKinnon made the first legal push for considering sexual harassment on college campuses a form of gender discrimination.[6] As a law school student at Yale in the mid-1970s, MacKinnon advised a group of undergraduate women to file a lawsuit after multiple experiences of sexual harassment, such as male professors propositioning them for sexual favors in exchange for higher grades. The legal argument behind *Alexander v. Yale* (1980) was that sexual harassment interfered with women's educational experience, and as such, was a violation of Title IX that mandates a gender equitable learning environment.[7] A federal court dismissed the case because most of the plaintiffs had graduated, but this legal loss was still a victory for MacKinnon and the students she advised. Yale created harassment reporting procedures and a grievance board to hear cases, and hundreds of other colleges and universities followed suit.

The Lehigh University Case (1986)

In 1986, 19-year-old Jeanne Ann Clery was a first-year student at Lehigh University, a school nestled in the scenic, rolling hills of rural Pennsylvania. Her parents, Constance and Howard Clery, encouraged their daughter to choose Lehigh University over Tulane University in New Orleans because they thought this East Coast campus would be safer. Fellow student Josoph M. Henry raped and murdered Clery in her third-floor dorm room in April of 1986. He was able to get into the building through doors that were propped open with pizza boxes.[8]

During Henry's trial, Jeanne's parents learned of the college's security lapses and also discovered that 38 violent crimes had occurred on or near the campus in the three years leading up to their daughter's death. The Clerys were also shocked to discover that campus administrators were not required to report campus crimes to incoming students and parents. They brought a $25 million lawsuit against Lehigh University and used the settlement proceeds to start Security on Campus, Inc., the most effective non-profit clearinghouse of information on campus crime.[9] This non-profit organization, now called The Clery Center, assists campus officials with the training and resources they need to get in compliance with crime prevention and reporting laws.

The Clery Center lobbied to pass legislation in the state of Pennsylvania mandating that schools report campus crimes. They went on to successfully lobby for passage of federal guidelines—the Jeanne Clery Disclosure of Campus Security Policy and Campus Crime Statistics Act of 1990, referred to as the Clery Act.[10] It applies to public and privates colleges and universities that receive funds from the federal government, such as financial aid.

Virtually every school out of the 7,500 institutions of higher education in the United States receives some sort of federal funding, whether they are public or private. The Clery Act requires campuses to maintain and report information about eight different types of crimes that occur on and near campus:[11]

1. Criminal Homicide
2. Sex Offenses
3. Robbery
4. Aggravated Assault
5. Burglary
6. Motor Vehicle Theft
7. Arson
8. Domestic Violence, Dating Violence, and Stalking[12]

Schools are required to maintain a daily crime log and publish an annual crime security report on October 1st of each year that furnishes the total number and locations of crimes that occurred on or near campus during the previous calendar year. Colleges are also required to issue Timely Warnings for crimes they consider to be an "ongoing threat" to the safety of the campus, for example, someone stealing laptops from dorm rooms. The Clery Act allows the ED to impose civil penalties against schools for up to $35,000 per infraction.[13] The ED can also suspend federal funds, including critical research dollars, from institutions that are not in Clery compliance.[14]

In 1992, the Clery Act was amended to include the Campus Sexual Assault Victims' Bill of Rights. This amendment requires that colleges and universities receiving federal funds must provide basic rights to both parties during the sexual assault adjudication process. More specifically, both the complainant (alleged victim) and the respondent (alleged perpetrator) must have the same opportunity to have other parties present; both parties must be informed of the outcome of proceedings, counseling options, and options for changing academic and living arrangements; and the complainant must be informed of his or her option to file a complaint with local law enforcement. In summary, the Sexual Assault Victims' Bill of Rights requires schools to notify complainants of their options, provide a fair adjudication, and provide support services.

The Clery Act and the Sexual Assault Victims' Bill of Rights were pivotal as the first national laws that specifically pertain to crime on campus, and sexual crime on campus, respectively. When the new CARM got under way in earnest in 2013, many school officials responded to heated activism with the claim that they were unaware of Clery mandates. Their ignorance of the issue is simply not plausible given that campus sexual violence was identified as a problem by researchers in 1957, established as an epidemic in data published and debated in the 1980s, and codified into law as a problem with the Clery Act in 1990. Claims by administrators that campus rape is a newly discovered problem are disingenuous.

The Evergreen State College Case (1995)

The other major law that applies to sexual violence on campus is Title IX, the educational amendments of 1972 that require that no student be subjected to discrimination in schools due to their sex.[15] In other words, schools are required to provide a gender equitable learning environment and the fact that female students face a much higher risk of sexual violence on campus means rape and sexual assault can preclude this equity. Title IX complaints in the 1990s and early 2000s established that this body of law, which was typically applied to gender equity in sports, could also be applied to sexual misconduct cases. In 2001, the Department of Education (ED)[16] formally included sexual misconduct as a violation of Title IX, and in 2011, the ED issued guidelines for how schools should address sexual misconduct. (We explore the legal landscape that was crucial to the new CARM in the following chapter in greater detail.)

Title IX was initially extended to sexual harassment cases in academia, and later, to sexual assault, which was considered a form of sexual harassment. The first known application to sexual assault was in 1995 when the ED found that Evergreen State College failed to provide a prompt and equitable resolution to a student's assault claim against a professor.[17] The case involved a student enrolled in a Quantum Theory Physics class that met once a week in the professor's home.[18] The student was also enrolled in a theater class, and she was flattered when the professor offered to look at a screenplay she had written. She met the professor at his house to receive feedback on the play, during which time he kissed her. The student told the professor she did not want to have a romantic relationship with him, but he persisted in romantically pursuing her. She filed a complaint against the professor, and the college found that the professor had made unwelcome sexual advances that "interfered with the student's academic environment." The professor rejected the allegations and refused to participate in a sanctions hearing. The college responded with a subsequent investigation in which they ruled in the professor's favor.

The ED found that the process the college used that ultimately ruled in the professor's favor violated the "preponderance of evidence" (more likely than not that the incident happened) standard set forth for Title IX cases. Additionally, the ED determined that Evergreen State College failed to consider the considerable power differential between the professor and the student in their finding. The college and the ED reached a resolution that Evergreen would implement new adjudication procedures to gain Title IX compliance. Very little was publicly known about this case at the time, so it did not incite a national wave of similar Title IX complaints involving sexual misconduct. It did, however, establish that Title IX could also be applied to sexual assault, considered a subset of sexual harassment.

The Eastern Michigan University Case (2007)

Another key development that was crucial to the new CARM was the 2008 revision to the Clery Act to protect crime victims and "whistleblowers" from retaliation from school officials. This amendment makes it unlawful for colleges and universities to retaliate against any individual for reporting a crime or revealing that their school is not in compliance with Clery.[19]

This change to the Clery Act was prompted by the tragic case of Laura Dickerson, an undergraduate student at Eastern Michigan University, who was raped and murdered in her dorm room by a fellow student in 2007.[20] It took university officials ten weeks to tell Dickinson's parents and the campus community the truth of what had happened, opting instead to say that she had died from natural causes and that there was "no reasons to suspect foul play."[21] Three university officials were fired over the cover-up, including the college president.[22] Dickerson's case not only strengthened existing Clery protections for whistleblowers, it also sent a clear message that colleges could no longer sweep these cases under the rug. The cover-up in Dickerson's case drew national outrage, and administrators at other colleges and universities took notice of the new environment of public accountability.

The Harvard Case (2002)

In 2002, pioneering feminist attorney Wendy Murphy used Title IX to overturn Harvard's requirement that survivors provide "independent corroboration" of their rape from a third party.[23] This case relied on legal arguments from MacKinnon in *Alexander v. Yale*, and was a game-changer in several ways. First, Murphy's Title IX complaint successfully overturned a provision that prevented the vast majority of rape cases to even be adjudicated at Harvard (since most sexual assaults and rapes are not witnessed by a third party). Secondly, Murphy's complaint also established the precedent that anyone could file a complaint on behalf of an aggrieved party, thereby taking the filing burden off the shoulders of survivors who may face public scrutiny and retaliation.[24] Murphy found a way for interested parties to advocate on behalf of injured parties who may not be in a good position to advocate for her- or himself. Prior to this time, many survivors were effectively barred from seeking justice because they were not able to juggle the trauma of their violation with classes and the drafting and filing of a federal complaint. Murphy's complaint also ensured that professionals with legal experience and training could get involved in filing federal complaints.

Murphy, an adjunct professor of sexual violence at the New England Law School, worked as a sex crimes and child abuse prosecutor prior to becoming an academic.[25] She founded the Victim Advocacy & Research group in 1992 to provide pro bono legal services to victims, and frequently appears as a legal analyst on CNN, Fox News, and MSNBC. Murphy was teaching at Harvard when she filed a complaint against the institution after hearing from survivors about the flawed adjudication process.

In 2010, Murphy filed new Title IX complaints against Harvard, Princeton, and the University of Virginia for troubling patterns in their handling of sexual assault/rape cases.[26] Her cases received favorable findings for survivors at Harvard and Princeton, and the Virginia case remains under investigation. In 2012, Harvard Law School student Kamilah Willingham filed yet another Title IX complaint against the institution for its handling of a 2011 sexual assault from a fellow law school student, and the ED again found the school in violation of Title IX.

Figure 3.1.   Wendy Murphy, Early CARM Architect. *Wendy Murphy*

The University of Madison-Wisconsin Case (2006)

For a decade after the Evergreen case, the ED opened only two Title IX cases per year that involved sexual assault/rape, and very few of these cases resulted in sanctions against schools.[27] A handful of intrepid survivor activists filed Title IX cases involving sexual violence during the 2000s, but with limited success. From 1998 to 2008, the ED found in favor of the university 19 times out of 24 complaints filed.[28] Few details are known about most of these cases since virtually every survivor was anonymous.

Laura Dunn was one survivor who filed a complaint in the 2000s and went public. In 2006, Dunn, a student at the University of Wisconsin, filed a Title IX complaint against the school for failing to conduct a timely investigation of her rape at the hands of two rowing crewmates.[29] The college took nine months to decide that they would not investigate the case because Dunn could not provide eyewitnesses to the rape other than those involved, a requirement that looked oddly similar to the Harvard standard that the ED had struck down in 2002. However, the ED ruled in the University's favor and determined that the school's nine month deliberation and failure to investigate were "reasonable."

Dunn's case became a lightning rod for critics of how administrations fail to hold perpetrators accountable. Dunn's advocate in the case was S. Daniel Carter, a longtime campus violence advocate who had worked for The Clery Center during its early years. Years earlier, he had developed the first national program to provide legal and other support services to campus rape survivors. After experiencing injustice at her college, Dunn would go on to complete a law degree and found the organization SurvJustice, a non-profit organization serving campus sexual assault survivors. Carter is on the SurvJustice board of directors. Both Dunn and Carter played a critical role in the build up to the new CARM.

The Tufts University Case (2009)

In 2009, Wagatwe Wanjuki filed a Title IX complaint against Tufts University for their failed handling of her report of an abusive relationship involving sexual assault.[30] Wanjuki reported that she was sexually assaulted multiple times by a fellow student with whom she was in a relationship, and that administrators failed to open an investigation or take any preventative action. Wanjuki was a social media pioneer in the new CARM—the first to use an online space to spread awareness of the problem. She started the blog "Raped at Tufts" that detailed her violation and the school's ensuing betrayal. Wanjuki later filed a Title IX complaint with the ED over her school's failure to investigate and adjudicate her complaint, but the Office for Civil Rights branch of the ED declined to investigate her case, citing a technicality in

Figure 3.2. S. Daniel Carter, Early CARM Architect. *S. Daniel Carter*

terms of when it was filed. In 2013, Wanjuki worked with other survivor activists to put pressure on the ED to respond more quickly to Title IX investigations, and in 2015, she founded Survivors Eradicating Rape Culture, a non-profit organization to combat campus sexual violence through social media campaigns.

The Notre Dame Case (2010)

In 2010, Notre Dame made national headlines after a rape survivor committed suicide. Lizzy Seeberg, a country music lover who was buried in her
cowgirl hat,[31] was a student at Saint Mary's College (a women's college
affiliated with Notre Dame University). She took her own life just ten days
after reporting that she was sexually assaulted by Prince Shembo, a Notre
Dame football player.[32] After reporting the incident, Seeberg faced a wave of
harassment from students and football fans who smeared her as emotionally
troubled and sexually aggressive.[33] A friend of Shembo sent Seeberg threat-

Figure 3.3.   Wagatwe Wanjuki, CARM Social Media Pioneer. *S. Wagatwe
Wanjuki*

ening messages, including one that said "Messing with Notre Dame football is a bad idea." [34]

Notre Dame dragged their feet in protecting Seeberg from harassment and in investigating the complaint. School officials did not interview Shembo until five days after Seeberg took her life—a full fifteen days after she filed the complaint. According to retired Notre Dame security officer, Pat Cottrell, the alleged perpetrator's status as a star athlete at a campus known for its football team played a role in the institutional response. Cottell told a reporter that if the alleged perpetrator was "Just a regular Joe, if they were working a job on campus, I could go there and say, 'Hey, I need to talk to you.'" But with athletes, "if they don't respond, they don't respond, and that makes it harder to do your job." [35]

After Seeberg's death, the local prosecutor decided not to bring charges, "as expected in a case without a living victim." [36] Shembo's lawyer continued to malign Seeberg's character by suggesting that she could not have been sexually assaulted because she was sexually aggressive ("she was being rather forward and dancing with the young man; she was dancing for him."). Shembo's lawyer also implied that Seeberg was racist (she was white, the football player was black), a liar, and was too mentally ill to be away at college. [37] National news attention raised public outrage at the retaliatory harassment Seeberg experienced and Notre Dame's failure to protect her and properly investigate the case. Shembo went on to play in the National Football League. [38]

The Yale University Case (2011)

On March 15, 2011, on the heels of Murphy's second Harvard complaint, Yale students Alexandra Brodsky and Hannah Zeavin filed a Title IX complaint against Yale University. [39] This complaint, filed on behalf of fifteen current and former students, detailed many troubling instances of a sexually hostile environment. For example, fraternity members gathered outside a frosh dorm yelling "No means yes, and yes means anal" and "My name is Jack, I'm a necrophiliac, I fuck dead women and fill them with my semen!"; a fraternity shouting "dick, dick, dick!" in front of the Yale Women's Center; a 2007 petition signed by 150 medical students alleging groping, verbal abuse, and rape; and an email ranking 53 first-year female students by "how many beers it would take to have sex with them." The ED promptly opened an investigation into Yale's handling of sexual violence, and the school entered a resolution agreement, the outcome of which was deemed insufficient two years later by the campus activists who filed the complaint.

A month after activists filed the Yale complaint, the ED issued the Dear Colleague Letter (DCL) detailing new guidelines for Title IX application to sexual assault/rape issues. Even though the Clery Act had been on the books for two decades, these new Title IX guidelines shifted the legal terrain. The timing of the DCL was fortuitous for the Yale University survivor activists, but it was not the catalyst for the DCL. Wendy Murphy's decade of Title IX activism prompted the ED to finally issue guidelines on how this body of law pertaining to equitable learning environments applies to campus sexual violence. After the DCL made it clear that the ED would now formally treat sexual violence as a Title IX issue, student activism around the issue started percolating across the nation. For example, in March of 2011, students at Dickinson College organized a march and a sit-in to demand college administrators provide greater transparency in the sexual assault adjudication process, a more effective rape prevention program, and expulsion for students found responsible for sexual assault and rape. [40]

The Amherst Cases (2012)

The Yale complaint received some press coverage, but media attention to campus rape reached its first high in October of 2012 when Amherst College sophomore Angie Epifano published a personal account of her rape in the student newspaper. Her critique mostly centered on the school's institutional betrayal after she reported her experience:

> I am sickened by the Administration's attempts to cover up survivors' stories, cook their books to discount rapes, pretend that withdrawals never occur, quell attempts at change, and sweep sexual assaults under a rug. . . . Why should we be quiet about sexual assault? "Silence has the rusty taste of shame."[41]

Epifano's letter inspired a massive outpouring of public attention and marked a turning point because it inspired so many other survivors to go public with their experiences. The more survivors spoke up, the more survivors were inspired to speak up. Social media allowed a student newspaper article to go viral, and Epifano's words served as a catalyst for many other survivors to find their public voice.

Earlier that same year, Trey Malone, a recent Amherst University graduate took his life in the wake of trauma from a rape he experienced at the school. In his suicide note, he blamed the school's institutional betrayal for amplifying his trauma:

> What began as an earnest effort to help on the part of Amherst, became an emotionless hand washing. In those places I should've received help, I saw none. I suppose there are many possible reasons for this. But in the end, I'm still here and so too is that night. I hold no ill will nor do I place an iota of blame upon my family. I blame a society that remains unwilling to address sexual assault and rape. One that pays some object form of lip service to the idea of sexual crimes while working its hardest to marginalize its victims. One

where the first question a college president can pose to me, regarding my own assault is, "Have you handled your drinking problem?"[42]

When Epifano's op-ed went viral, Malone's story also received attention given the overlap in how the school responded. Epifano's case was the first high-profile case to document the day-to-day trauma survivors may experience, and Malone's case was the first prominent case involving a male campus survivor. Online narratives of sexual violence and institutional betrayal are unique to the new CARM, and Epifano and Malone's voices caused a snowball effect of public survivorship.

First Wave of Complaint Filings (2013)

In January of 2013, University of North Carolina-Chapel Hill students Landen Gambill, Andrea Pino, and alum Annie Clark, filed Title IX and Clery complaints on behalf of 64 other students and alums alleging egregious mishandling of sexual assault/rape cases.[43] In February of 2013, over 300 students at Occidental College marched to demand that the college provide better transparency and adjudication of sexual violence on campus. By March of 2013, faculty and students at Occidental College filed Title IX and Clery complaints advancing claims of 37 survivors that the institution had failed to prevent and properly respond to instances of sexual violence.

In the summer of 2013, Occidental College faculty members Caroline Heldman and Danielle Dirks named and registered End Rape on Campus (EROC), the first CARM organization established to offer direct support for filing Title IX and Clery complaints. They launched the organization with a small group of student activists from schools across the country: Andrea Pino (UNC-Chapel Hill), Mia Ferguson (Swarthmore), Sophie Karasek (UC-Berkeley), Audrey Logan (Occidental College), Kristin Brown (Occidental College), and Annie Clark (UNC-Chapel Hill).[44] This organization initiated the first wave of federal complaints that drew intense public attention to the new CARM.

In addition to the UNC-Chapel Hill and Occidental College filings, survivor activists filed federal complaints against Swarthmore College (filed by Ferguson and Hope Brinn), the University of Southern California (filed by Alexa Schwartz and Tucker Reed), the University of California-Berkeley (filed by Karasek and Haley Broder), Dartmouth College (filed by Nastassja Schmiedt, Lea Roth, Nina Rojas, and others), the University of Connecticut (filed by Carolyn Luby), Vanderbilt (filed by Sarah O'Brien), Emerson (filed by Sarah Tedesco), the University of Colorado, Boulder (filed by Sarah Gilchriese), and Amherst College (filed by Epifano).

This emerging network of activists, connected via social media sites like Facebook, began to organize and strategize about the best ways to bring

Figure 3.4.   Mia Ferguson, Cofounder, End Rape on Campus. *Mia Ferguson*

attention to campus sexual violence. The first wave of filings was a tactic to gain legitimacy for the concerns of the movement, to demonstrate that campus violence is a national problem, and to garner media attention. And it worked. By late 2013, the coverage of campus rape increased eight times over (figure 3.7).[45]

Figure 3.5. Haley Broder, Activist Who Filed a Title IX Complaint Against UC-Berkeley. *Haley Broder*

Second Wave of Filings (2014)

A second wave of filings occurred in 2014 with the University of Texas Pan American (filed by Joanna Espinosa), the University of Akron (filed by Julia Dixon), Hobart & William Smith Colleges (filed by Jane Doe), Iowa State (filed by Jane Doe), Northeastern University (filed by Katherine Rizzo), Pace University (filed by Jane Doe), University of Tennessee at Chattanooga (filed by Molly Morris), and dozens of other institutions. By the end of 2014, the ED had 110 open Title IX investigations involving sexual misconduct.[46] By 2016, the number of Title IX investigations would top 200.[47] The strategic use of federal complaints to put the issue on the national agenda was highly effective, but it extended the average length of time for investigations

Figure 3.6.   Alexa Schwartz, Activist Who Filed a Title IX Complaint Against USC. *Alexa Schwartz*

from about one year to four years[48] (which means that most survivors from the first and second wave of filings are still awaiting the outcome of their investigation).

The Columbia University Case (2014)

In April of 2014, Emma Sulkowicz, a senior visual arts major at Columbia University, filed a complaint with the school that fellow senior, Paul Nungesser, had raped her in her dorm room two years prior.[49] The University's investigation found Nungesser "not responsible" through the campus adjudication process. Sulkowicz also filed charges with the New York Police Department, but withdrew the charges upon discovery that the case would extend well past her graduation date. In response to what Sulkowicz perceived as institutional betrayal from Columbia University, she created a senior thesis titled *Mattress Performance (Carry That Weight)*. This performance entailed carrying a 50-pound mattress—similar to the one on which she was raped—to and from class, and even across the platform at graduation. Hundreds of students helped her "carry that weight" during the project, and it garnered national media attention and the label "mattress girl."

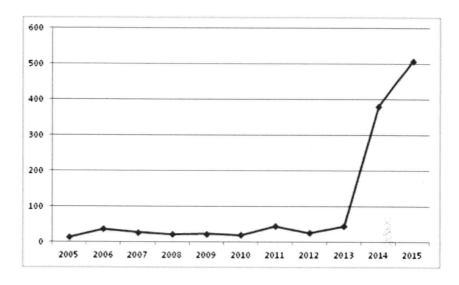

Figure 3.7.   Number of Stories about "Campus Rape" in U.S. Newspapers, 2005–2015. *Created by the authors*

Sulkowicz's performance raised awareness of the already prescient issue of campus rape even further. Her performance piece was the physical representation of the struggle that so many survivors were readily sharing in social media posts and media interviews, so it resonated with many students and survivor activists. The creativity of *Carry That Weight* drew more media attention than had been given to any previous Title IX filings. In short, "mattress girl" made campus rape water cooler conversation across the United States. This attention signaled that the new CARM was part of the national dialogue.

The University of Virginia Case (2014)

The momentum of the new CARM came to a rapid (albeit temporary) halt in late 2014 when *Rolling Stone* published "A Rape on Campus," an account of an alleged gang rape at the University of Virginia.[50] In the story, "Jackie" claimed that seven members of Phi Kappa Psi raped her as part of an initiation ritual. The story framed some of "Jackie's" friends and campus officials as cold and unsupportive after the rape. The fraternity immediately disputed the story, and some investigative news organizations looked into the case and quickly found discrepancies in "Jackie's" account that raised suspicion. Within a matter of weeks, many of the key facts that "Jackie" laid out were discredited and *Rolling Stone* retracted the story.

Figure 3.8.   Emma Suklowitz, "Mattress Girl," 2014. *Emma Sulkowicz, Mattress Performance (Carry That Weight), 2014–2015. Self-portrait in studio. Photo: Emma Sulkowicz*

Three lawsuits have been filed against the publication and author Sabrina Erdley: one by three fraternity members; another by the UVA chapter of Phi Kappa Psi; and a third by Nicole P. Eramo, an administrator who was portrayed in a negative light in the article.[51] The lawsuit brought by the fraternity members was dismissed because the story did not actually name any Phi Kappa Psi members, but the UVA chapter of the fraternity has filed a $25 million civil suit against *Rolling Stone* that is still under way. *Rolling Stone* settled with Eramo for an undisclosed amount in 2017.[52]

The UVA case set back the new CARM considerably. The backlash forces that shut down the campus anti-rape activism peak in the 1990s used this case as a means to discredit the entire movement and all survivors. As reporter Arielle Duhaime-Ross put it, "*Rolling Stone* just wrecked an incredible year of progress for rape victims."[53] Internally, CARM activists feared that this story would be *the* story of the movement for the foreseeable future, but this was not to be. While the UVA case made reporters more cautious about double and triple-checking sources and facts, they continued to report on the numerous narratives of rape from survivors who came public in the following years. Most notably, Tyler Kingkade of *The Huffington Post* (and later Buzzfeed) provided the most coverage of the campus rape epidemic, before and after the UVA case. Katie J.M. Baker from Buzzfeed also broke significant stories about sexual violence on campus at the start of the new CARM.

Campus Rape Documentaries (2014–2015)

Two teams of filmmakers began working on projects to tell the story of the campus rape epidemic and the new CARM in 2013.[54] Director Lisa F. Jackson worked with producer Marjorie Schwartz Nielsen to make *It Happened Here*, a heartfelt documentary that followed the stories of Angie Epifano (Amherst University), Sarah O'Brien (Vanderbilt University), Kylie Angell (University of Connecticut), Carolyn Luby (University of Connecticut), and Erica Daniels (University of Connecticut), all of whom were betrayed by their institutions. *It Happened Here* was released in 2014 and has been screened on hundreds of college campuses since.

A second campus rape documentary, *The Hunting Ground*, premiered at the Sundance Film Festival in 2015. It was created by director-producer team Kirby Dick and Amy Ziering whose previous film exposing the rape epidemic in the military, *The Invisible War*, was nominated for an Academy Award. *The Hunting Ground* focused on two out of the dozen or so survivors who launched the first wave of federal complaints in 2013. CNN aired *The Hunting Ground* several times in the fall of 2015, and the new publicity raised awareness of campus rape once again. The data provided in the film put to rest the backlash idea that the campus rape epidemic had been overstated. *The Hunting Ground* renewed the momentum of the new CARM that had slowed after the UVA case.

Stanford University Case (2016)

Public awareness of the campus rape epidemic peaked again in 2016 because of the Stanford rape case. This case involved a decorated athlete, an open-shut case of sexual violence, and Good Samaritans. Two international graduate students from Sweden intervened when they witnessed first-year Stanford student, Brock Turner, sexually violating a half-naked, unconscious woman behind a dumpster on campus.[55] Turner fled the scene, but the Swedes caught up with him and held him until police arrived. Turner had met "Emily Doe" (the survivor) at a party earlier that evening. During the trial, Turner would say he did not know how he and "Emily" arrived behind the dumpster, and "Emily" could not remember anything about the sexual assault. He was

Figure 3.9.   It Happened Here, Campus Rape Documentary, 2014. *http://www.ithappenedhere.org/*

Figure 3.10. The Hunting Ground, Campus Rape Documentary, 2015. *http://the-huntinggroundfilm.com/*

found guilty of three counts of felony sexual assault and faced up to fourteen years in prison.

During the sentencing phase, "Emily" read a victim's statement in court that would soon move a nation to tears. This statement detailed how the sexual assault had ruined her life, beginning with the following words:

> You don't know me, but you've been inside me, and that's why we're here today.
>
> On January 17th, 2015, it was a quiet Saturday night at home. My dad made some dinner, and I sat at the table with my younger sister who was visiting for the weekend. I was working full time and it was approaching my bed time. I planned to stay at home by myself, watch some TV and read, while she went to a party with her friends. Then, I decided it was my only night with her, I had nothing better to do, so why not, there's a dumb party ten minutes from my house, I would go, dance like a fool, and embarrass my younger sister. On the way there, I joked that undergrad guys would have braces. My sister teased me for wearing a beige cardigan to a frat party like a librarian. I called myself "big mama," because I knew I'd be the oldest one there. I made silly faces, let my guard down, and drank liquor too fast not factoring in that my tolerance had significantly lowered since college.
>
> The next thing I remember I was in a gurney in a hallway. I had dried blood and bandages on the backs of my hands and elbow. I thought maybe I had fallen and was in an admin office on campus. I was very calm and wondering where my sister was. A deputy explained I had been assaulted. I still remained calm, assured he was speaking to the wrong person. I knew no one at this party. When I was finally allowed to use the restroom, I pulled down the hospital pants they had given me, went to pull down my underwear, and felt nothing. I still remember the feeling of my hands touching my skin and grabbing nothing. I looked down and there was nothing. The thin piece of fabric, the only thing between my vagina and anything else, was missing and everything inside me was silenced. I still don't have words for that feeling.[56]

Turner's father, Dan Turner, submitted a letter to Judge Aaron Persky asking for leniency for his son that argued that Brock had already paid enough for "20 minutes of action."[57] Judge Persky gave Turner a six month sentence out of concern that a longer sentence would have a "severe impact" on the star swimmer's Olympic ambitions. These seemingly callous actions were widely covered in the press and drew considerable public outrage.

Stanford Law Professor Michelle Dauber was present in the courtroom, and upon hearing "Emily's" statement, she contacted Amy Ziering from *The Hunting Ground* who used her media contacts to publicly share the victim statement. *Buzzfeed* published Emily's statement in full, and news anchor Ashleigh Banfield read "Emily's" letter in full on CNN. "Emily's" statement was then widely disseminated by mainstream media outlets, and public outrage ensued. When Judge Persky sentenced Turner to six months, activists organized a petition to have him recalled from office that has garnered 1.3

million signatures to date.[58] Turner was met by a crowd of protesters when he was released after only three months, having served only half his sentence due to good behavior.

Lady Gaga Oscar Performance (2016)

These are the words of former vice president Joe Biden which were spoken at the 88th Academy Awards in 2016 where he introduced Lady Gaga:

> Despite significant progress over the last few years, too many women and men on and off college campuses are still victims of sexual abuse. Tonight, I'm asking you to join millions of Americans including me, President Obama, the thousands of students I've met on college campuses, and the artists here to-night to take the pledge. A pledge that says I will intervene in situations when consent has not or cannot be given. Let's change the culture. We must and we can change the culture so that no abused women and men like the survivors you will see tonight ever feel they have to ask themselves, "What did I do?" They did nothing wrong.[59]

Following these words, Lady Gaga performed the song "Til It Happens To You," which she co-wrote with Diane Warren, from the documentary *The Hunting Ground*.[60] Lady Gaga performed this song with a stage filled with 50 survivors, many of them new CARM activists. The emotional and power-ful performance put the CARM in the spotlight—roughly 34.4 million people watched the Academy Awards that night. Some of the survivors had written messages on their raised arms, while others displayed tattoos they had gotten in solidarity with one another. Lady Gaga also went public as a survivor the night of the performance, which was the first time her family had heard about her experience. The following day, she posted a photo on Instagram of her experience discussing her rape with her grandmother and her aunt. This post went viral and received a quarter of a million views.

Lady Gaga's emotional performance of "Till It Happens to You" with survivors, and the decision to be a public survivor, brought new attention to the new CARM. There is no good way to measure the impact of these actions, but we assume that Gaga's efforts reached a new, younger audience that was less aware of the issue of campus rape.

NEW CARM TOOLS

The new CARM put campus violence on the national agenda using federal complaints (Title IX and Clery), group lawsuits, and social media shaming.[61] Institutions of higher education are in a difficult position because they are mandated to reduce sexual violence, but each year they inherit a new group of mostly eighteen- and nineteen-year-olds who have grown up in a culture

ladygaga ● · Follow

ladygaga My grandmother (in the middle) and my Aunt Sheri (on the right) both called me the day after the Oscars because I never told them I was a survivor. I was too ashamed. Too afraid. And it took me a long time to even admit it to myself because I'm Catholic and I knew it was evil but I thought it was my fault. I thought it was my fault for ten years. The morning after the Oscars when I talked to my grandmother Ronnie, with tears in her eyes I could hear them welling through the phone she said to me "My darling granddaughter, I've never been more proud of you than I am today." Something I have kept a secret for so long that I was more ashamed of than anything-- became the thing the women in my life were the most proud of. And not just any women, the ones I look up to the most. #BeBrave #speakup

228,556 likes

Figure 3.11.   Lady Gaga's Instagram Post about Being a Survivor, 2016. *Instagram © /ladygaga*

that normalizes sexual violence against women, who are coming from high schools that teach them very little about sexual consent. These challenges, mingled with administrator concerns about school reputation, the high cost of good policies, and a lack of research on best practices for preventing sexual violence, mean that most colleges and universities fail to protect students and continue to betray survivors. The new CARM has focused attention on this problem in a way that no previous activist has, but this new normal did not come quickly or easily.

Yale students, staff, and faculty worked for five years on the issue internally before filing a complaint in 2011. According to Alexandra Brodsky from Yale University, "they were banking on our feminine forgiveness . . . we were supposed to be good little girls."[62] The Oxy Sexual Assault Coalition (OSAC) presented a seven-year timeline of work on the issue leading up to their filing of federal complaints in 2013.[63] U.C. Berkeley activist Sophie Karasek included alums from 1975 in her Title IX complaint with Haley Broder. She stated that schools "respond so poorly because they benefit from the culture of silence that has surrounded sexual assault for so long. It benefits them monetarily to make sure that survivors stay quiet and aren't aware of their rights."[64] Given the fact that most activists are students who typically spend four years on campus, it is no surprise that schools have been able to outmaneuver activists for decades. But activist use of online networking maintained pressure on institutions and government officials, and in 2014, the White House announced that campus rape was a national policy priority.

When it comes to federal complaints, to date, the ED has opened over 200 federal investigations into complaints involving sexual violence on college campuses. The lengthy (now four year) process and historically weak accountability mechanisms of the ED (given limited resources) make federal complaints more effective in putting the new CARM on the agenda, but not very effective in gaining justice for specific survivors. Early CARM activists were aware at the start of the shortcomings of Title IX and Clery complaints to truly hold institutions accountable. Nonetheless, federal complaints served the important functions of establishing campus sexual violence as a national problem and garnering mainstream media attention on the issue.

It is unclear whether the second primary tool of the new CARM—group lawsuits—has brought about institutional change when it comes to preventing campus rape. Students at the University of Connecticut, Occidental College, University of California–Santa Cruz, Baylor University, the University of Oregon, the University of Texas, and other institutions have settled lawsuits costing millions of dollars. In 2013 alone, students and alums from Swarthmore, the University of Southern California, Occidental College, and the University of Connecticut retained well-known women's rights attorney Gloria Allred to represent their interests.[65] To date, ten survivors settled with Occidental College for an undisclosed amount with the college and were required to sign a 15-page non-disclosure agreement that effectively silenced further activism around sexual assault issues.[66] In the spring of 2014, Occidental also settled for an undisclosed amount with three male survivors who alleged sexual battery and sexual assault at the hands of long-time athletic trainer John Sweet.[67] More survivors are filing civil cases over sexual assault/rape than in the past, and most of these cases target institutions that failed to prevent the attack, such as malls, nursing homes, and schools.[68]

In 2017, a graduate of Baylor University filed a lawsuit over her experience of sexual violence on campus, and the suit reports that the football team perpetrated 52 rapes over four years.[69] This case received ample media coverage and raised awareness about the right to sue institutions over their handling of sexual violence. Campuses have been settling with rape survivors over institutional betrayal for at least two decades,[70] and there is no doubt that the volume of cases filed by survivors has increased with the new CARM. With this said, litigation that results in survivors not being able to share the details of their case has also been used by schools as an effective silencing mechanism. On one hand, lawsuits mean that college and universities have to be more concerned about getting sued by survivors. On the other hand, settlements often allow institutions to cover up the full extent of their culpability.

The third primary tool of the new CARM is social media shaming. Wanjuki provided the template for new CARM activism moving forward—the online sharing of personal experience—that would make the efforts far more effective at raising awareness and bringing about policy change than previous efforts. Survivors can now take to social media to raise awareness of specific problems on their campus, and sharing from named and anonymous survivors enables activists to put a human face on the suffering from sexual violence. As we explore in the chapter on shifting technological landscapes, online organizing has made the new CARM effective in ways that nearly half a century of activism around this issue was not. Social media means activists can raise awareness of their plight in new and creative ways. Also, survivor activists can set the terms of the debate and frame the axes of public discussion in ways that mediates against the backlash.

WHOSE VOICES ARE HEARD?

Young people have often been at the forefront of major social movements that have "transformed human history," including the Civil Rights Movement, the Environmental Justice movement, the movement for LBGTQ rights, the Women's Movement, anti-war movements, and immigrant rights movements.[71] The first two authors have participated in anti-rape efforts for decades that were minimally effective, but it took the enthusiasm and hard work of a group of dedicated students to really launch what has unambiguously been the most successful effort to date to address campus sexual assault/rape.[72] The campus anti-rape movement flies in the face of stereotypes of young people being politically inactive "slacktivists." This movement reveals that young people can be innovative, effective agents of change, even on issues where others have been working for decades. Campus activists are using a sophisticated arrangement of formal political and legal tactics (lobbying, filing lawsuits, filing federal complaints, passing new laws, etc.) in tandem with unconventional political tactics (sit-ins, demonstrations, protests, online shaming campaigns, online petitions, etc.). Young people are more likely to engage in unconventional political participation than older generations, and the tactics of the new campus anti-rape movement reflect this.[73]

The networked nature of the movement lends to its diversity of membership. The new CARM is comprised of survivors and a diverse group of allies, including college students, alumni, faculty, a few administrators, bloggers, non-profit organizers, and others. As with most feminist efforts, most of the key players are women, but men and transgender individuals also have a strong voice in the movement.[74] LGBT individuals are also very active organizers, and, as with sexual violence in the United States more broadly, women of color are a leading force in the movement. As with other leaderless, networked movements, the anti-rape movement is highly self-reflexive, meaning that it is constantly questioning its processes and practices.[75] Issues of privilege, dominance, and identity-based disrespect are constantly brought up and grappled with in online movement forums. The new CARM has a class bias given the fact that schools have a strong class bias in terms of who can afford to attend,[76] and early movement activists mostly came from Ivy League schools and expensive liberal arts institutions. However, it quickly and purposefully expanded to public and private institutions of all sizes, rankings, and locations.[77]

Even though the movement is diverse in many ways, it is important to note that the most prominent voices in the struggle belong to white women. This bias stems from who is comfortable speaking and who is listened to the most. Survivors of color, men of all races, and LGBTQ individuals have greater barriers when it comes to speaking up. Coming forward as a survivor is never easy, but survivors who do not fit the media stereotype of a rape survivor (a heterosexual white woman) face even more intense scrutiny and severe and additional consequences for coming forward, outing themselves as victims and survivors, or standing up for themselves and others. We have witnessed firsthand the unique pressures women of color have faced when being the face of the movement—being fired outright, ostracized by the people they thought they could rely on the most, being repeatedly told that they need to support men of color, having administrators engage in protectionism for men of color over their needs, worrying about their families, worrying about their immigration status or those of their families. These structural and organizational issues "permit" only certain women or men (with privilege in various forms) to be able to be out in front.

Similar layers of silence deter male and LGBTQ survivors from being public about their experiences. Regardless of their sexuality, male survivors who are public about experiencing rape or sexual assault run the risk of being seen as weak, violable, feminized in a way that erodes their privileged male status. Male survivors of all races are less likely to report a sexual assault/ rape than female survivors.[78] Survivors are already stigmatized due to unconscious, deep-seated biases that assume they "asked for it" or could/should have done something to prevent their violation, but the additional stigma experienced by male survivors presents yet another barrier to being public about the assault.[79] Some LGBTQ survivors may feel pressure to suffer in silence because they don't want to make the community look bad.[80] Also, most campuses gear their support services to heterosexual female survivors, so heterosexual male survivors and LGBTQ students are not well served, and some service providers have a "serves you right" attitude due to homophobia.[81] Male survivors of color at the intersection of race and sexual status have a particularly difficult time being public about their sexual assault/rape. Despite these barriers, many women of color, men of color, white men, and LGBTQ survivors are speaking up and engaging in incredibly brave and effective work. Indeed, "youth who have to struggle the hardest develop the strongest connections to social movements [and] are also doing some of the most powerful organizing work."[82]

These intersectional silencing barriers are not the only factor in why white women are so prominently featured in media narratives of campus rape. This misrepresentation can be accounted for by the fact that white women are more likely to be listened to, believed, and thought of as sympathetic victims. Black women are stereotyped as domineering, strong, and promiscuous, and are subsequently more likely to be blamed for their sexual assault/rape than white women.[83] Sexual assaults/rapes against women of color are not seen as serious a crime as those involving white women.[84] News reporters are telling stories about people they think their listeners, watchers, and readers will care about, and Americans care more about white women than other survivors.

The first author watched the bias in action at a press conference in New York in June of 2013 when activists from seven different schools gathered. Reporters and photo journalists seemed disinterested in the activists of color who spoke, but when the mic was passed to a thin, conventionally attractive white woman, the sound of camera shutters broke the silence. These reporters did not know who this young woman was or her story, but they were waiting to tell it because of the way she looked. This bias can be effectively addressed if the white women who are garnering media attention insist that other activists are included, and if reporters make a concerted effort to include a diversity of voices in every story they publish.

CONCLUSION

Activists have been organized on college campuses for the past 50 years, but what is happening now is different. Survivor activists have pushed the movement forward by publicly sharing their stories, filing federal complaints, creating online survivor activist spaces, lobbying for better laws, drafting petitions, protesting and demonstrating, filing lawsuits, and many other tactics. The new movement is the most intense, comprehensive campaign against sexual violence on college campuses. Survivors of color, male survivors of all races, and LGBTQ survivors face greater barriers to reporting and speaking out about their experiences, and the movement is self-reflexive about these challenges. The question is whether it will be enough to effectively change powerful institutions of higher education that have been valuing male prerogative and power for centuries.

The new anti-rape movement has been unusually effective in framing this issue, putting it on the public agenda, and shaping the policy response, but the ultimate success of the movement cannot be accurately predicted. It could fail because of a social backlash, pushback from schools, co-optation by the schools and governmental institutions it is trying to reform,[85] the complexity of reform, the difficulty of changing campus culture, and myriad other reasons. On the other hand, the movement could succeed in achieving its dual goals of reducing gendered campus violence and addressing it in a fair and just manner when it occurs. The tenacity of campus activists and the force and attention of the White House and the ED suggest that success is far more likely than failure. The backlash today will be less successful than the backlash of the 1990s because of the force of the feminist blogosphere and the ability of activists to immediately respond in cyberspace. Also, the movement is unlikely to get co-opted by schools or the ED because of its networked, leaderless nature. Even if some individuals are co-opted, meaning that they get invited to "important" meetings where dialogue about the problem stands in for action on the problem, these individuals cannot speak on behalf of the movement or silence other activists.

Our examination of the new movement in this chapter begs the question of why, after nearly five decades of activism, has the new CARM succeeded in ways that previous activism has not. Campus rape has been part of the national conversation before, but it had never been a prominent theme on the national political agenda. The national wave of reform in response to the new CARM is unlike anything we have seen before in both its scope and depth.

Two primary factors make the new CARM the most effective peak of campus anti-rape activism: new legal tools and new technology. Efforts in the early 2000s brought about a new legal landscape that enabled survivor activists to make new claims on institutions pertaining to sexual violence. Additionally, the rise of new online communication technologies and social media enabled survivors to connect, go public, and shape the terms of the debate. We analyze the shifting legal and technological landscape in the following two chapters.

NOTES

1. Gwen Everett, "Lists Alleging Names of Sexual Assaulters Appears in Campus Bathrooms," *The Brown Daily Herald*, April 27, 2017, http://www.browndailyherald.com/2017/04/27/list-alleging-names-sexual-assaulters-appears-campus-bathrooms/.

2. Erin Gloria Ryan, "Here's the 'Rapist List' Flyer Being Anonymously Handed Out at Columbia," Jezebel, May 13, 2014, http://jezebel.com/rapist-list-mysteriously-appearing-in-columbia-universi-1575660992/1575819470.

3. Kate Dries, "University of Chicago Gets Its Own 'Rapist List,'" Jezebel, September 22, 2014, http://jezebel.com/university-of-chicago-gets-its-own-rapist-list-1637594348.

4. Interview with S. Daniel Carter, February, 2014.

5. The White House, "The President and the Vice President Speak on Preventing Sexual Assault," January 22, 2014. Accessed January 22, 2014. http://www.whitehouse.gov/photos-and-video/video/2014/01/22/president-and-vice-president-speak-preventing-sexual-assault#transcript.

6. Tyler Kingkade, "How a Title IX Harassment Case at Yale in 1980 Set the Stage for Today's Sexual Assault Activism," *The Huffington Post*, June 10, 2014. Accessed December 30, 2017, https://www.huffingtonpost.com/2014/06/10/title-ix-yale-catherine-mackinnon_n_5462140.html.

7. Nora Caplan-Bricker, "How Title IX Became Our Best Tool Against Harassment," *New Republic*, June 1, 2012. Accessed December 30, 2017, https://newrepublic.com/article/104237/how-title-ix-became-our-best-tool-against-sexual-harassment.

8. Ken Gross and Andrea Fine, "After Their Daughter Is Murdered at College, Her Grieving Parents Mount a Campaign for Student Safety," *People Magazine*, February 19, 1990. http://www.people.com/people/archive/article/0,,20116872,00.html.

9. "Our History," Clery Center for Security on Campus, 2014. http://clerycenter.org/our-history.

10. "Summary of the Jeanne Clery Act," Clery Center for Security on Campus, 2014. http://clerycenter.org/summary-jeanne-clery-act.

11. "Summary of the Jeanne Clery Act," Clery Center for Security on Campus, 2014. http://clerycenter.org/summary-jeanne-clery-act.

12. The initial Clery Act included only the first seven crime types. This eighth category was added in 2015.

13. Campus Safety, "Clery Act Fine Increases to 35K Per Violation," *Campus Safety Magazine*, 2012. http://www.campussafetymagazine.com/Channel/University-Security/News/2012/10/02/Clery-Act-Fines-Increased-to-35—000-Per-Violation.aspx.

14. Ibid.

15. U.S. Department of Education, "Title IX and Sex Discrimination," Office For Civil Rights. Accessed May 11, 2017, https://www2.ed.gov/about/offices/list/ocr/docs/tix_dis.html.

16. The DOE is the Department of Energy, while ED is the acronym for the Department of Education.

17. This information is based on an interview with S. Daniel Carter, February, 2014. We have no way of knowing whether there were earlier cases since the Department of Education

does not make this information public, and colleges and universities have a vested interest in keeping this information private.

18. Department of Education, "The Evergreen State College," *Office For Civil Rights*, April 4, 1995, https://www2.ed.gov/policy/gen/leg/foia/misc-docs/ed_ehd_1995.pdf.

19. Campus Safety, "Clery Act Needs Whistleblower Protection," *Campus Safety Magazine*, 2007. http://www.campussafetymagazine.com/article/clery-act-needs-whistleblower-protection/Clery_Act,_Director_of_the_Year,_Officers,_Podcast,_Title_IX0.

20. "Summary of the Jeanne Clery Act," Clery Center for Security on Campus, 2014. http://clerycenter.org/summary-jeanne-clery-act.

21. Russell Goldman, "School Accused of Covering Up Student's Murder," *ABCNews.com*, June 20, 2007. http://abcnews.go.com/US/story?id=3296170.

22. P. J. Huffstutter, "3 Lose School Jobs in Slaying Cover-up," *The Los Angeles Times*, July 17, 2007. http://articles.latimes.com/2007/jul/17/nation/na-dickinson17.

23. Wendy Murphy, "Using Title IX's 'Prompt and Equitable' Hearing Requirements to Force Schools to Provide Fair Judicial Proceedings to Redress Sexual Assault on Campus," *New England Law Review* 40, no. 4 (2006): 1007–1022.

24. Wendy Murphy, "The Harsh Truth about Campus Sexual Assault," *wendymurphylaw.com*, February 13, 2013. http://bit.ly/1laLrEd.

25. Wendy Murphy, "About Wendy Murphy," February 27, 2013, accessed May 8, 2017, http://www.wendymurphylaw.com/about/#more-11.

26. Murphy (2013).

27. The Center for Public Integrity, "A Lack of Consequences for Sexual Assault," 2010. http://www.publicintegrity.org/2010/02/24/4360/lack-consequences-sexual-assault-0.

28. Joseph Shapiro, "Campus Rape Victims: A Struggle for Justice," NPR Morning Edition, February 24, 2010, http://www.npr.org/templates/story/story.php?storyId=124001493.

29. Shapiro, (2010).

30. Wagatwe Wanjuki, "Raped at Tufts University," Blog, 2014. http://www.rapedattufts.info/.

31. Ryan Gorman, "Outrage at Football Fan with Sign 'Taunting' Girl who Killed Herself after Alleged Sexual Assault . . .But He Claims He Was Trying To 'Raise Awareness.'" *Daily Mail*, September 8, 2013, Accessed December 30, 2017, http://www.dailymail.co.uk/news/article-2415625/Lizzy-Seeberg-Outrage-football-fan-sign-taunting-girl-killed-herself.html.

32. Dom Cosentino, "This is What Happens When You Accuse a Notre Dame Football Player of Sexually Assaulting You." Deadspin, April 6, 2012. Accessed December 20, 2017, https://deadspin.com/5897809/this-is-what-happens-when-you-accuse-a-notre-dame-football-player-of-sexually-assaulting-you.

33. Ibid.

34. Melinda Henneberger, 2012. "Reported Sexual Assault at Notre Dame Campus Leaves More Questions Than Answers." *National Catholic Reporter*, March 26, accessed December 30, 2017, https://www.ncronline.org/news/accountability/reported-sexual-assault-notre-dame-campus-leaves-more-questions-answers, Internet Page 1.

35. Quoted in Ibid.

36. Henneberger (2012).

37. Ibid.

38. Tom Lighty and Rich Campbell, "Ex-Notre Dame Player's Remarks Reopen Wound," *Chicago Tribune*, February 24, 2014. Accessed December 20, 2017, http://articles.chicagotribune.com/2014—02—26/news/ct-seeberg-interview-met-20140226_1_lizzy-seeberg-tom-seeberg-seeberg-case.

39. Caroline Tan, "Up Close: Title IX, One Year Later," *Yale Daily News*, April 9, 2012, http://yaledailynews.com/blog/2012/04/09/up-close-title-ix-one-year-later/.

40. Anna North, "Students Stage Sit-In to Protest College Sexual Assault Policy," *Jezebel*, March 4, 2011, http://jezebel.com/5776436/students-stage-sit-in-to-protest-college-sexual-assault-policy.

41. Angie Epifano, "An Account of Sexual Assault at Amherst College," *The Amherst Student*, 2011, http://bit.ly/1laUKnL.

42. Trey Malone, suicide note reprinted by *The Good Men Project*, November 5, 2012, https://goodmenproject.com/ethics-values/lead-a-good-life-everyone-trey-malones-suicide-note/#ICFM7hoUxep8iatH.99. This note was reprinted with permission from Malone's family.

43. Tyler Kingkade, "University of North Carolina Routinely Violates Sexual Assault Survivor Rights, Students Claim," *The Huffington Post,* June 20, 2013, http://huff.to/1laVFEK.

44. "Our Team." *End Rape on Campus*, 2013. Accessed June 18, 2014, http://endrapeoncampus.org/our-team/.

45. This search was conducted using Nexis and the search term "campus rape." We found similar results using "campus" and "sexual assault" as the search words.

46. Jake New, "Justice Delayed," *Inside Higher Ed*, May 6, 2015, https://www.insidehighered.com/news/2015/05/06/ocr-letter-says-completed-title-ix-investigations-2014-lasted-more-4-years.

47. Tyler Kingkade, "There Are Far More Title IX Investigations of Colleges Than Most People Know," *The Huffington Post*, June 16, 2016, http://www.huffingtonpost.com/entry/title-ix-investigations-sexual-harassment_us_575f4b0ee4b053d433061b3d.

48. New (2015).

49. Roberta Smith, "In a Mattress, a Lever for Art and Protest," *The New York Times*, September 21, 2014, https://www.nytimes.com/2014/09/22/arts/design/in-a-mattress-a-fulcrum-of-art-and-political-protest.html?_r=0.

50. T. Rees Shapiro, "Hear U-Va.'s 'Jackie' Testify About Rolling Stone Rape Story," *The Washington Post*, October 26, 2016, https://www.washingtonpost.com/news/grade-point/wp/2016/10/26/hear-u-va-s-jackie-testify-about-rolling-stones-gang-rape-story/?utm_term=.fc11d5fa48ff.

51. Shapiro (2016).

52. Matthew Haag, "Rolling Stone Settles Lawsuit Over Debunked Campus Rape Article," *The New York Times*, April 22, 2017, https://www.nytimes.com/2017/04/11/business/media/rolling-stone-university-virginia-rape-story-settlement.html?_r=0.

53. Arielle Duhaime-Ross, "Rolling Stone Just Wrecked an Incredible Year of Progress for Rape Victims," *The Verge*, December 5, 2014, https://www.theverge.com/2014/12/5/7342317/rolling-stone-retraction-rape-blame-consent.

54. The first author worked with both teams of filmmakers. She appears in *The Hunting Ground* as an expert.

55. Stephanie Webber, "Brock Turner's Stanford Rape Case: Everything You Need to Know," *US Weekly*, June 7, 2016, http://www.usmagazine.com/celebrity-news/news/brock-turners-stanford-rape-case-everything-you-need-to-know-w209237.

56. Katie J. M. Baker, "Here is the Powerful Letter the Stanford Victim Read Aloud to her Attacker," *Buzzfeed*, June 3, 2016, https://www.buzzfeed.com/katiejmbaker/heres-the-powerful-letter-the-stanford-victim-read-to-her-ra?utm_term=.daLq52b688#.aiQPLp4r99.

57. Marina Koren, "Telling the Story of the Stanford Rape Case," *The Atlantic*, June 6, 2016, https://www.theatlantic.com/news/archive/2016/06/stanford-sexual-assault-letters/485837/.

58. "Remove Judge Persky from the Bench for Decision in Brock Turner Rape Case," *Change.org*, Accessed May 10, 2017, https://www.change.org/p/california-state-house-impeach-judge-aaron-persky.

59. VP Joe Biden pleads for end of rape culture at Oscars before introducing Lady Gaga and dozens of sexual assault victims on stage. Retrieved on May 5, 2017, from http://www.nydailynews.com/entertainment/oscars/joe-biden-pleads-rape-culture-oscars-article-1.2547155.

60. Nardine Saad, "Lady Gaga's Family Learns of Her Sexual Abuse after Emotional Oscars Performance," *Los Angeles Times*, March 2, 2016, http://www.latimes.com/entertainment/gossip/la-et-mg-lady-gaga-family-sexual-abuse-revelation-oscars-20160302-htmlstory.html.

61. Libby Sander, "White House Raises the Bar for Colleges' Handling of Sexual Assault," *The Chronicle of Higher Education*, April 29, 2014. Accessed April 30, 2014, http://chronicle.com/article/White-House-Raises-the-Bar-for/146255/.

62. Interview with Alexandra Brodsky, December, 2013.

63. "OSAC's 7-Year Timeline," *Oxy Sexual Assault Coalition,* 2013. Accessed June 3, 2014 http://oxysexualassaultcoalition.wordpress.com/timeline/.

64. Interview with Sophie Karasak, December, 2013.

65. CBS Philly, "Complaints Filed Against 4 Colleges Over Rapes, Including Swarthmore," *CBSPhilly.com,* May 22, 2013, http://philadelphia.cbslocal.com/2013/05/22/complaints-filed-against-4-colleges-over-rapes-including-swarthmore-college/.

66. John Wiener, "Rape Settlement at Occidental College: Victims Barred from Campus Activism," *The Nation,* September 19, 2013, http://www.thenation.com/blog/176270/rape-settlement-occidental-college-victims-barred-campus-activism#.

67. Jason Song, "Occidental College Reaches Agreement with Students Who Claimed Harassment," *The Los Angeles Times,* April 4, 2014, http://www.latimes.com/local/la-me-oxy-settlement-20140405-story.html.

68. Ellen Bublick, "Tort Suits Filed by Rape and Sexual Assault Victims in Civil Courts: Lessons for Courts, Classrooms and Constituencies," Arizona Legal Studies Discussion Paper 6, no. 16, (2006).

69. Sara Mervosh, "New Baylor Lawsuit Alleges 52 Rapes by Football Players in 4 Years, 'Show 'em a Good Time' Culture," *The Dallas Morning News,* January 27, 2017, https://www.dallasnews.com/news/baylor/2017/01/27/new-baylor-lawsuit-describes-show-em-good-time-culture-cites-52-rapes-football-players-4-years.

70. Diana Moskovitz, "Why Title IX Has Failed Everyone on Campus Rape," *Deadspin,* July 7, 2016, http://deadspin.com/why-title-ix-has-failed-everyone-on-campus-rape-1765565925.

71. Sasha Constanza-Chock, "Youth and Social Movements: Key Lessons for Allies," *The Kinder & Braver World Project,* December 17, 2012. Accessed June 10, 2014, http://cyber.law.harvard.edu/sites/cyber.law.harvard.edu/files/KBWYouthandSocialMovements 2012_0.pdf.

72. Higher levels of narcissism amongst Millennials may account for the sheer volume of activists in the new CARM. Today's students demanded change when they experienced the same violence that students have experienced for at least half a century. Most scholarship on narcissism emphasizes its downsides, but we see the empowerment of young people, and especially young women, in the face of commonplace sexual violence as a silver lining of historic rates of narcissism.

73. Dominique Apollon, "Millennials, Activism, and Race," *Applied Research Center,* 2012. Accessed June 20, 2014 http://www.arc.org/millenials.

74. Our analysis of the leadership of new CARM organizations indicates that the key players are racially diverse and include people of different genders and sexualities.

75. Manuel Castells, "Networks of Outrage and Hope: Social Movements in the Internet Age" *Polity,* (2012): 225.

76. Melissa Strong, "Educating for Power: How Higher Education Contributes to the Stratification of Social Class," *The Vermont Connection* 28, (2007): 51–59. Accessed March 2, 2014, http://www.uvm.edu/~vtconn/v28/Strong.pdf.

77. This conclusion is based on the observations of the first two authors who initially worked with students and faculty at elite private institutions, then public four-year institutions, and now students at two-year colleges. Survivors have gone public with their voices and activism in every type of institution of higher education.

78. Linda A. Foley, Christine Evancic, Karnik Karnik, Janet King, and Angela Parks, "Date Rape: Effects of Race of Assailant and Victim and Gender of Subjects on Perceptions," *The Journal of Black Psychology* 21, no. 1. (1995): 6–18.

79. Maya Shwayder, "The Same-Sex Domestic Violence Epidemic Is Silent," *The Atlantic,* November 5, 2013. Accessed June 10, 2014, http://www.theatlantic.com/health/archive/2013/11/a-same-sex-domestic-violence-epidemic-is-silent/281131/.

80. Ibid.

81. Ibid

82. Constanza-Chock (2012).

83. Roxanne A. Donovan, "Tough or Tender: (Dis)Similarities in White College Students' Perceptions of Black and White Women," *Psychology of Women Quarterly* 35, no. 3 (2011): 458–468.

84. See Foley et al. (1995).

85. Frances Fox Piven and Richard A. Cloward, *Poor People's Movements: Why They Succeed, How They Fail*, New York: Vintage Books, 1978.

Chapter Four

"You're Not Doing Enough"

The Shifting Legal Landscape

In 2013, after Andrea Pino went public about filing a federal Title IX complaint against the University of North Carolina-Chapel Hill, a dorm common area was vandalized with content intended to target her.[1] The vandal(s) dumped macaroni on the floor, poured cooking oil on the furniture, and drew several pictures of penises. They also left behind a knife they used to carve graffiti. The dorm area housed an exhibit featuring Pino that celebrated the courage of sexual assault survivors, and the vandal(s) defaced the exhibit with the word "whore" and a penis drawing.

In April of 2013, the Department of Education (ED) issued a Dear Colleague Letter (DCL) reminding college and university administrators that it is unlawful to retaliate against CARM activists. The DCL praised survivor activists—"Discriminatory practices are often only raised and remedied when students, parents, teachers, coaches, and others can report such practices to school administrators without the fear of retaliation. Individuals should be commended when they raise concerns about compliance with the federal civil rights laws, not punished for doing so."[2] The DCL went on to talk about existing laws protecting CARM activists from retaliatory acts: "The Federal civil rights laws make it unlawful to retaliate against an individual for the purpose of interfering with any right or privilege secured by these laws. . . . [We] will continue to vigorously enforce this prohibition against retaliation." This DCL is one of many new laws and new emphasis on or interpretations of existing laws that characterize the changing legal terrain of the new CARM.

The campus legal landscape is shifting in ways that now require schools to take sexual violence prevention more seriously. Campus activists are using new laws and new applications of old laws. As laid out in previous chapters, researchers first identified the sexual violence problem on college campuses in 1957, had a national debate about the issue with data that were published in 1985, and passed the first national law to address campus rape (the Clery Act) in 1990. Nonetheless, it took a new interpretation of an old law (Title IX from 1972) for campus officials to finally address the issue in a widespread and sustained manner.

The purpose of this chapter is to describe the shifting legal landscape that facilitated the rise of the new CARM and is now being shaped by it. Campus activists have three primary laws at their disposal to hold schools account-able. Title IX (1972) requires schools to provide a safe and equitable learning environment. The Clery Act (1990) mandates that colleges publish crime data, and The Campus Sexual Violence Elimination Act (SaVE) (2013) re-quires schools to implement programs to prevent sexual crimes on campus. Each of these laws contributes an important piece to the strongest legal patchwork of campus anti-rape laws we have ever had in the United States.

We begin this chapter with a description of the campus adjudication process. This background is necessary in order to understand the significance of these laws. In the second section, we describe and analyze Title IX, the Clery Act, and the SaVE Act to give readers a better understanding of avail-able legal tools. The third section focuses on taking action in the form of filing federal complaints and lawsuits. In the fourth section, we analyze school response to the new anti-rape movement with special emphasis on the financial and reputational constraints these institutions face. In the last sec-tion, we examine why law enforcement is not a viable replacement for cam-pus procedures at this point in time.

CAMPUS ADJUDICATION PROCESS

To fully understand the significance of different campus sexual assault laws, the reader needs a working knowledge of the typical campus adjudication process. Campuses use non-legal terms when referring to the victim (com-plainant) and the alleged perpetrator (respondent) since this is not a legal process. There are generally five stages of filing a formal complaint with a school: reporting, investigation, adjudication, sanctions, and appeals. The process varies widely from institution to institution, but all include these five tasks in their processes. We discuss the possible variations here.

Reporting Stage

In the reporting stage, complainants can file a confidential, anonymous, or formal complaint of sexual violence. Survivors who want to talk about their experience but do not want to formally report it often choose the confidential reporting option. Some complainants choose to file a confidential complaint with designated school employees who are exempt from reporting the incident to other campus officials. Members of the clergy and professional counselors are not required to act upon or share reports of sexual violence they receive from students, so anything a student shares with them can be kept in confidence.[3] This means that instances of sexual violence reported to clergy and professional counselors do not have to appear in annual security reports.

The second option is to report an incident of sexual violence anonymously; meaning that campus officials have been informed of an incident but the school does not have the complainant's name. Only about half of schools in the United States provide an anonymous reporting option,[4] even though this is recommended as a best practice by the ED.[5] Some schools offer anonymous on-line reporting forms where survivors can provide as much information about their experience as they would like, while other schools provide anonymous reporting boxes at different sites on campus. College officials do not formally act upon anonymous complaints, but they are required to report generic information about anonymously reported incidences in crime reports. If school officials receive multiple anonymous reports about a student, they may schedule a meeting to discuss this with the student in question, but anonymous reports cannot be the basis for judicial action against a student.

The third reporting option is to file a formal complaint in person with a college employee in charge of taking reports of sexual violence. Different departments can be tasked with taking reports—campus safety, the Title IX coordinator, the Dean of Students or someone in their office, health center staff, or a person or office specifically designated to handle these claims. For example, at Colorado College, students who have been sexually assaulted or raped are encouraged to call the Sexual Assault Response Coordinator,[6] whereas students at Ohio State University are encouraged to contact the University Police Division.[7] In response to the new CARM and revised federal guidelines, schools are now required to have a designated Title IX officer. This is the person who oversees sexual violence complaints on most campuses today.

As soon as a student files a complaint of sexual violence, the school is required to provide accommodations—counseling and academic support services, etc. Accommodations may also include "stay away" orders so that the complainant and respondent do not have to interact in classrooms, dorms, or dining halls during the complaint process. If both students are registered in the same course or live in the same fraternity or dorm, the Title IX office is tasked with coming up a solution to make sure that the complainant and the respondent do not interact with one another.

Investigation Stage

If a formal complaint has been filed, the process now enters the investigation stage. Only one-fourth of schools offer a formal information gathering or investigative process,[8] and of those, different schools handle investigations in different ways. Some handle it internally with one primary investigator, while others have a committee conduct the investigation. Some schools hire outside contractors to conduct the investigation. This phase involves gathering physical evidence (e.g., a rape kit, if available), written statements from the respondent and the complainant, and statements from witnesses. Some schools allow statements from medical and counseling professionals as well.

Adjudication Stage

Schools must provide an informal or formal adjudication process, and it violates Title IX for schools to require that students enter a mediation to resolve sexual assault complaints.[9] Once the incident has been investigated, these materials are typically shared with an adjudicator or a hearing panel that considers additional testimony from the complainant, respondent, and witnesses prior to rendering a decision. The adjudication phase varies widely from campus to campus in terms of the membership and size of the hearing panel and the procedures employed. Eighty percent of schools use the same disciplinary board for sexual violence as other violations of the student code of conduct.[10] Some schools use individual judges, others use small panels with three or fewer members, while others have as many as ten adjudicators making decisions. Hearing panels can be a mix of staff, administrators, faculty, and even students. For example, Columbia University includes students on its adjudication panels,[11] whereas Dartmouth College has one external investigator oversee investigations and adjudications.[12]

Schools are required to issue a finding of responsibility within two days of completing the adjudication process, and are required to inform both the complainant and the respondent of the outcome of the adjudication. Some schools allow legal representation during this stage of the process, but most schools explicitly forbid participants to use lawyers for the complaint process.[13] Approximately half of the respondents are found "responsible" for sexual assault in campus adjudications.[14]

In the past few years, some schools have adopted the "single investigator model" that merges the investigation and adjudication stages. In this model, the investigator(s) gather information from the complainant, respondents, and witnesses, and reaches a decision about whether the respondent is responsible for sexual violence.[15] (Since this is an administrative rather than legal proceeding, schools use the language "responsible" rather than "guilty.") There is no hearing component under the single investigator model, so the complainant and the respondent never appear together in person to debate the facts of the allegation. Instead, each party to the case provides a detailed account of the incident in question, they then review their statement, review the statement from the other party, and respond to the other party's statement. The investigator then typically meets with each party again separately to discuss discrepancies in their accounts before rendering a finding. The process then moves to another person or body to determine the appropriate sanction. The single adjudicator model is faster and less expensive than the investigation-adjudication model because it involves fewer people. It may also produce more reliable results since the single investigator is usually an expert on the subject (versus a committee of faculty and staff who receive a few hours of training). The single investigator model also ensures that the complainant will not have to interact with the respondent, an experience that many survivors describe as being stressful and triggering. The advantages of the single investigator model are apparent, but it is now being challenged on due process grounds in several court cases in which students assert that they have a right to a hearing with the complainant present.[16]

Sanctioning Stage

The last stage of the complaint process is the sanctioning stage. If the respondent is found responsible, sanctions are determined by the adjudicator/adjudication body, a school administrator who was not involved in the investigation or adjudication, or a committee assigned to make sanctioning decisions. The process varies widely across institutions, and sometimes differs within institutions. For example, at the Tufts University Public Health & Professional Degrees Program, the Dean convenes a panel to determine sanctions,[17] but in the Fletcher School of International Affairs at Tufts, the Dean determines the sanctions.[18] A year-long study by the Center for Public Integrity found that, of respondents who are found responsible for sexual assault, schools permanently expelled only 10% to 25%.[19] In the vast majority of cases, students found responsible for sexual assault stay on campus or are allowed to return to campus after a suspension. Given that approximately half of respondents are found "responsible," only 5% to 12% of all formal complaints of sexual assault on college campuses result in an expulsion. When coupled with reporting statistics (12% are reported) and false and unfounded reporting statistics (ranging from 2% to 7%),[20] this means that out of every 100 rapes that occur on college campuses, 12 are reported to campus authorities, 11 are truthful or "founded" filings, in six cases the perpetrator is found responsible, and 1 perpetrator is expelled. If being expelled is the yardstick for campuses taking sexual violence seriously, then only about 1% of perpetrators who commit sexual battery, sexual assault, and rape are held accountable.

Appeals Stage

Schools are required by the ED to provide a formal appeals process that is open to both the complainant and the respondent. Schools are far more likely to keep the respondent informed during the process than the complainant. [21] The ED mandates that everyone involved in the complaint process receive training, and they suggest that the complaint process take no more than 60 days from start to finish. [22] Our work with survivor activists across the nation indicates that few cases are resolved within this timeframe, with most cases extending the better part of the school year.

Even though laws regulating campus response to sexual violence have been on the books for decades, campus administrators mostly used ad hoc approaches to the problem until the new CARM raised public awareness that shone a spotlight on the issue that politicians were eager to do something about. This means that best practices for prevention, adjudication, and accommodations have yet to be thoroughly researched and implemented. According to an April 2013 national study conducted by Students Active for Ending Rape (SAFER), half the students surveyed rated their school a C or lower in terms of handling sexual assault. Only 9.8% rated their school an A. [23] According to Kevin Kruger, the president of Student Affairs Administrators in Higher Education, schools are taking sexual violence much more seriously today. "We had become a little complacent about thinking this is a societal problem, and we were not doing enough about it. [Survivors said] 'You're not doing enough,' and they were right." [24]

CAMPUS SEXUAL VIOLENCE LAWS

Three major bodies of law exist that mandate how campuses are supposed to respond to the sexual assault. These laws are enforced by two different offices within the ED. The Clery Act and the SaVE Act, which is essentially an update to Clery, are enforced by the Clery Act Compliance Division of the ED. Title IX is enforced by the Office for Civil Rights within the ED. In this section, we describe the history and content of each of these laws, and analyze how they have been used by survivor activists to hold schools accountable in the new anti-rape movement.

Title IX (1972)

Sophia's Experience—Faculty Activism

As a college professor, I expect students to come forward today to talk about their personal problems, but I was not prepared for the year that 17 students told me about their sexual assaults and rapes. It started with two students that came into my office. They told me about a sexual predator—their shared rapist, a man that was still on campus because the college merely gave him a warning and an assignment to read a book. He was still on campus and would possibly rape other women, so I knew I had to do something because my school had failed these students so miserably.

I worked with the two student victims on a letter to the student newspaper. We published it anonymously, but word got out that I was willing to help survivors. And that's what my life became that year. My teaching suffered. My research just didn't get done. Instead, I learned about student's rights under Title IX, and I passed along that information to the 17 students who reached out to me. I also let them know about all of the support resources, both on and off campus, and gave them my cell phone number in case of emergencies, and there were plenty of emergencies. They called me crying that another friend had been raped. They called me saying they wanted to kill themselves.

At the end of that year, the students got together and filed a Title IX complaint and the federal government decided to open an investigation. When lawyers came to campus to take statements, I told them about all of the students who had come to me, many thinking they had nowhere else to turn. One investigating attorney assured me that the school would have to change its approach to sexual assault.

It's been three years and not much has changed. We have a Title IX office now, but the person in charge is not trusted by the students, so they still come to me for help. The new Title IX officer keeps everything in house, but the students that seek my help say that rapists are still allowed to stay on campus. The university says it's doing more, but most students still don't seem to even know what consent or sexual assault is. They go through an online training during their first year, but the program is so campy that students treat it like a joke. I don't know what would actually bring about change, but I know that we're a long way off, regardless of what my university says.

The first major body of law that campus anti-rape activists have used is Title IX, part of the 1972 Educational Amendments to the Civil Rights Act of 1964. Title IX exists because of three women. It was the 1950s and Edith Green dreamed of being an electrical engineer, but no schools would accept a woman. Patsy Mink wanted to become a doctor but women were not accepted at the 20 schools to which she applied. Bernice Sandler could not get hired for a full-time professorship after earning her doctorate because she was a woman. [25] These three women would go on to become members of congress who worked together in the early 1970s to champion Title IX legislation. This law prohibits discrimination on the basis of sex in educational programs that receive federal financial assistance. Representative Mink (D-HI) and Senator Birch Bayh (D-IN) were the official sponsors of the bill, and it was signed into law by President Nixon with bi-partisan support during the height of the Women's Movement.[26] Title IX was originally enacted to address hiring and employment practices for university employees, but has since been best known for increasing the number of women in collegiate sports.[27]

During its 40 years, the impact of Title IX has been dramatic, although women have yet to achieve parity with men on most measures in higher education.[28] Title IX has mostly eliminated the more obvious forms of gender discrimination for students in higher education, and has somewhat addressed the more subtle forms of discrimination found in differential financial aid packages, housing accommodations, and sexual harassment. Title IX has brought about seismic change in the number of female students, faculty, and administrators. Women now outnumber men in the ranks of undergraduate students.[29] For faculty, women earned only 14% of Ph.D.s in 1970, and today they earn nearly 50% of these degrees and comprise nearly 40% of the professorate.[30] The number of female college presidents jumped from 3% to 23% during this same time (which is a significant improvement, but nowhere near gender parity).[31]

Women's participation in Division I sports also rose from 15% in 1970 to 44% today.[32] The success of Title IX is undeniable in many areas, but gender discrimination persists in higher education, especially for female students who are far more likely to be assaulted/raped than their male peers.[33]

As noted in the previous chapter, Title IX has been applied to sexual assault cases in the past that have resulted in rulings from the ED that schools have to investigate complaints, provide accommodations for complainants, and provide a fair process for the complainant and the respondent,[34] but the ED would not formally recognize sexual violence as a gendered barrier to an equitable learning environment until 2001, and it would not be followed in any significant way until 2011. In April of 2011, the ED issued a directive known as a Dear Colleague Letter (DCL)[35] stating that, "The sexual harassment of students, including sexual violence, interferes with students' right to receive an education free from discrimination and, in the case of sexual violence, is a crime." The ED added that it is the responsibility of institutions of higher education "to take immediate and effective steps to end sexual harassment and sexual violence," which sent a signal to schools that the 2001 policy would now be the focus of their enforcement. This clear application of Title IX classifies school failure to properly address sexual assault issues a civil rights issue, and states that sexual violence creates an inequitable learning environment for female and male students. In other words, because female students face higher assault/rape rates, their learning experience is not the same as their male colleagues. As noted above, the Office for Civil Rights (OCR) is tasked with Title IX enforcement pertaining to campus sexual violence.

The DCL of 2011 sent up a warning flare to schools that they have to get serious about tackling campus rape. It specifies that once a school knows or should have reasonably known of sexual violence, they have to take immediate action to determine what happened, and take prompt and effective steps to prevent its recurrence and address its effects. Considering that every college campus has issues of sexual violence, this means that every school is now obligated to reduce sexual violence on campus under federal law. In other words, colleges and universities are required to provide preventative programming to educate students about assault/rape, and to take actions that will prevent it from happening again, such as enforcement of sanctions that will deter future sexual assaults and rapes. Schools are also mandated to address the effects of assault/rape, including providing survivors with adequate resources to continue their academic pursuits.

The Dear Colleague Letter of 2011 also delineates specific school responsibilities during the adjudication process. Schools are mandated to protect the complainant during the investigation, including shielding her or him from the alleged assailant and making sensible safety accommodations. Schools also have to have a grievance procedure that allows both parties the same opportunity to present evidence and witnesses, notify both parties of the outcome of the complaint, and give both parties the same right to appeal findings. Many of these Title IX provisions overlap with The Clery Act, reinforcing that these policies and practices should now be a priority for schools.

The Dear Colleague Letter also mandates that schools use the "preponderance of evidence" (POE) standard of proof in assault/rape adjudication—that it is more likely than not that the assault/rape occurred. The Preponderance of Evidence (more likely than not that it happened) standard is lower than the Clear and Convincing (75% sure it happened) and Beyond Reasonable Doubt (95% sure it happened) standards that are used in a court of law. About 80% of colleges and universities were using the POE standard prior to the DCL, so for most schools, this stipulation did not require a policy change.[36]

The POE standard has drawn fire from critics who believe that the standard is rather low as the basis for making life-altering decisions. Defenders respond that the ED could mandate this lower standard of evidence because American men are 32 times more likely to be killed by lightning than they are to be falsely accused of rape.[37] Also, only 2% of incapacitated and 13% of forcible assault/rape survivors report these crimes to campus or local law enforcement authorities, which means that the vast majority of perpetrators are never held accountable.[38] The POE standard is also a potent tool for schools to effectively deal with students who are serial rapists since a higher standard would allow more of these serial offenders to stay on campus.[39] (According to Swartout and colleagues, 10.8% of college men will perpetrate rape before or during their time in college, and of those men, 27.2% commit more than one rape.)[40]

One particularly controversial aspect of Title IX is a new interpretation from institutions of higher education that faculty must report incidences of sexual misconduct to school administrators when survivors disclose this information. This new interpretation came from an agreement that the ED reached with the University of Montana in 2013 that imposed a faculty reporting requirement.[41] The American Association of University Professors studied the law and this interpretation, and concluded that "Title IX does not require such a broad sweep," but this has not stopped colleges and universities across the United States from interpreting it in this way. Proponents of mandatory faculty reporting, namely school administrators and the Department of Education, see it as a positive because campuses can get a more accurate sense of what their student body is experiencing. Critics of mandatory faculty reporting, namely, faculty, are concerned that it takes decision-making power away from sexual assault survivors and requires faculty to betray the trust of students who have confided in them.[42] Faculty groups at institutions across the country pushed back against this interpretation in 2015 and 2016, but with little success. Mandatory faculty reporting is now policy for virtually every campus in the United States.

On May 1, 2014, the ED did something unprecedented when they issued a list of 55 schools under investigation for alleged mishandling of assault/rape by the OCR.[43] Survivor activists had been calling for this type of transparency for years, and the ED finally responded to that call with this list. The list of 55 illustrated the size and national scope of this problem as well as the fact that schools of all types are facing issues—from Ivy League institutions to small, liberal arts colleges to major state research institutions to community colleges. This act of transparency signals a strong commitment from the OCR to hold schools publicly accountable and to respond to the work of campus activists. Today, over 200 schools have open investigations of potential Title IX violations pertaining to sexual violence.

The Clery Act

The Clery Act, passed in 1990, requires that schools maintain a daily crime log and release annual crime reports that include statistics on sexual violence each year. It also requires schools to issue a timely warning if there is a threat on campus. The Sexual Assault Victims' Bill of Rights, a 1992 amendment to the Clery Act, details basic rights to fair procedures and support services (figure 4.1).

Academic research has established that passing a policy is not a guarantee that it will be implemented, and the Clery Act is a prime example of that.[44] Even though the Act has been on the books for over two decades, only one-third of schools are in full compliance with this federal law.[45] Four-year colleges and historically black institutions are doing a better job of reporting sexual crimes, but most institutions have a long way to go in terms of achieving promising practices. A 2009 report by the Center for Public Integrity found vast underreporting of sexual assault data because of confusion about reporting requirements, failure to gather data, and institutional exploitation of loopholes such as the counselor and clergy exemption.[46] Three-quarters of two- and four-year institutions report zero sexual assaults in their Annual Security Reports (!)[47]

Until the new CARM, few school officials had a working knowledge of Clery because it was not effectively enforced.[48] The Clery Act Compliance Division of the ED has been underfunded and understaffed since its inception in 2010, and because it was not actively holding schools accountable, busy school officials and resource-strapped institutions allocated their time and resources elsewhere. In the last few years, the Clery Division of the ED doubled its staff and received a moderate funding increase.[49] The Clery Division holds particular importance in preventing sexual violence because it can levy a fee of $35,000 for each violation of the law.

Starting in 2013, the ED starting levying considerably more fines and higher fines against institutions found in violation of the Clery Act.[50] In the first 22 years of Clery, the ED issued an average of three fines a year, but in 2013, they issued eight fines ranging from $82,500 to $280,000. Of particular note are the fines levied against Lincoln University of Missouri for failing to maintain a crime log and produce an annual crime report ($275,000),[51] Dominican College of Blauvelt for failing to properly classify and disclose crime statistics ($262,500),[52] and Yale University for underreporting campus crimes ($165,000).[53] The ED is also instigating more department-initiated compliance reviews (as opposed to responding to a Clery complaint that an

- **Survivors shall be notified of their options to notify law enforcement.**

- **Accuser and accused must have the same opportunity to have others present.**

- **Both parties shall be informed of the outcome of any disciplinary proceeding.**

- **Survivors shall be notified of counseling services.**

- **Survivors shall be notified of options for changing academic and living situations.**[xliv]

Figure 4.1. *Sexual Assault Victims' Bill of Rights.* Created by the authors

institution is noncompliant), and they increased the Clery fines in 2013.[54] The ED has continued this trend with stiffer penalties in 2014 and 2015, and in 2016, they levied the largest Clery fine to date—$2.4 million against Pennsylvania State University in the case of Jerry Sandusky, a coach whom administrators knew was raping children on campus for years.[55] It is worth noting that the Clery Act fines are but a fraction of the operating budgets and endowments of institutions of higher education, so in and of themselves, they are hardly a deterrent. The Clery division has yet to pull federal financial aid or research funds from a college or university.

The Campus SaVE Act (2013)

Congress passed the Campus Sexual Assault Violence Elimination (SaVE) Act in 2013, by far the most comprehensive law to date pertaining to campus sexual violence.[56] New CARM activists Laura Dunn and S. Daniel Carter were integral to its passage.[57] SaVE was included as an amendment in the reauthorization of the Violence Against Women Act, and it went into effect in 2014. It is essentially a major overhaul of the Clery Act, and its provisions are enforced by the Clery division of the ED. Campus SaVE requires schools to address sexual assault and rape, but also intimate partner violence, stalking, dating violence, and domestic violence. It mandates that campuses report these crimes in their Annual Security Report.[58] Anti-retaliation provisions were strengthened again in the Campus SaVE Act. [59]

Campus SaVE goes further than any existing laws by explicitly holding schools responsible for providing programs to reduce and prevent sexual violence.[60] Schools are now required to offer prevention programming for all incoming students and new employees that includes a clear definition of consent, the process for reporting, risk reduction advice, and bystander intervention training. Schools are also responsible for providing on-going student and employee training and information on how to recognize abusive behavior. According to attorney Carter, who was instrumental in drafting both the original Clery Act and updated Campus SaVE Act, "Much of what was in the old law [Clery Act] focused on treating the symptoms. The Campus SaVE Act will focus on inoculating against the disease."[61]

Campus SaVE also mandates standard procedures for processing complaints of sexual violence, including letting students know of their right to report to local authorities in writing, their right to receive legal advocacy and mental health services, their right to request (and receive) a change in living, academic, transportation, and working situations, honoring restraining orders on campus, disclosing sanctions for sexual violence, and detailed information about the investigation and adjudication process. The Campus SaVE Act mandates greater transparency about policies and procedures, and encourages colleges and universities to undertake research on best practices for preventing and responding to sexual violence (which means little unless the government allocates federal funds for said research).

Campus activists have the strongest tools they have ever had in the fight against sexual assault and rape, much of it due to the dedication of Vice President Joe Biden and President Barack Obama. The Obama White House was instrumental in putting campus rape on the national policy agenda. Obama announced the creation of a task force during a press conference in January of 2014.[62] This task force was directed to raise awareness of the problem, inform survivors about resources, and assist colleges and universities in devising effective prevention and response plans to gain compliance with federal laws.[63] Later that year, the White House published the *Not Alone* report that detailed campus sexual assault issues, and launched the "It's On Us" campaign to encourage bystander intervention. To date, more than 300,000 people have taken the pledge to intervene, and 48 states have active chapters of the "It's On Us" campaign.[64] The "It's On Us" website provides considerable resources, guidelines, and best practices for campus administrators who want to improve their institution's handling of sexual violence.

Other major legislation has been proposed in recent years that would have sweeping effects—the Campus Accountability & Safety Act (CASA) proposed by Senator Gillibrand (D-NY) that would raise standards for survivor support and institutional transparency, and increase fines;[65] and the Hold Accountable and Lend Transparency (HALT) Act sponsored by Representative Jackie Speier (D-CA) that would considerably increase funding for the ED to enforce existing laws.[66] To date, these bills have not received enough support for consideration in or passage by Congress, and they are unlikely to for the foreseeable future. In the final chapter of this book, we examine what the Donald Trump presidency means for the issue of campus rape.

STUDENTS RESPOND

The shifting legal landscape has given survivor activists critical tools in the effort to prevent campus rape, especially the Title IX DCL of 2011 and the Clery update of 2013. In this section, we describe the process of filing a federal complaint and initiating a lawsuit against a school for its handling of sexual violence.

Filing a Federal Complaint

The new CARM caused filings of federal complaints to increase over 1,000 percent from 2010 to 2015.[67] This action is typically taken after years of internal lobbying of administrators to change campus culture, policies, and procedures.[68] Campus activists at Swarthmore,[69] Dartmouth,[70] Amherst,[71] Occidental College,[72] the University of Southern California,[73] U.C. Berkeley,[74] U.N.C. Chapel Hill,[75] Vanderbilt University,[76] Columbia University,[77] U.C. Boulder,[78] and the University of Oregon[79] were very public in filing Clery complaints. Their federal complaints alleged similar problems—schools failing to accurately report rates of sexual violence in daily crime logs and annual security reports; failing to provide adequate support services to survivors; not informing students of their right to go to local authorities; and inequitable adjudication processes. In the fall of 2013, while under investigation by the ED, officials at the University of Southern California and Occidental College admitted that they under-reported Clery numbers in previous years.[80]

Activists also went public in filing Title IX complaints against Yale University,[81] U.C. Berkeley,[82] U.C. Boulder,[83] Columbia University,[84] Swarthmore,[85] Harvard,[86] Princeton,[87] the University of Virginia,[88] U.N.C. Chapel Hill,[89] the University of Connecticut,[90] the University of Southern California,[91] Occidental College,[92] Amherst,[93] Vanderbilt University,[94] Johns Hopkins University,[95] and other schools. These complaints had great overlap in student experiences: schools discouraging survivors from reporting their rape; failing to provide adequate survivor support services; unfair adjudication processes; light sanctions for students found "responsible" for rape; and lack of effective prevention efforts. Below, you will read the story of David Atkins. David was a student representative on the Greek Council at his university. His story sheds light on how a university can use its power to discourage students from reporting. Many elements of Title IX overlap with The Clery Act, so it was no surprise when the OCR opened a Title IX investigation into Dartmouth University after campus activists filed a Clery complaint against the school.[96]

David's Experience—Students as Mandated Reporters?

When I was an undergraduate student, I was on the Greek Council for my university. It's been a few years and I do not remember the exact title of the office, but during the spring semester of 2015 the Greek Council was informed that the Department of Education's Title IX office was going to meet with us.

On the day of the meeting it was just the Council and the representative. No one from the school was present. The representative said the school was going to make certain positions of student leadership mandatory reporters of sexual assault, starting with Greek Executive positions like the Council and the officers of each student organization. It would start with us but the intention was to spread to sport captains and other student club and organization leaders.

At first thought, this might have sounded like a good idea. But as I thought about it more, it sounded like an attempt to merely collect numbers on sexual assault rather than prevent. This was not an attempt to bring justice for survivors. It was not a way to provide resources for survivors. It was simply about administrative practice.

I was concerned that this would negatively affect the Greek Council's relationships with fellow students. As leaders of any organization on campus we try to do our best to help and care for our fellow students. This sense of care is what I liked most about my university. The small size of the campus allowed us to cultivate a genuine community of students who cared for each other.

There were many times during my tenure as a student where I tried to help fellow students through rough stretches of their lives. This was especially true of younger students. I remember in my first and second year how having the ear of an older student was invaluable. I tried to make myself available to any and all of my friends, not just fellow student leaders.

After the meeting with this Title IX representative, I realized that any of the conversations I had with fellow students that started to move toward the topic of sexual assault that I would have had to disclose that I was a mandated reporter. I recognized that any conversation I had with a fellow student about sexual assault would most likely end the minute I mentioned my role. The school wouldn't get its datum and more importantly, a fellow student who needed help or just needed to talk about what happened to them and/or what they should do would have been unable to do so. I was worried that we would be taking friends from survivors when they need them most.

As a council, we were concerned by the willingness to push a duty to report onto members of student organizations. Unlike resident assistants and other individuals who work for the university, student organization members are not employed by the school. The Greek Council therefore had an issue with the potential liability involved or our involvement in investigations. We were not trained like actual Title IX office staff, faculty members, or Project Safe staff.

We voiced these concerns to the representative. She said she would look into them but in the meantime wanted us to sign on to an agreement to be a mandatory reporter. We said we would not until she answered our questions. She never got back to us. The school administration never said anything to us about it. To my knowledge nothing has come of this since then. The entire scenario and the point of it all remains elusive.

The process for filing Clery and Title IX complaints is relatively straightforward and does not require a lawyer since it is an administrative, not a legal, procedure. The ED offers an easy process for online filing. It requires that the complaint(s) outline the ways in which her or his school has violated Title IX or Clery and list the protected class(es) of student affected. Several new CARM organizations have formed to provide free assistance to help campus activists file complaints: Know Your IX, End Rape on Campus (EROC), and SurvJustice. These organizations provide templates for both Clery and Title IX complaints and assistance with every step of the filing process. SurvJustice is the only one of the three that is staffed by attorneys and can provide legal assistance, if needed.

The majority of federal complaints filed in recent years include multiple complainants, but a complaint can also be filed by one person. Survivors have the choice of being named or remaining unnamed in their complaint, and while more survivors are going public with their names, some choose to remain anonymous. The ED specifies that a complaint can be filed by anyone who thinks that a school is in violation, so survivors can file or a person or organization can file a complaint on their behalf. For example, in December of 2013, the American Civil Liberties Union filed a Title IX complaint against Carnegie Mellon on behalf of a sexual assault survivor.

As noted above, the Clery division enforces the Clery and Campus SaVE acts, and OCR enforces Title IX. The Clery division can assess fines for noncompliant schools whereas the OCR has the power to pull federal funds from institutions. To date, the OCR has never pulled funds from a school over sexual assault noncompliance, instead negotiating voluntary resolution agreements to get into compliance. In July of 2013, campus activists from across the nation rallied outside the ED's offices in Washington, D.C., to deliver a petition with 175,000 signatures calling for stronger enforcement of Title IX for assault/rape. The petition noted that the "ED's willingness to accept colleges' promises to change their ways—rather than levy sanctions and publicly declare offending schools as 'noncompliant'—isn't working."[97] The OCR signaled that it is stepping up enforcement efforts in the spring of 2014 when it threatened to pull federal funding from Tufts University for continued noncompliance. Tufts responded by signing an agreement to get into compliance, and no funds were pulled, but this stand-off between OCR and a school sent a strong message that the legal landscape is shifting for institutions.[98]

SCHOOL RESPONSE

Colleges and universities have varied widely in their response to the new CARM and intensified federal scrutiny, but all of these institutions have similar concerns when it comes to campus rape—balancing student safety with economic and reputational concerns. Whether they are public or private, institutions of higher education rely on student tuition dollars, state and federal funds, and donations from alums and supporters to stay in "business." Colleges and universities are fundamentally money-driven institutions, and the quality of product they provide (education) is heavily dependent upon their reputation. In fact, students say that school reputation is the most important factor in deciding where to attend college, more important than formal rankings.[99] It is no surprise, then, that college administrators go to great lengths to protect their institution's reputation. Protecting the institution in this way is perhaps the most important duty of a college president. In this section we explore the most common institutional responses to the shifting legal landscape of the new CARM: risk management, crisis management, and retaliation.

Risk Management

The Dear Colleague Letter (DCL) of 2011 inspired campuses across the country to revise their sexual assault policies and procedures, but for the most part, these changes focused on reducing legal risk. Campuses hired risk management organizations, like the National Center for Higher Education Risk Management (NCHERM) and the American Council on Education (ACE), to curtail new legal pressures. ACE represents 1,800 colleges and universities in the United States.[100] and membership in NCHERM has doubled in the past decade[101] as more schools use risk management strategies to "manage" sexual assault issues.

Critics say that a risk reduction approach prioritizes reputation over student safety. One example of this is a spring 2014 webinar, hosted by ACE.[102] During this webinar, ACE actively discouraged schools from completing a survey from Senator Claire McCaskill (D-MO) on how their campus handles sexual violence, and included a slide with the language "Avoid mistakes: Congressional investigations bring collateral risks, such as litigation or regulatory risks, public relations risks and reputational harm. Remember: What will play well on TV?"[103] Their slide and contextual conversation laid bare campus consideration of reputation as the most important factor in how to respond to survivor activism and sexual violence concerns more broadly.

In similar fashion, NCHERM president Brett Sokolow came under fire in 2014 for defending male students found responsible for rape, stating that they are "simply being punished" for having drunken sex.[104] Aside from promoting the myth that campus rape is mostly drunken miscommunication instead of a crime, Sokolow's comments defy most state laws that define sex as rape if one party is incapacitated. Sokolow has taken on eleven of these cases.[105] It is telling that the leader of the most popular risk management firm for sexual assault issues in the United States has sided against survivors. NCHERM offers specific trainings to "OCR-proof" schools, but this risk management approach is not effective since a majority of schools under investigation by the ED are current or former NCHERM members.[106]

Crisis Management

With the first big wave of federal complaints, many colleges also chose to hire attorneys to run public relations campaigns to clean up their college's image. One popular "fixer" is Gina Maestro Smith, an attorney who is hired by schools to quell the crisis that ensues when campus activists allege mishandling of sexual assault/rape.[107] As the managing member of a "scandal clean-up crew,"[108] Smith has been retained by over 50 colleges in recent years to handle sexual assault issues, including UNC Chapel Hill, Amherst, UC Berkeley, and Occidental. Smith's team is hired by campus administrators for around $1,100 an hour to come to campus and host educational forums with students, faculty, administrators, alums, and parents.[109] Campus activists widely report that instead of making serious changes to improve campus safety, Smith and other "fixers" "encourage their schools to crack down on activists instead of rapists and to adopt boilerplate policies instead of calling out inept administrators."[110] Schools hiring crisis management firms to manage their public relations in response to survivor activism speaks volumes to the reputational pressures college presidents and other administrators are under.

Retaliation

Janine's Experience—Institutional Retaliation

When I spoke out about students not being treated fairly after experiencing rape on our campus, I faced a level and type of retaliation that I did not expect. Many fellow faculty members judged me as being too outspoken, and I was censured at a faculty meeting for bringing up the issue. The chair of my department suddenly started giving me the worst teaching times, and I was told to teach certain required courses instead of my areas of expertise. The Dean suddenly pulled a grant I had received, citing a lack of funds. A request for additional conference funds was denied—for the first time in eight years. Several friendly faculty members told me that one administrator jokingly referred to me as a "bitch" to a table of university people at a social func-

tion. The college president told the Board of Trustees that I was a trouble-maker, and the president's spouse disparaged me to students who sat at her table during a graduation lunch.

My character assassination made me feel on edge every time I came to campus. I wasn't sure when I was going to encounter a faculty member ignoring me or an administrator walking to the other side of the quad to avoid me, so I barely come to campus. When I do walk onto the grounds that I used to love, I listen to loud music in my ear buds. This retaliation has made me hate my profession, but it's given me new life in the classroom. I pour all of my energy and time into teaching, and my students are a source of constant joy.

Institutions do not like to be told the truth about how or why they do so little to protect rape survivors. Dig down a theoretical and historical layer or two and it becomes obvious. They don't want to be told that they are patriarchal institutions that have long privileged male students over female students, straight men over gay men. They don't want to be told that the high rate of sexual violence experienced by female and LGBT students is an informal but powerful way of sending the message that these students don't really belong. Retaliation is just a way of silencing the truth tellers who unmask the patriarchal, heteronormative power dynamics of the university.

Some administrators have responded to campus activists with public denunciations and other forms of retaliation. The ED issued another Dear Colleague Letter in April of 2013 warning schools not to retaliate against students, faculty, or anyone else who files complaints or speaks out about issues of sexual misconduct.[111] The letter states that "Individuals should be commended when they raise concerns about compliance with federal civil rights laws, not punished for doing so." University of Connecticut President Susan Herbst responded to a federal complaint by publicly stating that activists who claimed that the university was dismissive of sexual assault reports were "astonishingly misguided."[112] Occidental College President Jonathan Veitch issued a public statement chastising activists for embarrassing the college by speaking out about sexual violence.[113] Jobs for two students of color were eliminated after they were vocal about administrators' handling of sexual assault issues, and faculty advocates had their laptops seized by the college.[114] Additionally, the Dean of Students, Barbara Avery, and college attorney Carl Botterud called a mandatory meeting of select male athletes to respond to campus anti-rape activists.[115] After about an hour of sharing stories of his sexual experiences during college and telling these male athletes that they had a high threat of being falsely accused of rape, the college attorney ended their first meeting with the words "fuck em," referring to survivor activists.[116] Occidental College faculty made a historic move in May of 2013 when they issued votes of no confidence for Botterud and Avery.[117] Neither administrator was sanctioned or fired for their actions.

UNC Chapel Hill student Landen Gambill faced retaliation after filing a Title IX complaint when the school filed honor code charges against her, claiming that she created an "intimidating" environment for her alleged abuser, a man she has never publicly named.[118] These charges were dropped amidst intense public pressure, and UNC officials denied this was in retaliation for filing a federal complaint. At the University of Connecticut, complainant Carolyn Luby received rape threats after speaking out about sexual assault/rape issues.[119] One person approached her in person and said "I hope you get raped by a husky," while another emailed her to say "you sure are pretty enough to rape." When she reported these incidents to campus safety, they suggested she wear a hat so she wouldn't be recognized on campus.

Faculty members have also faced retaliation for their work on campus sexual assault issues. Harvard anthropology professor Kimberly Theidon was denied tenure despite full support from her department and a stellar research and teaching record.[120] She attributes this to retaliation for being publicly supportive of campus activists. Heather Turcotte, an untenured member in the Women, Gender, and Sexuality Studies Department at the University of Connecticut sued the college for terminating her contract after she publicly criticized President Herbst's response to students filing a sexual assault complaint.[121] In the spring of 2014, University of Oregon officials besmirched the professional reputation of psychology professor Jennifer Freyd, the foremost expert in the world on issues of institutional betrayal pertaining to sexual assault.[122] University officials rejected her request to conduct a campus climate survey as recommended by the White House, stating that her personal biases would lead to sub-par research. Faculty members from across the nation are reporting similar silencing of and retaliation for their work on sexual assault issues which prompted the formation of the activist network Faculty Against Rape (FAR) in the spring of 2014.[123] The targeting of faculty members makes sense from an institutional perspective considering that faculty members are often at a college for decades whereas student activists graduate every four years.

These responses from administrators—risk management, crisis management, and retaliation—are predictable in light of economic and institutional constraints. College administrators have limited time and resources, and until recently, they have not been under pressure to make campus rape prevention a priority. This pressure came upon schools rather suddenly, and they are necessarily playing defense, responding to a crisis that carries severe reputational impact. Every residential, co-ed campus in the United States has issues addressing sexual assault/rape, and many administrators publicly refuse to acknowledge this fact because of knee-jerk defensiveness, but this admission is a basic starting point in reform.[124] In addition to being in a defensive mode that does not lend itself to true reform, most schools lack the financial and human resources to implement major, effective change in campus policies and procedures. It will likely take the better part of a decade for most colleges and universities to implement best practices for campus rape.

WHY NOT LAW ENFORCEMENT?

One persistent question about campus rape that pertains to the shifting legal landscape is whether it should be handled by local law enforcement rather than schools. The answer is no for three reasons. First, as laid out in this chapter, schools have a legal obligation to address sexual violence that is distinct from the criminal code. Secondly, given that one-in-three campus rapists will rape multiple times, and criminal adjudication of rapes takes several years, the timeline of criminal proceedings does not work to keep the campus community safe. Given that students often take a year or more to report a sexual violation against them, rape trials would probably extend well past the survivor's graduation. Thirdly, laws specific to sexual violence on campus (Title IX, Clery, SaVE) were passed because the criminal justice system has such a dismal record prosecuting sexual violence. If the legal system processed more rape cases more quickly, law enforcement would be a viable option for student survivors, but it simply does not.

The criminal justice system is essentially broken when it comes to punishing perpetrators of sexual violence. According to a recent analysis of Department of Justice data, only 3% of rapists will ever spend a day in jail.[125] Only 40% are reported to police, and of those, only 10% will lead to a felony conviction with slightly fewer seeing the inside of a jail cell.[126] In 2011, the *Chicago Tribune* published the results of a five year study involving 171 alleged campus sex crimes at six Midwestern universities.[127] Twelve of the accused perpetrators were arrested, and only four were convicted. The *Tribune* concludes that such low arrest and conviction rates reflect a "trend [that] leaves untold numbers of college women feeling betrayed and vulnerable, believing that their allegations are not taken seriously."[128]

Law enforcement authorities are hampered in prosecuting this crime because most sexual assaults and rapes are not witnessed by a third party,[129] physical evidence may look similar for consensual sex and rape, the standard of reasonable doubt (95%) is high, and the burden of proof is on the survivor to prove she or he was raped instead of the defendant proving that she or he obtained consent. Additionally, trauma impairs the prefrontal cortex which is crucial to decision making and memory, so survivors may come off as less believable to authorities when they report the crime.[130] Survivors often recount their crime with little emotion and are unable to give a linear account of events due to impaired brain functioning. Furthermore, widely held rape myths work against reporting,[131] arrest, and conviction rates for rape, including the myth that only stranger rape and interactions that result in physical damage constitute "real" rape.[132] Prosecutors have broad discretion in whether to prosecute a case or not,[133] and they tend to be more concerned about their win-loss record than pursuing justice in cases that will be hard to win.[134]

We have worked with over two dozen campus survivors in the past five years who have reported their rapes to police. None of these cases resulted in a successful prosecution, and the experience is often retraumatizing. The district attorney in California closed student Tucker Reed's case without taking an official statement from her, and despite the fact that she had a recorded conversation with her alleged perpetrator apologizing for raping her.[135] When student Morgan Carpenter filed a rape claim in New York, the DA said, "Well, I met him. He's really cute. Maybe you just had a weak moment and you thought maybe you could get away with it."[136] The first author worked with a survivor who was raped in the spring of 2013. This survivor awoke in the middle of a rape in a fraternity house, kicked off her assailant, ran into the street half clothed, and called the police. Her rape kit indicated serious physical damage that would not heal for weeks. The district attorney refused to press charges, citing a lack of physical evidence. Another student who was raped in the spring of 2014 in her off-campus apartment went straight to the police to report her rape and was told there "was nothing" they could do about it. She then documented the rape through a series of text messages and a recorded conversation in which the alleged perpetrator admitted holding her down, forcing her to have sex, and seeing the "pain on your face." The district attorney refused to move the case forward due to a lack of witnesses and physical evidence, and even accused the survivor of "flirting" with the alleged perpetrator by contacting him to obtain his admission of the crime. After her experience with the police, Columbia University student Emma Sulkowicz said she would discourage other survivors from doing so. "If you want to go to the police, this is what to expect: You'll be verbally abused. But at least no one will yell at you for not going to the police and getting verbally abused. Just take your pick."[137]

Many campus processes for adjudicating sexual violence are not in compliance with federal law, but in comparison, the criminal justice system is far worse for survivors. Schools have one primary advantage over law enforcement: the preponderance of evidence standard that is a better fit with crimes that typically do not involve witnesses or physical evidence, and for a crime that has very low false reporting rates. The preponderance of evidence standard is fitting given that students who perpetrate sexual violence on campus receive sanctions similar to students who plagiarize or vandalize campus property. In the rare instance when students who perpetrate violence are expelled, the only notation on their transcript is "separated from the university," and some perpetrators transfer schools prior to the outcome of the adjudication process, so most avoid accountability altogether. At some point in the future, activists will successfully reform the criminal justice system to treat sexual violence as a serious crime, but until that time, law enforcement is not a viable option for campus survivors seeking justice.

CONCLUSION

The new CARM has re-energized the enforcement of existing laws and produced new laws that increase institutional accountability. In this chapter, we described the three major laws survivor activists use to hold schools accountable—Title IX, the Clery Act, and the Campus SaVE Act. Each of these laws contributes an important piece to the strongest legal patchwork of campus anti-rape laws we have ever had in the United States. Clery mandated that schools document the problem of sexual violence on campus and offer survivors support, while Title IX requires a fair and swift response to survivors, and SaVE mandates that schools prevent sexual violence.

We covered a variety of related topics in this chapter to better understand the larger legal context of campus rape. We described variations in the five stages of the campus adjudication process: the reporting stage, investigation stage, adjudication stage, sanction stage, and the appeal stage. Some of the more recent developments in campus adjudication were covered, including the new single investigator model that more campuses are adopting each year. We also looked more closely at the process for filing a Title IX or Clery complaint using examples from recent years. The ED has made this online filing process straightforward and simple. It does not require a lawyer or an understanding of legal issues to file a federal complaint. Today, several organizations exist to support students in the filing process, including SurvJustice, EROC, and Know Your IX.

In this chapter, we also analyzed school response to the new CARM and the corollary shifting legal landscape. Schools have mostly responded with risk management strategies to reduce the likelihood of getting sued, crisis management strategies to contain the potential for reputational damage, and retaliation against survivor activists to silence institutional critics. We provided some contemporary examples of survivor activists—both students and faculty—who have faced retaliation for their work in the new CARM. Early activists, meaning those who pushed the issue in 2013 and before, faced the brunt of this retaliation, although institutions continue to use retaliation as an intimidation and silencing mechanism today.

In the last section of this chapter, we analyzed why law enforcement cannot replace the campus adjudication process. In short, the criminal justice system does such a poor job of prosecuting these cases that it is not a viable alternative for campus survivors. Most cases are not prosecuted for a variety of non-meritorious reasons, and the few that are typically take years for an outcome. Furthermore, institutions have a legal obligation to provide timely and equitable justice for survivors under laws that are separate from criminal statutes, so schools have an independent obligation to process cases of sexual violence. Campus sanctions for rape look similar to sanctions for plagiarism because this is an administrative procedure, so the lower preponderance of evidence standard makes sense given this context.

The new CARM has both employed and advanced legal strategies to tackle sexual violence on college campuses. The legal landscape continues to shift as new federal laws are proposed, the ED issues new guidelines, and campuses determine how they will implement existing laws. Also, new CARM activists have turned their sights to legislation at the state level, for example, successfully establishing a "yes means yes" standard of consent in California and New York.[138] We anticipate that the legal landscape will continue to swing and shift for many years to come as the various stakeholders in the fight to reduce sexual violence jockey to advance their interests. In the next chapter, we focus on the shifting technological landscape that made the new CARM possible.

NOTES

1. Tyler Kingkade, "UNC 'Courage Project' Vandalized by Person without Courage," *The Huffington Post*, August 28, 2013, http://www.huffingtonpost.com/2013/08/28/unc-courage-project-vandalized_n_3831667.html.

2. "Dear Colleague Letter," U.S. Department of Education, Office for Civil Rights, April 24, 2013, https://www2.ed.gov/about/offices/list/ocr/letters/colleague-201304.html.

3. "The Handbook for Campus Safety and Security Reporting," U.S. Department of Education, 2011, http://www2.ed.gov/admins/lead/safety/handbook.pdf, p. 77.

4. "Sexual Assault on Campuses: What Colleges and Universities Are Doing About It," National Institute of Justice, 2005, https://www.ncjrs.gov/pdffiles1/nij/205521.pdf.

5. U.S. Department of Education, 2011, p. 208.

6. "Sexual Misconduct Response & Resources," Colorado College, accessed June 10, 2014, http://www.coloradocollege.edu/other/studentguide/pathfinder/college-policies/sexual-misconduct-resources.dot.

7. Ohio State University, "Reporting Sexual Assault," accessed June 10, 2014, http://dps.osu.edu/police/campus_safety/reporting_sexual_assault.php.

8. National Institute of Justice, "Sexual Assault on Campuses"

9. Office for Civil Rights, "Dear Colleague Letter: Sexual Violence," Department of Education, April 4, 2011, http://www2.ed.gov/about/offices/list/ocr/letters/colleague-201104.pdf.

10. National Institute of Justice, (2005).

11. Samantha Cooney and Emma Bogler, "Q&A with Administrators: Recent Changes to Sexual Assault Adjudication Processes," *The Columbia Daily Spectator*, March 3, 2014, http://columbiaspectator.com/news/2014/03/03/qa-administrators-recent-changes-sexual-assault-adjudication-processes.

12. Dartmouth, "Proposed Sexual Assault Policy Q&As," Office of the President, accessed on June 12, 2014, http://www.dartmouth.edu/~president/sap/sapqa.html.

13. Libby Sander, "Federal Negotiators Agree to Allow Lawyers in Campus Sex-Assault Hearings," *The Chronicle of Higher Education*, April 2, 2014, http://chronicle.com/article/Federal-Negotiators-Agree-to/145665/.

14. Kristen Lombardi, "A Lack of Consequences for Sexual Assault," *The Center for Public Integrity*, February 24, 2010, http://www.publicintegrity.org/2010/02/24/4360/lack-consequences-sexual-assault.

15. Melanie Bennett, "Sexual Misconduct Adjudication: The Single Investigator Model," *EduRisk*, April, 2016, https://www.edurisksolutions.org/blogs/?Id=2801.

16. Ibid.

17. "Sexual Misconduct Adjudication Process," Tufts University, Public Health & Professional Degree Programs, accessed on July 3, 2014, http://publichealth.tufts.edu/Student-Services/~/media/PHPD/PDFs-A/Student%20Services/PHPD_SexualMisconductAdjudicationProcess.pdf.

18. "Sexual Misconduct Adjudication Process," Tufts University, The Fletcher School, accessed July 3, 2014, http://fletcher.tufts.edu/Students/StudentHandbook/Appendices/~/media/Fletcher/Student%20Handbook/SMAP.pdf.

19. Lombardi (2010).

20. "False Reporting: Overview," *National Sexual Violence Resource Center, Department of Justice, Office on Violence Against Women*, 2012, http://www.nsvrc.org/sites/default/files/Publications_NSVRC_Overview_False-Reporting.pdf.

21. National Institute of Justice (2005).

22. "Dear Colleague Letter: Sexual Violence," U.S. Department of Education, Office for Civil Rights, April 4, 2011, http://www2.ed.gov/about/offices/list/ocr/letters/colleague-201104.pdf.

23. Tyler Kingkade, "College Sexual Assault Policies Get Mediocre Grade from Students in Survey," *The Huffington Post*, May 10, 2013, http://www.huffingtonpost.com/2013/05/10/college-sexual-assault-policies-survey_n_3211272.html.

24. Quoted in Juliet Eilperin, "Biden and Obama Rewrite the Rulebook on Campus Sexual Assault," *Washington Post*, July 3, 2016, https://www.washingtonpost.com/politics/biden-and-obama-rewrite-the-rulebook-on-college-sexual-assaults/2016/07/03/0773302e-3654-11e6-a254-2b336e293a3c_story.html?utm_term=.bab85f9fc80c.

25. Feminist Majority Foundation, "The Triumphs of Title IX," accessed January 13, 2016, http://www.feminist.org/education/TriumphsOfTitleIX.pdf.

26. Ibid.

27. "Fast Facts: Title IX," National Center for Education Statistics, Institute of Education Sciences, 2014, http://nces.ed.gov/fastfacts/display.asp?id=93.

28. Caryn Musil Mctighe. "Scaling the Ivory Towers: Title IX has Launched Women into the Studies, Professions, and Administrative Jobs of their Dreams," accessed January 14, 2016, http://www.feminist.org/education/TriumphsOfTitleIX.pdf.

29. Musil Mctighe (2016), p.44.

30. Ibid.

31. Ibid.

32. Jennifer Hahn, "Schoolgirl Dreams," accessed January 14, 2016, http://www.feminist.org/education/TriumphsOfTitleIX.pdf, p.47.

33. Robin Hattersley Gray, "Sexual Assault Statistics," *Campus Safety Magazine*, March 5, 2012, http://www.campussafetymagazine.com/article/Sexual-Assault-Statistics-and-Myths.

34. Christopher Kaiser, "Celebrating Title IX and Its Relevance to Our Work," *Speaking Out*, accessed June 13, 2014, http://taasa.org/blog/category/sexual-assault-laws/Speaking.

35. U.S. Department of Education (2011).

36. Stacy Teicher Khadaroo, "Feds Warn Colleges: Handle Sexual Assault Reports Properly," *The Christian Science Monitor*, September 2, 2011, http://www.csmonitor.com/USA/Education/2011/0902/Feds-warn-colleges-handle-sexual-assault-reports-properly.

37. Charles Clymer, "Men are 32X More Likely to be Killed by Lightning than Falsely Accused of Rape," *Blogspot*, January 5, 2014, http://charlesclymer.blogspot.com/2014/01/men-are-32x-more-likely-to-be-killed-by.html.

38. Christopher P. Krebs, Christine H. Lindquist, Tara D. Warner, Bonnie S. Fisher, and Sandra L. Martin, "College women's experiences with physically forced, alcohol- or other drug-enabled, and drug-facilitated sexual assault before and since entering college," *Journal of American College Health* 57, no. 6 (2009): 639–647.

39. David Lisak and Paul M. Miller, "Repeat Rape and Multiple Offending Among Undetected Rapists," *Violence and Victims* 17, no. 1 (2001): 73–84.

40. Kevin M. Swartout, Mary P. Koss, Jacqueline W. White, Martie P. Thompson, Antonia Abbey, and Alexandra L. Bellis, "Trajectory Analysis of the Campus Serial Rapist Assumption." *JAMA Pediatrics* 169, no. 12, (2015): 1148–1164.

41. Tyler Kingkade, "Professors Are Being Forced to Reveal Sexual Assault Confidences, Like It or Not," *The Huffington Post*, May 11, 2016, accessed December 30, 2017, https://www.huffingtonpost.com/entry/mandatory-reporting-college-sexual-assault_us_57325797e4b016f37897792c.

42. Colleen Flaherty, "Endangering a Trust." *Inside Higher Ed*, February 4, 2015, accessed December 30, 2017, https://www.insidehighered.com/news/2015/02/04/faculty-members-object-new-policies-making-all-professors-mandatory-reporters-sexual.

43. "U.S. Department of Education Releases List of Higher Education Institutions with Open Title IX Sexual Violence Investigations," U.S. Department of Education, May 1, 2014, http://www.ed.gov/news/press-releases/us-department-education-releases-list-higher-education-institutions-open-title-i.

44. Peter DeLeon and Linda DeLeon, "What Ever Happened to Policy Implementation? An Alternative Approach," *Journal of Public Administration Research and Theory* 12, no. 4 (2002): 467–492.

45. National Institute of Justice (2005).

46. "Campus Sexual Assault Statistics Don't Add Up," Center for Public Integrity, December 2, 2009, http://www.publicintegrity.org/2009/12/02/9045/campus-sexual-assault-statistics-don-t-add.

47. Center for Public Integrity (2009).

48. Sara Lipka, "Ignorance and Low Priority of Clery Act Violations May Extend Beyond Penn State," *The Chronicle of Higher Education*. July 1, 2012, http://chronicle.com/article/IgnoranceLow-Priority-of/132839/.

49. Tyler Kingkade, "Senators Push for More Staff at Agency to Investigate Sexual Abuse at Colleges," *The Huffington Post*. April 4, 2014, http://www.huffingtonpost.com/2014/04/04/agency-sexual-assault-investigations-mccaskill-gillibrand_n_5092748.html.

50. Rebecca Lacher and Pedro A. Ramos, "U.S. Department of Education Levies More Fines for Clery Act Violations," *Mondaq*, January 30, 2014, http://www.mondaq.com/united-states/x/289764/Education/US+Department+Of+Education+Levies+More+Fines+For+Clery+Act+Violations.

51. Sara Lipka, "Lincoln U. of Missouri faces $275,000 Fine for Clery Act Violations," *The Chronicle of Higher Education*, November 11, 2013, http://chronicle.com/article/Lincoln-U-of-Missouri-Faces/142929/.

52. Christine L. Peterson, "The Clery Act: Costs of Noncompliance," North Carolina Bar Association, November 14, 2013, http://educationlaw.ncbar.org/newsletters/educationlaw-nov2013/clery.

53. Tyler Kingkade, "Yale Faces $165,000 Clery Act Fine for Failing to Report Sex Offenses on Campus," *The Huffington Post*, May 15, 2013, http://www.huffingtonpost.com/2013/05/15/yale-clery-act_n_3280195.html.

54. Lacher and Ramos (2014).

55. Hayley E. Hanson, "The Department of Education Announces the Largest Clery Fine in History—$2.4 million," *Higher Education Legal Insights*, November 4, 2016, http://www.highereducationlegalinsights.com/2016/11/the-department-of-education-announces-the-largest-clery-fine-in-history-2-4-million/.

56. "The Campus Sexual Violence Elimination (SaVE) Act," Clery Center for Security on Campus, 2014. http://clerycenter.org/campus-sexual-violence-elimination-SaVE-act.

57. Tyler Kingkade, "College Sexual Assault Victim Advocates Hail VAWA," *The Huffington Post*, March 1, 2013, http://www.huffingtonpost.com/2013/03/01/college-sexual-assault-vawa_n_2786838.html.

58. "New Campus Obligations Under Violence Against Women Act," *American Council on Education*, March 20, 2013, http://www.acenet.edu/news-room/Pages/MEMO-New-Campus-Sexual-Assault-Policies-and-Procedures-Under-Violence-Against-Women-Act.aspx.

59. "Non-Retaliation," *The Clery Center*, Jean Clery Act Information, accessed May 12, 2017, http://www.cleryact.info/non-retaliation.html.

60. Cody Carroll, "New Campus Regulations under Campus SaVE Address Sexual Violence," April 29, 2014, http://www.tcu360.com/campus/2014/04/32272.new-regulations-under-campus-SaVE-act-address-sexual-violence.

61. As quoted in Carroll (2014).

62. Jackie Calmes, "Obama Seeks to Raise Awarness of Rape on Campus." *New York Times*, January 22, 2014, accessed December 30, 2017, https://www.nytimes.com/2014/01/23/us/politics/obama-to-create-task-force-on-campus-sexual-assaults.html?_r=0.

63. The White House, "The Second Report of the White House Task Force to Protect Students from Sexual Assault," January 5, 2017, https://www.whitehouse.gov/sites/whitehouse.gov/files/images/Documents/1.4.17.VAW%20Event.TF%20Report.PDF.

64. Eilperin (2016).

65. Tyler Kingkade, "Senators Fight for a Vote on Campus Rape Rules." *The Huffington Post*, April 26, 2016. Accessed December 30, 2017, https://www.huffingtonpost.com/entry/senators-campus-rape-bill_us_571f8a2ae4b01a5ebde359f7.

66. Allie Bidwell, "Bipartisan Bill Would Boost College Accountability on Sexual Assault." *U.S. News and World Report*, June 4, 2015, accessed December 30, 2017, https://www.usnews.com/news/articles/2015/06/04/bipartisan-house-bill-would-boost-funding-for-campus-sexual-assault-investigations.

67. Allie Bidwell, "College Sexual Violence Complaints Up 1,000 in 5 Years," *U.S. News and World Report*, May 5, 2015, https://www.usnews.com/news/blogs/data-mine/2015/05/05/college-title-ix-sexual-violence-complaints-increase-more-than-1-000-percent-in-5-years.

68. "OSAC's Efforts," *Oxy Sexual Assault Coalition*, accessed June 13, 2014, http://oxysexualassaultcoalition.wordpress.com/timeline/ and "News and Updates," *Student Coalition Against Rape (SCAR)*, Accessed June 13, 2014, http://studentcoalitionagainstrape.wordpress.com/about-us/ as examples of lengthy internal campaigns at Occidental College and the University of Southern California, respectively.

69. Jenny Lu, "Students Announce Second Federal Complaint Against Swarthmore," *Daily Gazette*, April 26, 2013, http://daily.swarthmore.edu/2013/04/26/19921/.

70. Tyler Kingkade, "Dartmouth Under Investigation for Handling of Sexual Harassment Complaints," *The Huffington Post*, July 23, 2013, http://www.huffingtonpost.com/2013/07/23/dartmouth-investigation-sexual-harassment_n_3639096.html.

71. Tyler Kingkade, "Amherst, Vanderbilt Accused of Botching Sexual Assault Complaints," *The Huffington Post*, November 14, 2013, http://www.huffingtonpost.com/2013/11/14/amherst-vanderbilt-sexual-assault_n_4271138.html.

72. Tyler Kingkade, "Occidental College Subject of Federal Investigation Over Sexual Assault Response," *The Huffington Post*, May 8, 2013, http://www.huffingtonpost.com/2013/05/08/occidental-federal-investigation-sexual-assault_n_3240402.html.

73. Tyler Kingkade, "USC, Occidental Admit Underreporting Campus Sex Offenses," *The Huffington Post*, October 10, 2013, http://www.huffingtonpost.com/2013/10/10/usc-occidental-sex offenses_n_4073117.html?utm_hp_ref=college.

74. Jason Felch and Jason Song, "UC Berkeley Students File Federal Complaints over Sexual Assault," *The Los Angeles Times*, February 26, 2013, http://articles.latimes.com/2014/feb/26/local/la-me-ln-berkeley-students-complaint-20140226.

75. Tyler Kingkade, "UNC Faces Federal Investigation into Retaliation Complaint by Sexual Assault Survivor," *The Huffington Post*, July 7, 2013, http://www.huffingtonpost.com/2013/07/07/unc-investigation-retaliation_n_3555886.html.

76. Kingkade, "Amherst, Vanderbilt Accused" (2013).

77. Eliana Dockterman, "Students File Title IX Assault Complaint Against Columbia University," *Time*, April 24, 2014, http://time.com/76762/students-file-title-ix-sexual-assault-complaint-against-columbia-university/.

78. Tyler Kingkade, "University of Colorado-Boulder Faces New Claim of Mishandling Sexual Assaults," *The Huffington Post*, August 28, 2013, http://www.huffingtonpost.com/2013/08/28/cu-boulder-federal-complaint-sexual-assult_n_3826702.html?utm_hp_ref=college.

79. Tyler Kingkade, "University of Oregon Facing Federal Complaint for Hiding Gang Rape Report," *The Huffington Post*, May 15, 2014, http://www.huffingtonpost.com/2014/05/15/university-of-oregon-complaint-rape_n_5331120.html.

80. Kingkade, "USC, Occidental Admit" (2013).

81. Claire Gordon, "Title IX Complaint Against Yale Has a Case," *The Huffington Post*, April 1, 2011, http://www.huffingtonpost.com/claire-gordon/yale-sexual-harassment-title-ix_b_843273.html.

82. Felch and Song (2013).

83. Kingkade, "University of Colorado-Boulder" (2014).

84. Dockterman (2014).

85. Lu (2013).

86. For information about the 2011 Title IX filing, see Travis Andersen, "Harvard Faces Title IX Inquiry," *The Boston Globe*, April 25, 2011, http://www.boston.com/news/education/higher/articles/2011/04/25/harvard_law_faces_title_ix_inquiry/. For information about the 2014 Title IX filing, see Madeline Conway and Steven Lee, "Undergraduates Challenge College's Sexual Assault Policy Under Title IX," *The Harvard Crimson*, April 3, 2014, http://www.thecrimson.com/article/2014/4/3/title-ix-complaint-college/.

87. Raymond W. Ollwerther, "University Subject of Federal Title IX Probe," *Princeton Alumni Weekly*, June 1, 2011, http://paw.princeton.edu/issues/2011/06/01/pages/6913/index.xml.

88. Melissa Hipolit, "Feds. Investigate U.Va., W&M Over Sexual Assault Complaints," CBS 6 News. May 2, 2014, http://wtvr.com/2014/05/02/feds-investigating-uva-wm-for-handling-of-sexual-assault-complaints-1/.

89. Kingkade, "UNC Faces Federal" (2013).

90. Tyler Kingkade, "UConn Failed to Investigate Sexual Assault Reports and Protect Victims, Complaint Claims," *The Huffington Post*, October 21, 2013, http://www.huffingtonpost.com/2013/10/21/uconn-sexual-assault-complaint_n_4133713.html.

91. Kingkade, "USC, Occidental Admit" (2013).

92. Kingkade, "Occidental College Subject" (2013).

93. Kingkade, "Amherst, Vanderbilt Accused" (2013).

94. Kingkade, "Amherst, Vanderbilt Accused" (2013).

95. Carrie Wells, Erica L. Green, and Justin Fenton, "Johns Hopkins University Under Fire for Not Disclosing Alleged Rape," *The Washington Post*, May 3, 2014, http://www.washingtonpost.com/pb/local/johns-hopkins-university-under-fire-over-not-disclosing-alleged-rape/2014/05/03/c86582b4-d305-11e3-8a78-8fe50322a72c_story.html.

96. Kingkade, "Dartmouth Under Investigation" (2013).

97. "Department of Education: Hold Colleges Accountable That Break the Law by Refusing to Protect Students from Sexual Assault," *ED Act Now, Change.org*, accessed June 15, 2014, http://www.change.org/petitions/department-of-education-hold-colleges-accountable-that-break-the-law-by-refusing-to-protect-students-from-sexual-assault.

98. Jessica Testa, "Tufts University and Federal Government in Standoff over Sexual Assault Policies," *Buzzfeed*, April 2, 2014, http://www.buzzfeed.com/jtes/tufts-university-and-federal-government-in-stand-off-over-se.

99. Robert Morse, "Students Say Rankings Aren't Most Important Factor in College Decision," *U.S. News and World Report*, January 27, 2011, http://www.usnews.com/education/blogs/college-rankings-blog/2011/01/27/students-say-rankings-arent-most-important-factor-in-college-decision.

100. Sarah Mimms, "Lobbyists Warn Colleges that Participating in Sexual-Assault Survey Could Make Them Look Bad," *National Journal*, June 5, 2014, http://

www.nationaljournal.com/congress/lobbyists-warn-colleges-that-participating-in-sexual-assault-survey-could-make-them-look-bad-20140605.

101. Eric Kelderman, "Risk Managers Extend Their Turf to Every Corner of Campus," *The Chronicle of Higher Education*, November 22, 2009, http://chronicle.com/article/Campus-Risk-Managers-Extend/49226/

102. Mimms (2014).

103. Dana Bolger, "When Schools Put their Brands Before Assaulted Students," *Al Jazeera America*, June 10, 2014, http://america.aljazeera.com/opinions/2014/6/college-sexual-violencerapeeducationtitleixbranding.html.

104. Katie Baker, "College Sexual Assault Guru Stands Up for Accused Rapists," Buzzfeed. May 1, 2014, http://www.buzzfeed.com/katiejmbaker/college-sexual-assault-guru-stands-up-for-accused-rapists.

105. Robin Wilson, "Opening New Front in Campus-Rape Debate, Brown Student Tells Education Department His Side," *The Chronicle of Higher Education*, June 12, 2014, https://chronicle.com/article/Opening-New-Front-in/147047/.

106. Bolger (2014).

107. Katie Baker, "Rape Victims Don't Trust the Fixers Colleges Hire to Help Them," Buzzfeed, April 25, 2014, http://www.buzzfeed.com/katiejmbaker/rape-victims-dont-trust-the-fixers-colleges-hire-to-help-the.

108. "Safety Monitor," The American Lawyer. Accessed June 15, 2014, http://www.americanlawyer-digital.com/americanlawyer-ipauth/201309ip?pg=15#pg15.

109. Arielle Laub, "Gina Smith and Leslie Gomez to Take on Occidental's Sexual Assault Policy," *Occidental Weekly*, April 9, 2013, http://occidentalweekly.com/news/2013/04/09/gina-smith-and-leslie-gomez-to-take-on-occidentals-sexual-assault-policy/.

110. Baker, "Rape Victim's Don't Trust the Fixers" (2014).

111. U.S. Department of Education, "Dear Colleague Letter: Retaliation" (2013).

112. Kathleen Megan, "Herbst Calls Allegation That UConn Is Indifferent to Reports of Sexual Assault 'Astonishingly Misguided,'" *The Courant*, October 23, 2013, http://articles.courant.com/2013-10-23/news/hc-uconn-herbst-title-ix-complaint-trustees-1024-20131022_1_uconn-president-susan-herbst-sexual-assault-sexual-violence.

113. Jason Felch and Jason Song, "Occidental College Chief Asks for Reconciliation After Accusations," *The Los Angeles Times*, September 20, 2014, http://articles.latimes.com/2013/sep/20/local/la-me-0921-occidental-sexual-assaults-20130921.

114. This information was included in the Occidental College Title IX and Clery complaints.

115. Jessica Ogilvie, "Rape at Occidental College: Official Hush-Up Shatters Trust," *The LA Weekly*, June 27, 2013, http://www.laweekly.com/2013-06-27/news/rape-occidental-college/.

116. Ibid.

117. Tyler Kingkade, "Occidental Faculty 'No Confidence' Vote Rebukes Administrators for Handling of Sexual Assault," *The Huffington Post*, May 6, 2013. http://www.huffingtonpost.com/2013/05/06/occidental-faculty-sexual-assault-no-confidence_n_3220863.html.

118. Katie McDonough, "UNC Faces Federal Charges Over Complaint by Sexual Assault Whistle Blower," *Salon*, July 8, 2013, http://www.salon.com/2013/07/08/unc_faces_federal_charges_over_complaint_by_sexual_assault_whistle_blower/.

119. Soraya Chemaly, "UConn Student Receives Rape Threats After Suggesting School Address 'Frightening' Atmosphere for Women," RH Reality Check, May 1, 2013, http://rhrealitycheck.org/article/2013/05/01/uconns-mascot/.

120. Marcella Bombardieri, "Harvard Professor Challenges Denial of Tenure," *The Boston Globe*, June 13, 2014, http://www.bostonglobe.com/metro/2014/06/12/harvard-professor-challenges-tenure-denial/E64ruokHoD1WpokjwsbR3M/story.html.

121. Jacqueline Rabe Thomas, "UConn Prof Says Her Support of Outspoken Student May Cost Her Her Job," *The Connecticut Mirror*, November 13, 2013, http://ctmirror.org/uconn-prof-says-her-support-outspoken-student-may-cost-her-her-job/.

122. Josephine Woolington, "Scholar's Sexual Violence Study Rejected," *The Register-Guard*, June 11, 2014, http://registerguard.com/rg/news/local/31703535-75/sexual-survey-freyd-violence-university.html.csp.

123. Callie Beusman, "Colleges Fire and Silence Faculty Who Speak Out About Rape," Jezebel, June 13, 2014, http://jezebel.com/colleges-silence-and-fire-faculty-who-speak-out-about-r-1586169489.

124. Ibid.

125. "Why Will Only 3 Out of Every 100 Rapists Serve Time?" *Rape, Abuse & Incest National Network,* accessed on July 16, 2014, https://rainn.org/get-information/statistics/reporting-rates.

126. Ibid.

127. Todd Lighty, Stacy St. Clair, and Jodi S. Cohen, "Few Arrests, Convictions in Campus Sex Assault Cases," *Chicago Tribune*, June 16, 2011. http://articles.chicagotribune.com/2011-06-16/news/ct-met-campus-sexual-assaults-0617-20110616_1_convictions-arrests-assault-cases.

128. Ibid.

129. Bowen Bowcott, "Rape Myths Not Behind Low Conviction Rate, Says Leading Family Lawyer," *The Guardian*. March 25, 2013, http://www.theguardian.com/society/2013/mar/25/rape-myths-low-conviction-rate.

130. Rebecca Ruiz, "Why Cops Don't Believe Rape Victims?" Slate, June 19, 2013, http://www.slate.com/articles/news_and_politics/jurisprudence/2013/06/why_cops_don_t_believe_rape_victims_and_how_brain_science_can_solve_the.html.

131. Nicole M. Heath, Shannon M. Lynch, April M. Fritch, and Maria M. Wong, "Rape Myth Acceptance Impacts the Reporting of Rape to the Police: A Study of Incarcerated Women," *Violence Against Women* 19, no .9 (2013): 1065–1078.

132. Kimberly A. Longsway and Louise F. Fitzgerald, "Rape Myths: In Review," *Psychology of Women Quarterly* 18, no. 2, (2012): 133–164.

133. Cassia Spohn and David Holleran, "Prosecuting Sexual Assault: A Comparison of Charging Decisions in Sexual Assault Cases Involving Strangers, Acquaintances, and Intimate Partners," *National Institute of Justice*, 2004, https://www.ncjrs.gov/pdffiles1/nij/199720.pdf.

134. Tyler Kingkade, "Prosecutors Rarely Bring Charges in College Rape Cases," *The Huffington Post*, June 17, 2014, http://www.huffingtonpost.com/2014/06/17/college-rape-prosecutors-press-charges_n_5500432.html.

135. Ibid.

136. Ibid.

137. Claire Gordon, "Why College Rape Victims Don't Go to the Police," *Al Jazeera America,* May 14, 2014, http://america.aljazeera.com/watch/shows/america-tonight/articles/2014/5/19/why-college-rapevictimsdonatgotothepolice.html.

138. Proponents of the "yes means yes" standard argue that it shifts the assumed responsibility for preventing rape away from women by requiring both parties to actively consent to sexual activities, but in practice, many young people find it difficult to communicate during sexual activity. For more on this debate, see Jennifer Medina, "Sex Ed Lesson: 'Yes Means Yes,' But It's Tricky," *The New York Times*, October 14, 2015, https://www.nytimes.com/2015/10/15/us/california-high-schools-sexual-consent-classes.html?_r=0.

Chapter Five

"Going Public"

The Shifting Technological Landscape

Sarah Tedesco did not intend to "go public" about her experience at Emerson College, but a friend's ex-boyfriend sent a copy of the complaint to A Voice for Men, a men's rights organization. A Voice for Men promptly published her Title IX complaint on their website and listed Sarah's name as a complainant (but redacted the names of her alleged perpetrators). She had wanted to remain anonymous to avoid the pitying gazes of other students on Emerson's picturesque urban campus and the inevitable harassment from online trolls. But once the damage was done, Sarah embraced the idea of being a "public survivor"—someone who tells their story of rape again and again in public forums in order to help other survivors find their voice, and to advance the cause of the new Campus Anti-Rape Movement (CARM). Sarah used her new public survivor platform to post social media commentary about specific cases of campus rape. She also appeared on a Dateline special about college sexual violence and was interviewed by over a dozen reporters who wrote print pieces on the movement. Sarah joined a small army of public survivors who collectively and strategically put the new CARM on the national agenda, facilitated by the advent of new communication technologies in the last decade.

The purpose of this chapter is to analyze how relatively new communication technologies have facilitated the organizing and effectiveness of the new CARM. We begin this chapter with a look at an emerging body of literature on new networked social movements. Then, we apply existing research on networked movements to the new CARM to better understand this movement, and to advance our knowledge of networked movements through analysis of this recent case. Next, we focus on the connection between technology use and movement effectiveness. We conclude that internet activism played a key role in the success of the new CARM relative to previous student activism on this issue through the building of community, providing a forum for public survivorship, garnering mainstream media coverage, and allowing better message control by the movement. We close this chapter with an analysis of where CARM is in terms of the standard stages of social movements in order to better understand what comes next for the movement.

NEW NETWORKED SOCIAL MOVEMENTS

The new CARM is what sociologist Manuel Castells calls a new networked movement—a decentralized, leaderless(full) social movement where activists come together around shared problems and goals through new communication technologies.[1] The Global Justice Movement was the first networked movement in the United States,[2] aimed at curbing corporate globalization and ameliorating its role in global poverty. In 1999, the Global Justice Movement drew 50,000 activists to Seattle to protest the World Trade Organization, dubbed the "Battle in Seattle" in the press, and the city was overwhelmed with the unanticipated numbers.[3] The Seattle Police Department had projected only a fraction of attendees because organizers had used "hidden" online means to mobilize activists. The large and surprising size of the Battle in Seattle epitomizes a key difference between classic social movements that use conventional methods to mobilize members (e.g., mailers, phone lists, face-to-face outreach, etc.) and networked social movements that use new communication technologies (e.g., Tweets, Slack channels, private Facebook groups, etc.). Online communications that emerged in the 1990s, and social media capabilities that came about in the mid-2000s, have changed the way social movements emerge, mobilize their members, and communicate their message. Sociologists Victoria Carty and Jake Onyett find that new mass communication technologies "have played a critical role in the organization and success" of new networked social movements relative to classic social movements (that involve more face-to-face organizing).[4] Since the Battle in Seattle, new networked social movements have sprung up across the globe. Recent prominent examples of networked movements in the United States include the Occupy Wall Street movement of 2011 in response to the global economic crisis caused by Wall Street, and #BlackLivesMatter, a movement that came about in 2013 to address violence against and systemic racism aimed at black Americans. These social movements differ in their policy focus, but they all share the same basic horizontal structure, shaped by the use of social media tools to connect activists to one another and to reach a wider audience through mass communication technologies.

Scholars disagree about whether the networking of social movements has a net positive or negative impact on democracy.[5] On one side are scholars who argue that this new technology demeans political discourse and participation.[6] This debate is situated within a larger discussion of free speech and other democratic implications of the internet more broadly. Some political theorists see online communication as a threat to democracy because it can be used by governments and corporations at the expense of citizen interests.[7] Political theorist Benjamin Barber argues that political leaders and economic institutions can and do use online communications to manipulate citizens in ways that are difficult to detect,[8] and political writer Evgeny Morozov concludes that the internet poses a threat to democracy because it can be employed as a tool by authoritarian governments.[9] Techno-sociologist Zeynep Tufekci finds that the mundane organizing necessary for classical social movements caused them to coalesce more tightly, and to build more resilience that new networked social movements lack.[10] In other words, she is suggesting that online networking tools might produce short-lived campaigns but not social movements that can sustain themselves over time.

Other scholars conclude that online organizing technologies have positive impacts for democracy because they enhance citizen political participation, improve political information,[11] facilitate communication between ordinary people,[12] and provide a "space" for political deliberation.[13] Tufekci adds that the internet and social media lower the bar for entry into social movement organizing, enabling novice activists to start hashtag campaigns and mobilize rallies in ways that used to take months of tedious planning by veteran activists.

Castells and anthropologist Jeffrey Juris conclude that networked movements are generally more successful than classical movements since activists are organizing "under the radar" and do not have to rely on mainstream media to shape the terms of the debate. Juris argues that networked movements organize more quickly and with greater flexibility than classic social movements, and can thus be more effective in achieving goals. [14] Political scholar Merlyna Lim finds evidence of this greater relative success in her study of the Egyptian uprising in Tahir Square in 2011. Lim argues that this movement was made possible by social media networks that allowed activists to expand their networks, communicate behind the scenes, and mobilize resources beyond Egypt's borders.[15] She further finds that social media made the movement more effective in that leaders were able to control the framing of the issue and transmit unifying symbols.

Our analysis of the new CARM contributes to the active scholarly debate about the democratic merits of new networked political organizing. We enter this debate with CARM as a case study, which allows us to further our understanding of networked social movements as well as our knowledge of the CARM. Our analysis in this chapter confirms that online technology facilitates grassroots activism, which improves democracy as measured by citizen voice and participation in the political process and policymaking. Our findings suggest that new networked movements not only move faster and are more flexible in responding to external threats than classic social movements, but they are also more effective because they can reach a wider audience.

THE NETWORKED NATURE OF THE NEW CARM

In this section, we analyze the new CARM as a case study within the larger literature on new networked social movements. Special attention is paid to how the movement is structured, the fact that it is a student movement, the demographics of movement participants, and technology use by movement participants and leaders to connect to one another, mobilize members for actions, and attract public attention.

CARM Structure

The new CARM is distinct from half a century of previous activism on this issue in that, as a new networked movement, much of the day-to-day organizing is done online using new communication technologies. The movement is decentralized, lacking formal leadership, and relies on new communication technologies to mobilize activists. The CARM has no central organization or governing body running the movement; no single activist or organization launched the movement or is leading the movement. The most prominent CARM activists jockey for public attention for their work, but no person or group of people is guiding the movement with a set mission, goals, strategies, or tactics. Instead, activists are organizing petitions, protests, and other movement events, and other activists across the nation are supporting them in their efforts. We do not know the size of the movement because most of the organizing takes place through "hidden" online networks, but judging by the size of political actions, it appears quite large. For example, a Change.org online petition in 2013 to compel the Department of Education to better enforce Title IX guidelines received 174,000 signatures,[16] and a 2017 Change.org petition to recall Aaron Persky, the judge who gave Stanford rapist Brock Turner a light six-month sentence, garnered 1.3 million signatures.[17]

Movement work in the new CARM is concentrated in decentralized nodes[18] where some activists and organizations work on lobbying Congress and the White House for new laws (e.g., Promoting Awareness| Victim Empowerment), as others work on filing federal complaints (End Rape on Campus), representing survivors in lawsuits (SurvJustice), running media awareness campaigns (UltraViolet), providing resources to survivor activists

(Know Your IX), putting pressure on the ED to enforce Title IX and Clery (ED Act Now), and developing best practices for schools (Faculty Against Rape). The new CARM has employed a mixture of grassroots, legal, and policy strategies.

The new CARM is a leaderless movement, or, rather, a movement with many leaders. While recognizing the strength of leaderless, horizontal networked organizing, Tufekci argues that it also often results in informal leaders with relatively larger numbers of followers on social media, jockeying for influence, which produces conflict within the movement. This has certainly been the case with the new CARM in which there is an enduring struggle for individual prominence. As with all classic social movements and new networked social movements, the new CARM is both collaborative and competitive.

A Student Movement

The new CARM is predominately a student movement, although a fair number of faculty and staff, and feminist activists outside of institutions of higher education, have been active in the movement. Young people have often been at the forefront of major social movements that have "transformed human history," including the Civil Rights Movement, the Environmental Justice movement, the movement for LBGTQ rights, different feminist movements, anti-war movements, and immigrant rights movements.[19] Part of the reason the new CARM has been so successful is the enthusiasm and hard work of a group of dedicated students, in concert with faculty and university staff willing to risk their careers, to launch what has been the most successful effort in five decades of activism to address campus sexual violence. The new CARM shows that young people can be innovative, effective agents of change, even on issues where others have been working for decades. Campus activists are using a sophisticated arrangement of legal and policy tactics (lobbying, filing lawsuits, filing federal complaints, passing new laws, etc.) in tandem with more direct political actions (sit-ins, demonstrations, protests, online shaming campaigns aimed at institutions of higher education, online petitions, etc.) to advance their concerns.

Demographics of the Movement

Like other networked social movements, the form of the new CARM is related to the type of activist who is comfortable with new online and social media technologies—young people with economic resources. That the anti-rape movement is largely composed of young people cannot be disentangled from its status as a student-dominated movement. While similar to other movements in many ways, Philip Altbach argues that student movements are shaped by "specific aspects of campus life—an age-graded population, a fairly close community, common social class backgrounds and other elements."[20] The age of student CARM participants is also linked to social media use. Young people are much more likely to use online tools compared to older people, so it is unsurprising that a contemporary social movement composed of mostly students is a networked movement.[21] CARM participants also tend to be socioeconomically privileged. While access to the technology necessary to engage in a networked movement has become more democratized (e.g., access to a computer), college students tend to have greater resources than the average American and have disproportionate access to this technology.[22]

While CARM activists are disproportionately young, female college students, the networked nature of the movement also lends to its diversity of membership. The network is composed of campus sexual assault survivors and a diverse group of allies, including other college students, alumni, faculty, a few administrators, bloggers, non-profit organizers, and a broader feminist network. As with most feminist causes, most of the key players are women, but men and transgendered individuals also have a strong voice in the movement.[23] LGBT individuals are also active CARM organizers, and, as with sexual violence in the United States more broadly, women of color are a strong force in the movement.[24] The CARM has a class bias given the fact that schools have a strong class bias in terms of who can afford to attend, [25] but in our observations of the movement, many of the most prominent voices of the movement are first generation college students and self-identified "poor kids." Early movement activists tended to be students from mostly Ivy League schools and expensive private institutions,[26] but the movement quickly expanded to public and private institutions of all sizes, rankings, and locations.

Technology Use

New technologies enable CARM organizers to network and share resources in ways that were previously impossible. Prior to the new CARM, campus activists were organizing in small, relatively isolated groups, working on programs and policies on their individual campuses. Many assumed that their experiences of institutional betrayal were unique,[27] but through social media sharing, they learned that virtually every campus mishandles sexual violence. Today, CARM activists stay connected in real time via Facebook, Tumblr, Twitter, Google+, Skype, Snapchat, and so on.

New technologies also facilitate survivor support, an important part of the social movement. When a survivor comes into the vast online network of CARM activists and organizations, they are connected to a network of shared information from organizers and experts across the country. Survivors can be instantly connected to informational resources and templates that have been used on other campuses, and the anti-rape network provides ample coaching and other forms of support through Google Hangout conversations, text messages, and many other communication tools. Survivors are networking in ways that help them cope with post-traumatic stress disorder and other symptoms of trauma by seeking help from fellow survivors and supportive allies in times of crisis. They can easily and quickly get referrals for services and online resources for how to best cope after an experience of sexual violence. Campus activists have developed an informal counseling network where they share their fears and anxieties and assist one another in obtaining professional counseling, when needed. Survivors also help one another with their homework and offer advice for survivor-friendly educational faculty members and institutions. New communication technologies are facilitating activist and survivor connections that are vital to the work and self-care of CARM activists. One of the key modes of communication are secret Facebook groups where survivor activists connect with each other and stay current with movement activities. The largest private CARM Facebook group, IX Connection, has over 800 members at hundreds of colleges and universities across the United States. CARM activists have also formed secret Facebook pages for LGBT survivors, survivors of color, and male survivors of all races.

TECHNOLOGY AND CARM EFFECTIVENESS

In this section, we explore how new communication technologies are behind the heightened success of the CARM compared to activism on this issue in the previous four decades. We find that online networking has made this new peak of anti-sexual violence efforts more effective through hidden networks, promoting public survivorship, controlling the message, and garnering press coverage. We discuss each of these in turn.

Hidden Networks

The new CARM is more effective than previous anti-sexual violence efforts on campus because its "hidden" network is vast and constantly expanding, and it connects previously isolated individual activists and groups.[28] New communication technologies enable organizers to connect and collaborate quickly and cheaply. Activists use the network to share stories of violence and institutional betrayal with one another, collaborate on ideas for public shaming campaigns, share templates for Title IX and Clery Act complaints, and brainstorm nuts and bolts strategies for organizing.[29] Twenty years ago, during the first peak of campus activism, organizers had to rely on national media outlets to learn about activism at other schools, and telephone conversations were the primary means of communication. As S. Daniel Carter points out, describing the early 1990s activism in trying to get the Clery Act passed, "My long distance phone bills were outrageous." Today, any student with access to a computer can tap into the new CARM network to get resources, advice, and support.

The decentralization of the new CARM network also improves movement success because it lowers the chance that organizers will be coopted by the institutions they seek to reform.[30] Sociologists Frances Fox Piven and Richard Cloward argue that social movements often lose their force because the institutions and political leaders with whom they are struggling for concessions effectively co-opt movement leaders. "Political leaders . . . will try to quiet disturbances not only by dealing with immediate grievances, but by making efforts to channel the energies and angers of the protesters into more legitimate and less disruptive forms of political behavior, in part by offering incentives to movement leaders or, in other words, by coopting them."[31] The new CARM is a leaderfull movement, so if one titular movement leader (e.g., a survivor whom the press or a documentary film has elevated) is co-opted, there are hundreds more to carry out the work of the movement. In new networked social movements, one person cannot speak on behalf of the movement.

The hidden nature of the CARM network is also key to the movement's success in that it introduces a degree of unpredictable risk for institutions and organizations that stand in opposition to the movement. Hundreds of thousands of activists can be rapidly mobilized to confront a specific concern or institution (e.g., the Stanford rape case), and lawmakers and campus administrators cannot easily predict or contain the impact of CARM actions once they become the target of a CARM action. We believe that the unpredictable nature of the "hidden" network has been the impetus for some administrators to take action to reduce sexual violence sans student activism on their campus. We know of college presidents who have taken pre-emptive measures to inoculate against the new CARM spreading to their campus in the form of student organizations, protests, Tumblr campaigns, and federal complaints. Both the "hidden" and networked aspects of the new CARM, made possible by new online technologies, have been instrumental in its effectiveness.

Public Survivors

The new CARM is also effective because social media enables survivors to share intensely personal and painful stories that used to be hidden. Until 2013, survivors generally did not speak out about their experiences, and news organizations had a tacit agreement that they would not publish the names of survivors. Fast forward a few years and scores of survivors are naming themselves and sharing their experience in online forums, social media, and news outlets. In 2011, Grace Brown started "Project Unbreakable" on Tumblr to document rapists' statements to survivors. This Tumblr encourages healing through art, and it has received submissions from over 2,000 survivors holding posters with quotes from their attackers and other people in their lives, including "'You can't stop me now' he said with his hand around my neck" and "That's what happens to little girls that get drunk—my Mother—I was 13." Dana Bolger started the online magazine "It Happens Here" in 2012 to document issues of sexual assault at Amherst College. In 2012, Mount Holyoke College senior Ali Safran began the "Surviving in Numbers" Tumblr and started a non-profit with the same name after her sexual assault. Tufts University student Wanjuki was a social media pioneer in the anti-rape movement when she started chronicling her sexual assault and the school's betrayal in 2009 on her blog. Tucker Reed at the University of Southern California followed Wanjuki's model with her blog "Covered in Bandaids" that chronicled her assault and the adjudication process at her university. Online sharing capabilities means survivors can now go public, either anonymously or named, in ways of their own making and design.

This dramatic shift in rates of public survivorship may eventually erode the social stigma that comes with being a survivor. When survivors started to "go public" in large numbers in 2013, this had a snowball effect of inspiring a massive outpouring of public survivorship. In networked social movements, Castells notes that "Enthusiastic networked individuals, having overcome fear, are transformed into a conscious, collective actor."[32] Online technologies hold exceptional importance to the new CARM because, prior to social media, survivors were routinely bullied into silence by institutional actors and even fellow students who shamed and victim-blamed them. The new CARM normalized public survivorship, which means American society is less tolerant of survivor bullying, victim blaming, and stigmatization. Of course these unfair, sexist responses to survivors persist, but they are less frequent and met with pushback if posted on social media. Public survivorship has become so acceptable that millions of women and gender nonconforming individuals shared experiences of sexual harassment/violence in the 2017 #MeToo social media campaign, as we discuss in further detail in the concluding chapter.

Message Control

New communication technologies have also enabled the success of the new CARM by improving movement participants' ability to control the message. Networked activism means that campus activists can shape the terms of the debate through social media, theoretically shaping the outcome of the debate. According to Castells, networked activists "produce and share their own DIY [do it yourself] information, and resist, 'talk back' to, or otherwise critique and intervene in prevailing social, cultural, economic, and political conditions."[33] In other words, social media is a powerful tool in conveying movement messages and counteracting opposing messages.

Better message control is evident in the messaging strategies and content of the new CARM. Instead of waiting for the press to cover campus rape, early CARM activists took to social media to share their stories, frame the issues as a pressing national concern, and demand policy reform and better policy enforcement. Organizers used social media to put the topic on the public agenda, and to shape it as a national public health crisis, rather than waiting for journalists to pay attention to the issue or frame it in less urgent ways. Campus sexual violence could have easily just been a blip on the public radar had it been framed as an issue that only affects college students.

Message control is also crucial to weathering the backlash that has already begun against the new CARM. The backlash of today is likely to be less successful than the backlash of the 1990s because of the force of the feminist blogosphere and the ability of activists to immediately respond in cyberspace. To date, CARM activists have been able to counteract backlash arguments in real time with data and testimonials. Backlashers will not be able to paint campus rape as simply drunken miscommunications as they did in the 1990s peak of activism. We analyze the backlash in greater detail in the last chapter.

Press Coverage

CARM activists used new communication technologies to draw the attention of the press that was so crucial to igniting the national dialogue about sexual harassment/violence that began in 2013. Similar to Occupy Wall Street and the Arab Spring, social media sharing attracted the attention of mainstream media outlets. As survivors shared their stories online and rapidly filed a slew of federal Title IX complaints (both of which were facilitated by online technologies), news organizations started to cover campus rape. The nation's leading newspapers provided extensive, on-going coverage of movement efforts (*The New York Times, The Los Angeles Times,* the *Washington Post*) as well as popular news blogs (The Huffington Post, Slate.com, The Daily Beast, CNN.com, MSNBC.com, Bloomberg.com) and the feminist blogosphere. Al Jazeera America ran a series of stories on campus assault/rape that culminated in a Sexual Assault Town Hall in Washington, D.C., in 2013. The movement has also received coverage in news outlets in other countries, including *The Guardian* in the U.K., *The Times of India, China Daily,* and *The Sydney Morning Herald.* Numerous film and television crews from other countries have visited college campuses across the United States to interview survivor activists.

As noted earlier in this chapter, CARM activists did not wait for the press to pay attention to this issue, but when they did, they took the movement to the next level in terms of raising public awareness. The intense media interest in sexual harassment/rape that began in 2013 was fueled by the presence of newsworthy "events" that were strategically timed by activists in the CARM network. For example, CARM activists spaced out the filing of federal complaints to maximize news coverage and hosted rallies and press conferences in locations that would pull the most press. Jarring survivor stories, many initially posted online, were also "events" that drew press coverage. Online technologies were the reason that so many different survivor stories were told. Were the new CARM a classic social movement, its leaders would have worked with reporters to determine which survivor stories to feature, which means that only a handful of stories would have been shared again and again.

POLITICAL TIMING

We attribute much of the success of the new CARM to new technologies that facilitated online collaboration and allowed survivor stories to pierce public consciousness, but fortuitous political timing also played a role. In short, technological development converged with a favorable political environment to produce the effectiveness of the new CARM. President Barack Obama and Vice President Joe Biden, a long-time advocate who has worked to eliminate all forms of violence against women, were highly supportive of the goals of the new CARM. It seems unlikely that the CARM would have had similar champions in the White House during the George W. Bush Administration, and as we discuss further in the last chapter, the Trump Administration is openly hostile to the work of the new CARM. In the next section, we analyze whether the movement is in a better position to advance the cause under a hostile administration since it is no longer an emergent movement.

MOVEMENT STAGES

The Campus Anti-Rape Movement is now half a decade old, which means it is no longer emergent. It has arrived as it were, which means the shape and composition of the network have changed. Most of the early activists were undergraduate college students when they first got involved. Some have gone onto law school or graduate school and are now professionals and experts in the movement. Others have moved on with their lives and are working in jobs that have nothing to do with preventing sexual violence. Some faculty activists, many of whom have been working on these issues for decades, have faced retaliation and have left their institutions or the profession, while others plug away as stalwart CARM activists. The beauty of new networked social movements is that they are never one type of group or organization. They are constantly shifting, and the new CARM is evidence of that. The ranks of the CARM have been replenished with new students who learn about high rates of sexual violence on their campus and join the movement to change that. This has kept momentum relatively high, although that has dropped in measurable ways in recent years. In this section, we apply a standard model of social movement maturation to understand how the CARM has shifted and where it is likely to go.

Historian Jonathan Christensen documents that social movements typically move through four stages: emergence, coalescence, bureaucratization, and decline.[34] In the emergence stage, potential movement participants identify a problem but have yet to organize around it. Widespread discontent builds around the issue during this stage, often fomented through media coverage and public discourse. The new CARM was in the emergent stage for most of the 2000s, with a small group of dedicated activists filing federal complaints and lawsuits to bring attention to the issue and change policies, but a full-blown social movement was yet to form. Then, in 2013, buoyed by online communication technologies that allowed survivor activists to connect and a favorable political environment, the new CARM coalesced into a social movement.

For classic social movements, the coalescence stage typically requires a critical mass of organizers to come together around an issue, often concentrated in one or a few locations. For new networked social movements, the emergence stage takes place online. For the new CARM, the "hidden" network coalesced into a movement with more clearly defined discontent, organized tactics and strategies, and mainstream "popularity." During 2013 and 2014, CARM activists connected online to plan events, stage protests, launch campaigns, and start organizations. During this time, the movement network took shape and different nodes of the network became more distinct, organized around specific movement tasks. For example, one node of the network mostly worked to help survivors file federal Title IX and Clery complaints while a second node formed to connect survivors to legal representation. Other network nodes worked on survivor support resources, developing online organizing tools, and other work that was vital to establishing the contours and missions of the movement.

We argue that the new CARM moved from the coalescence stage to the bureaucratization stage in 2016. The bureaucratization stage is marked by the establishment of formal, sustainable organizations that tackle different pieces of the problem that instigated the social movement. The shape of the new CARM has shifted, from a scrappy network of (mostly student) activists to a loosely connected group of non-profit organizations run by professionals with advanced degrees and experience advocating against sexual violence. Virtually all of these professional leaders were early CARM organizers. A surprising number of early CARM activists have gone on to law school to gain legal tools for anti-sexual violence work, including Laura Dunn (University of Madison-Wisconsin), Alana Murphy (Occidental College), Alexandra Brodsky (Yale), Carly Mee (Occidental),[35] and Dana Bolger (Amherst).

Most of the non-profit CARM organizations were founded in the years leading up to 2016, but in our estimation, this is the year that all of the most prominent organizations founded by movement actors professionalized, meaning they acquired a full-time staff and more stable funding. The nodes of the CARM that organically came together in the coalescence stage are more distinct today because of the formation of formal organizations.[36] It remains to be seen whether the movement will maintain the loose knit horizontalism that defined its flexibility early on, or whether this flexibility is needed as the movement marches forward. The remainder of this section describes the primary CARM non-profits.

In the summer of 2013, Dunn and Carter worked with Wanjuki, Brodsky, Bolger, John Kelly (University of Maryland), and others to create ED Act Now, a network of organizations lobbying for better enforcement of existing laws from the ED. Their highest profile event to date was to stage a protest outside of the Department of Education building in Washington, D.C., in May of 2014 during which they delivered a petition with over 100,000 signatures demanding that the ED better enforce existing laws and guidelines.[37] ED Act Now continues to lobby the ED for better enforcement of federal laws pertaining to campus sexual assault.

In August of 2013, End Rape on Campus (EROC) was cofounded by a small group of faculty and student activists to assist survivors in filing federal Title IX and Clery complaints. EROC's leadership has turned over several times since its founding, but it continues to assist student survivors with federal complaints, resources, and organizing advice. Also in August of 2013, Bolger and Brodsky launched Know Your IX to provide on-line resources for students to learn about their rights and federal laws pertaining to campus sexual violence. Today, Know Your IX is the most comprehensive site for survivor activists. It offers resources for survivor support, getting involved in the new CARM, filing lawsuits and federal complaints, and a host of other pertinent issues.

Dunn founded SurvJustice in late 2013, an organization dedicated to reducing the "prevalence of sexual violence by assisting survivors, empowering activists, and supporting institutions."[38] SurvJustice offers legal assistance for sexual assault survivors in civil, criminal, and campus proceedings. When Dunn filed her Title IX complaint against the University of Wisconsin-Madison in 2004, Carter offered her legal assistance in the matter. In 2013, both Carter and Dunn worked on the content for The Campus SaVE Act.[39]

Figure 5.1.   Dana Bolger, Cofounder, ED Act Now. *Dana Bolger*

In June of 2014, a group of professors formed Faculty against Rape (FAR), led by Simona Sharoni (SUNY Plattsburgh), Caroline Heldman (Occidental College), Jennifer Freyd (University of Oregon), Carol Stabile (University of Oregon), and William Flack (Bucknell College). This organization assists faculty who advocate on behalf of survivors, and offers guidance for professors who experience institutional retaliation. The FAR website provides resources for best faculty ally practices, the latest research on reducing campus sexual violence, and legal resources for faculty.

In 2016, Kamilah Willingham and Wagatwe Wanjuki cofounded Survivors Eradicating Rape Culture, an organization founded to address the concerns of marginalized survivors. This organization launched the #JustSaySorry campaign urging schools to apologize to survivors whom they have betrayed. This hashtag campaign encourages survivors across the country to burn items with their school logo—sweatshirts, hats, etc., and to post these videos of their protest burnings online.

All of these new CARM non-profits are still relatively small organizations, not rigid bureaucracies that have lost their activist edge. In this sense, even though the movement has bureaucratized, it has not suffered the fate of many movements that slow down during this phase. The decline of the new

Figure 5.2. William Flack, Cofounder, Faculty against Rape. *William Flack*

CARM, which is the last phase of social movements, is not on the horizon as of yet, and it may not be for quite some time given the renewed steam of the new CARM, inspired by the broader #MeToo Movement for which it laid the groundwork.

CONCLUSION

The new CARM has been more successful than four decades of previous campus anti-rape activism due in part to new communication technologies

Figure 5.3.   Kamilah Willingham, Cofounder, Survivors Eradicating Rape Culture. *Kamilah Willingham*

that enabled the emergence of a vast national networked movement. Activists in previous peaks were relatively isolated in their efforts to make change, but today, CARM activists connect online with ease in ways that require few resources. The new CARM has also benefitted from the political environment of the Obama Administration that was both sympathetic to and supportive of survivors. Today, the CARM faces a hostile political environment with the Trump Administration. His administration has already reversed many of the Obama-era reforms that CARM helped to enact. In terms of the maturation of the movement, the new CARM has moved through the emergence and coalescence stages to the bureaucratization stage, defined by the presence of not-for-profit organizations that are the new shape of the movement. The next social movement stage is decline, and the new CARM is not yet showing signs of this.

The CARM is one case study, but we believe it to be representative of contemporary networked social movements in terms of their ability to harness new communication technologies in unusually effective ways. Social media connects activists and allows them to more successfully set the agenda, control the message, and defend against backlash forces. Lim attributes the success of the Arab Spring to mostly invisible, online organizing and activists' ability to control the framing of the issue. In a similar vein, the #BlackLivesMatter (#BLM) movement in the United States has succeeded in raising public awareness of the issue of officer involved shootings of black Americans through online organizing and a streamlined message. Similar to the new CARM, #BLM has achieved what decades of activism on the issue of police brutality have failed to achieve. Today, every major city has an online network of BLM activists who are mobilized in response to calls for local and national action. Also, the ease with which activists can take and post video of police brutality has elevated the urgency of the situation by showing that officer involved shootings represent a pattern of behavior that violates the civil liberties of fellow Americans. Online technology in general, and social media in particular, have dramatically changed grassroots organizing in ways that scholars are just beginning to understand.

NOTES

1. Manuel Castells, *Networks of Outrage and Hope: Social Movements in the Internet Age*. Cambridge, UK: Polity Press, 2012.

2. Jeffrey Juris. "Networked Social Movements: Global Movements for Global Justice" in *The Network Society: a Cross-Cultural Perspective*, Manuel Castells, Ed., Northamton, MA: Edward Elgar Publishers, (2004): 341–362.

3. Christine E. Selig, "Transforming Our World: U.S. Grassroots Organizations and the Global Justice Movement," *Grassroots Global Justice Publications*, 2010. http://ggjalliance.org/system/files/TransformingOurWorld_Final_hiRes.pdf.

4. Victoria Carty and Jake Onyett, "Protest, Cyberactivism and New Social Movements: The Reemergence of the Peace Movement Post 9/11," *Social Movements Studies* 5 no. 3, (2007): 229–249.

5. Merlyna Lim, "Clicks, Cabs, and Coffee Houses: Social Media and Oppositional Movements in Egypt, 2001–2011," *Journal of Communication*, 62 (2012): 231–248.

6. Donald Gutstein, *How the Internet Undermines Democracy*. Toronto, Canada, 1999. Anthony G. Wilhelm, "Virtual Sounding Boards: How Deliberative Is On-line Political Discussion." *Information, Communication and Society* 1 , no. 3, (1998): 313–338.

7. Benjamin Barber, *Jihad vs. McWorld: How Globalism and Tribalism Are Reshaping the World*. New York, NY: Ballantine Books, 1996; Evgeny Morozov, *The Net Delusion: The Dark Side of Internet Freedom*. New York, NY: PublicAffairs, 2011.

8. Barber, *Jihad v. McWorld*.

9. Morozov, *The New Delusion*.

10. Zeynep Tufekci, *Twitter and Tear Gas: The Power and Fragility of Networked Protest*, New Haven, CT: Yale University Press, 2017.

11. Brian Hague and Brian Loader, *Digital Democracy: Discourse and Decision Making in the Information Age*. London, England: Routledge, 1999.

12. Dorothy Kidd, "Which would you rather: Seattle or Porto Alegre?" Paper presented at the "Our media" pre-conference of the International Association for Media and Communication Research, Barcelona, 2002.

13. Clay Shirky, "The Political Power of Social Media: Technology, the Public Sphere, and Political Change," *Foreign Affairs* 90, no. 1 (2011): 28–41.

14. Jeffrey S. Juris, "The New Digital Media and Activist Networking within Anti–Corporate Globalization Movements," *The Annals of the American Academy of Political and Social Science* 597 no. 1 (2005): 189–208.

15. See Lim, "Clicks, Cabs . . ."

16. "Petition: Department of Education: Hold colleges accountable that break the law by refusing to protect students from sexual assault." Know Your IX, 2013. *Change.org,* https://www.change.org/p/department-of-education-hold-colleges-accountable-that-break-the-law-by-refusing-to-protect-students-from-sexual-assault.

17. Maria Ruiz, "Petition: Remove Judge Aaron Persky from the Bench for Decision in Brock Turner Rape Case," *Change.org,* 2017. https://www.change.org/p/california-state-house-impeach-judge-aaron-persky.

18. Manuel Castells, *Networks of Outrage* (2012): 221.

19. Sasha Constanza-Chock, "Youth and Social Movements: Key Lessons for Allies." The Kinder & Braver World Project. December 17, 2012. Accessed June 10, 2014, http://cyber.law.harvard.edu/sites/cyber.law.harvard.edu/files/KBWYouthandSocialMovements2012_0.pdf.

20. P. G. Altbach, "Student Political Activism," In *International Higher Education: An Encyclopedia,* edited by P. G. Altbach, New York and London: Garland, (1991): 247–260.

21. Valerie M. Sue and Lois A. Ritter, *Conducting Online Surveys,* Thousand Oaks, CA: Sage, 2012.

22. Henry Jenkins, Sangita Shresthova, Liana Gamber-Thompson, and Arely Zimmerman, *By Any Media Necessary: The New Youth Activism,* New York, NY: NYU Press, 2016.

23. This assessment is based on our interactions with movement organizers.

24. Of the eight members of the 2013/14 Oxy Sexual Assault Coalition, six identified as LGBT or "queer," four were people of color, and one was a man. National gatherings of activists reflected similar racial and sexual diversity.

25. Melissa Strong, "Educating for Power: How Higher Education Contributes to the Stratification of Social Class."*The Vermont Connection* 28, (2007):51–59. Accessed March 2, 2014, http://www.uvm.edu/~vtconn/v28/Strong.pdf.

26. Murphy, 2013. "The Harsh Truth."

27. Interview with Alexandra Brodsky, December, 2013.

28. These networks are mostly hidden because activists find one another and communicate online through private means.

29. Amanda Hess, "How the Internet Revolutionized Campus Anti-Rape Activism," Slate.com, 2013, http://www.slate.com/blogs/xx_factor/2013/03/20/occidental_college_sexual_assault_case_how_the_internet_revolutionized_campus.html.

30. Frances Fox Piven and Richard A. Cloward, *Poor People's Movements: Why They Succeed, How They Fail.* New York: Vintage Books, 1978.

31. Ibid., p. 300.

32. See Castells, *Networks of Outrage,* p. 219

33. Leah A. Lievrouw, *Alternative and Activist New Media.* Cambridge, UK: Polity Press (2011): 5.

34. Jonathan Christiansen, "Four Stages of Social Movements," EBSCO Research Starters, 2009. Accessed June 10, 2014, http://www.ebscohost.com/uploads/imported/thisTopic-dbTopic-1248.pdf.

35. Willingham was a law student when she was raped at Harvard, but her experience of institutional betrayal caused her to go into public interest law with an emphasis on sexual violence.

36. Doowon Suh, "Institutionalizing Social Movements: The Dual Strategy of the Korean Women's Movement," *The Sociological Quarterly* 52, no. 3, (2011): 442–471.

37. Dylan Mattews, "Student Activists Push Obama to Act on Sexual Assault. This is Where They Want to Go From Here," *Vox,* May 7, 2014. Accessed January 1, 2018, https://www.vox.com/2014/5/7/5690682/student-activists-pushed-obama-to-act-on-sexual-assault-this-is-where.

38. SurvJustice. "About Us." 2013. Accessed June 18, 2014, http://survjustice.org/about-us.

39. Taylor Harvey, "Victim into Advocate: One Sexual Assault Survivor's Fight for Justice," *The Daily Cardinal.* April 11, 2013. Accessed June 19, 2014, http://host.madison.com/daily-cardinal/news/campus/victim-into-advocate-one-sexual-assault-survivor-s-fight-for/article_fddc55ea-a277-11e2-8f72-001a4bcf887a.html.

Chapter Six

"Women Should Avoid Dressing Like Sluts"

Campus Rape Prevention Programs

Sheron stepped up to the mic, shaking, and unfolded the piece of paper in her hand. Her voice barely came out when she started to read:

> A year ago, I stood where you stood. I was at this march to support my best friend who spoke out being raped her first week on this campus. Tonight I am speaking for myself. Devon W. raped me in November after a football game. I was too drunk to stand up, and I trusted him to take me to my dorm room. I didn't want to be here tonight, but everyone should know the kind of "friend" Devon is. I say his name tonight so that no one will ever have to say his name at this march again.

Sheron stepped down and handed the mic to another student to share her experience of sexual violence with the tearful audience of fellow survivors and supporters.

This annual ritual of speaking out publicly at Take Back the Night (TBTN) events occurs on hundreds of college campuses each year. TBTN marches are typically hosted during Sexual Assault Awareness Month in April. TBTN is but one of many programs planned by university students, faculty, and staff to address campus rape. Such programs are typically sponsored by gender equity offices or student organizations, and colleges and universities tout these events in their annual security reports as evidence that they take sexual violence seriously.

Five decades of activism from students, faculty, staff, and alums have produced a plethora of programs to address sexual violence on college campuses. Efforts to combat campus rape have evolved as laws and our understanding of the perpetration of sexual violence evolve. Campuses moved from having no programs prior to the 1970s to early programs centered on stranger rape and self-defense. In the 1990s, the campus approach shifted to acquaintance rape and the development of more effective communication and a focus on consent. The 2000s saw a shift to bystander training modules in first-year orientations as the dominant approach. Despite decades of research on sexual violence, and many policies and programs designed to eradicate the problem, the incidence and prevalence of campus sexual assault remains alarmingly high. Though many of these policies and programs are designed with prevention as a main goal, most actually focus on awareness of the problem.

In previous chapters, we discussed how the new CARM amplified various awareness campaigns. It promulgated a fervor among activists and allies alike to "do something." The CARM was successful at bringing a new sense of awareness to the epidemic, but so far, it has fallen short of producing results that measurably decreased rates of sexual violence. While some CARM activists worked on improvements to federal laws, most of the gains achieved through CARM activism have been related to reactions to campus sexual violence *after* it occurs. Indeed, much of the debate surrounding campus rape has focused almost exclusively on investigating, adjudicating, and punishing those who commit campus sexual assault. Questions of whether campus administrators or local police departments should have jurisdiction, or whether alleged offenders are granted due process rights, lose sight of an important and often unaddressed issue. Prevention of sexual violence does not occur via reactions to assaults that have already occurred. Reactionary policies are not the answer to this epidemic.[1] Prevention is.

We begin this chapter with a definition of prevention, including the nuances of what the term actually means. Then we examine existing programs that have been utilized across the United States on college campuses, and discuss the literature on their effectiveness. Finally, we return to the ideal definition of prevention and best practices for how to decrease sexual assault perpetration on campuses.

WHAT IS PREVENTION?

The Centers for Disease Control and Prevention (CDC) advocates for a public health approach to preventing sexual violence by addressing concerns before victimization ever occurs.[2] In order to prevent sexual violence from ever happening in the first place, we must understand the many factors that contribute to victimization. In other words, campus sexual violence can only be understood through a complex constellation of variables. Simplistic, one-factor answers are appealing, but the truth of the matter is that if colleges and universities want to eradicate sexual violence, they must use multiple and varied tools that span the continuum from individual to environmental factors.

The public health approach to preventing sexual violence can be tailored for use on college campuses. Regardless of where or how strategies are implemented, a public health approach to prevention has at least three levels. In fact, the CDC delineates three prevention categories.[3] Primary prevention refers to strategies that stop sexual violence before it ever happens. Secondary prevention targets the immediate and short-term impacts of victimization after it occurs, including the time period when survivors are in acute crisis mode. Tertiary prevention focuses on the prolonged consequences that survivors of sexual violence face and the treatment strategies used for individuals who perpetrate these crimes. Most conversations about the prevention of sexual violence focus on single-factor primary prevention strategies, but all of these levels must be engaged for institutions of higher education to effectively reduce sexual violence. We now turn to a description of existing prevention programs on college campuses and their effectiveness.

CAMPUS PROGRAMS

Institutions of higher education employ three general types of programs to address sexual violence: awareness raising events, prevention programs, and survivor support programs. In this section, we describe the origins of these programs and provide a basic overview of their content. We also present critiques that have come up over the years about how these events are designed and implemented. Lastly, we include an assessment of the effectiveness of these programs.

Awareness Raising Events

This section lays out the origins and intentions of campus events created to raise awareness of sexual violence. Students and other activists create many of their own programs to raise awareness, but the most popular events are Take Back the Night, the Clothesline Project, the Vagina Monologues, Denim Day, Walk a Mile in Her Shoes, and Slut Walk. We discuss these programs in the order in which they were established.

Take Back the Night

TBTN events take place on more campuses than any other sexual violence awareness program. The first TBTN march took place in the streets of San Francisco in 1973, but it did not specifically focus on sexual violence. Instead, the first march protested pornography and the serial murders of women of color in Los Angeles in the years leading up to the event.[4] TBTN marches were reframed as actions against sexual violence after microbiologist Susan Alexander Speeth was raped and murdered while walking from work to her home in Philadelphia in October of 1975.[5] A spontaneous TBTN march was held to push back against the violence directed at women in public spaces, and similar marches were held in New York City, San Francisco, Belgium, Rome, and West Germany in the years following Speeth's death. TBTN derives its name from a memorial statement that was read by activist Anne Pride at the march for Speeth.

Early TBTN marches were organized in response to specific, high-profile incidences of sexual violence against women in public spaces, but over time, this action became an annual event to publicly stand against sexual violence. TBTN marches now take place across the globe in cities, on military bases, in high schools, and on thousands of college campuses each year. These events are the most visible public display against sexual violence both on and off campus. TBTN events typically take place on campus during Sexual Assault Awareness Month (SAAM) in April. SAAM was established in 2001 by the National Coalition Against Sexual Assault.[6] The typical TBTN event involves a candlelight vigil, a rally, a march through or around campus, and an open mic speak-out where survivors publicly share their experiences. Some marches are planned during the day, and participants typically march with signs that include statements and statistics about sexual violence (see figure 6.1). Other marches take place at night, a symbolic act that signals that people should not be afraid to walk the streets after dark. Most early TBTN marches were spaces exclusively for women, but over the years, most have been opened to men and gender nonconforming individuals based on the recognition that they can be survivors, too. Today, most TBTN marches are open to allies as well as survivors.

The Clothesline Project

Many campuses feature the Clothesline Project during SAAM, a display of t-shirts with survivor stories.[7] This is another public forum where survivors can speak out about their experiences. The Clothesline Project was created in 1990 by the Women's Defense Agenda, a group of feminist activists in Cape Cod, Massachusetts.[8] They created the Clothesline Project in response to a newly published statistic that 58,000 American soldiers died in the Vietnam War, while 51,000 women were killed by domestic violence during that same time period. The symbolism of the clothesline derives from the idea that women exchange information with one another about their lives, politics, and so on while hanging out their laundry. The first program began with 31 shirts hanging on a piece of twine at a TBTN march.[9] It drew substantial press

Figure 6.1.   Take Back the Night March at New Mexico State University, Alamogordo, 2010. *Allen S., April 23, 2010*

coverage and activists across the globe set up their own Clothesline installations. Today, an estimated 500 projects take place each year in five countries with over 60,000 shirts involved.[10]

The Clothesline Project initially revolved around domestic violence, and many installations still center on this theme, but on college campuses, installations also share stories, quotes, and statements pertaining to sexual violence. This awareness-raising event usually involves a gathering where students design their t-shirts in a supportive group setting. Some campuses save t-shirts from previous years and add to their Clothesline installation each year.

Students who participate in The Clothesline Project have the freedom to share their experience however they would like, but the color of the t-shirt is significant. White shirts are reserved for women who were killed by violence, while yellow or beige shirts represent women who have been assaulted or battered. Survivors of rape and sexual assault hang shirts that are red or pink, and survivors of childhood sexual abuse hang blue or green shirts.[11] In recent years, lavender t-shirts have been added to signify people who are violated because of their sexual orientation.

The Vagina Monologues

Many schools across the nation organize performances of The Vagina Monologues in February to raise awareness and money for local domestic violence and rape crisis centers.[12] The Vagina Monologues is a play written by Eve Ensler that features a series of monologues about sexual experiences (consensual and non-consensual), sex work, reproduction, body image, genital mutilation, and other issues of sexuality. Each monologue features the voice of a different woman so the content is delivered from a first-person perspective—of a college rape survivor, a young girl who is sexually abused, an elderly woman who fears orgasm, a sex worker, a survivor of female genital mutilation, etc.

Ensler first staged the play in 1996 off-Broadway at the HERE Arts Center in New York.[13] A public rape survivor, Ensler turned her experience into one of the most effective political art campaigns in existence. In the original run, Ensler starred in The Vagina Monologues, and word-of-mouth buzz created momentum to expand performances of the play. It was soon performed on college campuses throughout the United States, organized by campus activists (not theater departments). In 2001, Whoopi Goldberg was joined by a cast of celebrities to perform the play in Madison Square Garden in New York and the play became a staple part of the national conversation around sexual violence.

The original monologues were based on interviews Ensler conducted with over 200 women about their sexual experiences. The common theme of vaginas emerged in the interviews, so she named the play accordingly, as a celebration of the vagina. Within two years of the play's launch, Ensler reframed The Vagina Monologues away from being a celebration of women to a focus on the sexual violence they experience. She included new monologues more specifically focused on this theme, and in 1998, she launched the V-Day campaign to raise money and awareness of the global issue of sexual violence against women. To date, The Vagina Monologues have raised over $100 million for organizations working against sexual violence.[14]

The Vagina Monologues performances take place on or around St. Valentine's Day each year. College students work with a faculty or staff advisor to bring the production to the stage. It is a time- and energy-intensive process that involves selecting the preferred monologues for the performance (new monologues are added every few years), casting the play, costuming, set design and creation, marketing, a busy rehearsal schedule, and managing the play the night of the performances. Campuses often perform the play two or more weekends, and the proceeds go to local rape crisis or similar anti-sexual violence organizations.

The Vagina Monologues is not without its critics. In the early years, the play came under fire for its narrow depiction of the experience of mostly white, Western women.[15] Ensler responded by adding monologues featuring women of color and non-Western women. The Vagina Monologues has long faced resistance from administrators at Catholic campuses for its racy content.[16] In 2015, The Vagina Monologues came under fire for not including content on the experiences of transgender women who do not have a vagina.[17] Some campuses have altered the play to feature the voices of transgender women, while others have dropped the play entirely in lieu of other programming. Ensler responded to this most recent criticism by pointing out that The Vagina Monologues has incorporated a monologue based on an interview with a transgender woman for the last decade, and that she supports the creation of new plays to feature the voices of women "with and without vaginas."[18] Even with the pushback from different quarters over the years, The Vagina Monologues continues to be performed on hundreds of college campuses each February to raise money for and awareness of sexual violence prevention.

Denim Day

Since 1999, campuses have marked Denim Day USA on a day in April by asking community members to wear a pair of blue jeans. This awareness campaign was inspired by a ruling by the Italian Supreme Court that a victim could not have been raped because she was wearing tight jeans.[19] The court concluded that she must have helped her rapist remove her jeans, and thus consented to the rape. The day after this ruling, female representatives in the Italian parliament wore jeans to work to demonstrate their solidarity with the victim. Denim Day was established as an annual public awareness event by Patricia Giggans, the Executive Director of the Los Angeles-based organization Peace Over Violence. On college campuses, students, faculty, staff, and administrators are encouraged to wear blue jeans to make a statement about destructive rape myths that prevent survivors from getting justice in the legal system.

In 2014, Denim Day partnered with lifestyle and jean company GUESS? The company spread the word about Denim Day through its 400 retailers in the United States and through social media inviting customers to join this action. To date, GUESS? has reached over 11 million customers with this anti-sexual violence message through Denim Day events.[20] The company also expanded the campaign to Denim Day Canada and Denim Day Europe. Even though Denim Day has existed for nearly two decades, it has become far more popular in the 2010s with the help of GUESS? and social media. The #DenimDay hashtag trends each year and participants are encouraged to post photos of their jeans with a message about sexual violence on social media sites.

Walk a Mile in Her Shoes

Walk a Mile in Her Shoes (WMHS) is a men's walk that takes place in cities and on college campuses across the globe each year to raise awareness of the role men can play in preventing rape and sexual abuse.[21] Many of the men who march don red high heels as a way of demonstrating their solidarity with women in preventing sexual violence—a literal enactment of walking in women's shoes. WMHS takes place in hundreds of locations each year as part of The International Men's March to Stop Rape, and is increasingly popular on college campuses. In addition to raising awareness about issues of sexual violence, WMHS also raises money for local rape crisis centers, domestic violence shelters, and sexual violence prevention programs.

WMHS was founded by Frank Baird in 2001 on a dare. Baird was working as a volunteer Rape Crisis Advocate at a California trauma center, and he wanted to come up with a way to get more men involved in the work. Baird recruited a small group of men to march wearing heels in a public park to show their support for sexual assault survivors, and the media attention garnered by this act spurred an international movement. Baird continues to be involved in the planning of WMHS marches.

Some activists have publicly criticized WMHS over the years for mocking femininity, trivializing sexual violence, and excluding gender queer individuals.[22] For example, UNC-Chapel Hill student Peter Vogel penned an open letter to the campus when his fraternity decided to host a WMHS march in 2015. He wrote that the march "is inappropriately festive for an event that addresses violent crime. Furthermore, as many individuals and organizations on campus have pointed out, people of all gender identities, not just women, are survivors of these crimes. What's more, not all women wear heels, and some men do!"[23] Vogel went ahead and participated in the event, but his fraternity altered the format to make it a more serious and inclusive event.

Slut Walk

Another program aimed at raising awareness of sexual violence is SlutWalk, an international movement where scantily clad women march against using any aspect of women's appearance to justify sexual violence against them. SlutWalk originated in Toronto in January of 2011 after Police Constable Michael Sanguinetti told a group of students that "women should avoid dressing like sluts in order to not be victimized."[24] His words reinforced the rape myth that women deserve to be raped if they are wearing revealing clothing, and that women can avoid sexual violence by wearing the "proper" attire. Heather Jarvis and Sonya Barnett, two college students that heard the constable's remarks, immediately organized a march from Queens Park to the Toronto police headquarters. Jarvis and Barnett used social media to spread the word, and the first SlutWalk attracted thousands of participants.[25]

Figure 6.2.   Walk a Mile in Her Shoes, Roanoke College, 2013. *Albert Herring,*
October 3, 2013

Since that time, SlutWalks have taken place in over 70 cities in the United
States, India, South Korea, and Brazil.

SlutWalk has faced criticism from some quarters since its inception.
Some feminists are critical of SlutWalk attempts to reclaim the word "slut,"
and for reinforcing the celebration of women as sexual objects.[26] Also, hundreds of black women signed an open letter to SlutWalk organizers about the
racial implications and the social impossibility of black women reclaiming
the "slut" label. But regardless of the controversy, SlutWalks have become a
staple of Sexual Assault Awareness Month on many campuses in the United
States. Some young feminists see SlutWalk as a more contemporary, less
institutionalized version of TBTN marches. But to date, TBTN marches remain the most common annual anti-sexual violence event on college campuses.

Program Effectiveness

In general, awareness campaigns and events are crucial to informing people
about how sexual violence impacts the lives of so many individuals. As noted
above, some awareness programs are not inclusive and reinforce harmful
stereotypes, so not all awareness programs are equally effective in their
design and implementation. Awareness programs are especially important

Figure 6.3.   Slutwalk, New York City, 2011. *David Shankbone, October 1, 2011*

for college students since a new group comes in each year, bringing their rape culture myths and practices from high school and the broader culture. These programs can also furnish an important healing space for sexual assault survivors. Some scholars argue that opportunities to participate in and/ or view such public displays of emotion promote empowerment.[27] Other scholars note that it is the power of emotion, or what Jill Gregory and her colleagues call affective power, that promotes the ability to make change.[28] Additionally, most of these awareness programs have a fundraising component that funnels resources to local rape crisis centers, women's shelters, and similar organizations.

To sum up, awareness programs are important because they educate each new generation of students about the problem, empower survivors, get people involved in addressing the issue, and tangibly benefit sexual violence prevention programs in the local community. These outcomes are significant in getting people to pay attention and do something about campus sexual violence, but they do not prevent this violence from happening. We now turn our focus to campus prevention programs.

Prevention Programs

Colleges and universities have developed or purchased various programs aimed at reducing or preventing sexual violence on campus. This section provides a general overview of the most frequently used prevention efforts—orientation programs and self-defense courses.

Orientation Programs

Orientation programs are events that all incoming first-year students are required to attend before classes begin. Orientations occur at a critical moment because they take place at the start of the "red zone," the first few weeks of the fall semester where first-year female college students face a higher risk of sexual violence.[29] Orientation programs vary from online programs to a one day or multiple day event, depending upon the size, mission, and resources of the institution. Historically, orientation programs have been offered at the beginning of the academic year, with programming that lasts anywhere from forty-five minutes to two hours.[30]

The purpose of orientation programs is to familiarize students with campus operations (e.g., where to go for what), introduce students to the culture and norms of the particular campus, and educate students on the perils of campus life (e.g., alcohol and drug abuse and sexual violence). In her review of early programming models, psychologist Kim Breitenbecher noted that most of these programs focused on debunking rape myths, providing prevalence data, discussing sex role socialization, identifying risky dating behaviors, and promoting empathy for rape survivors.[31] Orientation content is delivered in many different forms—written materials, review of the campus sexual violence policy, guest speakers, videos, films, musicals, comedy sketch performances, interactive exercises, discussion groups, and so on.

The University of California system adopted the first rape prevention module in its orientation program in 1976,[32] but many campuses did not include a sexual assault prevention component until the new CARM put the issue on the national agenda in 2013. Today, virtually all four-year college orientation programs at least briefly introduce students to the subject of sexual violence, and many two-year colleges are adopting orientations that speak to this issue.[33] The Campus Sexual Violence Elimination (SaVE) Act of 2015 recommends that all institutions of higher education provide sexual violence harassment prevention training to new students and employees. Here, we describe different types of orientation programs, including peer-to-peer training, online training, and bystander programs.

Some orientation programs use a peer-to-peer model. Claire Walsh created the first peer education group, Campus Organized Against Rape (COARS), in 1982 at the University of Florida, and variations on that model have been replicated on campuses since.[34] Peer-to-peer programs are typically led by junior or senior students who have had extensive training on issues of sexual violence. For example, the Get Explicit 101 program at the University of Oregon employs a "train the trainer model" where students get training on sexual violence prevention that they then use to train other students.[35] Peer-to-peer orientations and trainings take advantage of the fact that students may be more receptive to hearing about and discussing sexual practices with their peers. These programs also take advantage of the fact that male students tend to care about what other male students think of them, so older male peers can influence their behavior. For example, the Mentors in Violence Prevention (MVP) program employs masculine peer pressure by pairing upper-class male students with incoming male students to lead discussions about drinking, healthy masculinity, and preventing sexual violence.[36]

Many colleges and universities have adopted online violence prevention training programs in the last few years. The rapid adoption of online trainings occurred in response to the attention and pressure brought by the new CARM, coupled with technological advances. To date, at least nine online sexual violence prevention programs are being used by hundreds of educational institutions, including RealConsent, Haven, and Think About It.[37] Virtually all of these programs include bystander training, a focus on empathy for sexual assault survivors, content challenging rape myths, and an examination of the link between alcohol and sexual violence. The format varies widely, but they all include narratives, videos, and interactive exercises. Online training modules enable larger campuses to reach a large number of students and allow all campuses to require students to think about issues of sexual violence prior to coming to campus. Some campuses offer these trainings on an optional basis, but most institutions that use online training make them mandatory for incoming students by requiring completion before they can register for classes.

Little academic research is available on the effectiveness of online orientation trainings since they have only been in existence for a few years, but one study shows promise for these programs. Public health professor Laura Salazar and colleagues evaluated one online orientation program used by college students at a large, Southern university, and found significant improvement in knowledge, attitudes, and behaviors.[38] In a six-month follow-up survey, male students who went through the online orientation had better knowledge of consent and legal knowledge of what constitutes rape and sexual assault than male students who had not gone through the training. Male students who completed the online training were also more willing to intervene in situations where sexually violent language or behavior is used, and reported lower rates of perpetration of sexual violence. Further research is needed on multiple campuses and with different online programs to assess whether these trainings are effective at reducing rates of sexual violence on campus.

Many campuses are also using bystander training in their orientation curriculum, as recommended by the Campus SaVE Act.[39] Developed by educator Jackson Katz in the early 1990s, bystander training educates students about how they can help fellow students they see headed for a sexual assault situation. They are based on the premise that third party witnesses can intervene when they see risky situations. For example, bystander training empowers witnesses to step in if they see a fraternity brother walking an inebriated woman upstairs to his room at a party. Bystander education seeks to increase the number of individuals who would intervene,[40] but it also conveys to potential rapists that other students are on the lookout for predatory behavior.

The proliferation of bystander education and training programs to prevent sexual assault on college campuses began about a decade ago, but the emergence of such programs actually began several decades ago.[41] There are several bystander education and training protocols available, the original and most theoretically sophisticated being Katz's *Mentors in Violence Program.*[42] The two most prominent programs used today are *Bringing in the Bystander* and *Green Dot,*[43] but schools also use *The Men's Program* and *The Women's Program,*[44] and *The Men's Project.*[45] Bystander education programs share common goals, but approach them in different ways. Most programs focus on changing community attitudes and creating additional allies and helpers who will intervene when they see potentially troubling behavior. Trainees learn how they can promote and create safe environments by responding in risky situations and challenging the status quo.[46]

Evaluations of bystander intervention have shown initial promise in preliminary studies, though some of the findings are mixed. These mixed findings may be the result of the particular aspect of bystander intervention that is being studied. For example, most of the studies on bystander education focus on whether programming impacts rape myth acceptance. While several studies have found a reduction in rape myth acceptance,[47] at least three found no effect.[48] Similarly, a few studies have found that bystander training increases self-reported responsive bystander actions,[49] but these findings have not been consistent.[50] Some scholars argue that while these findings are noteworthy, they do not measure actual bystander behavior. A program or training may decrease rape myth acceptance or increase one's sense of responsibility to intervene, but such increases or decreases do not necessarily equate to actual changes in behavior. McMahon and her colleagues point out that no research to date has considered the difference between bystander behavior and bystander opportunity.[51]

Unfortunately, when bystander intervention programming has been studied using rigorous evaluation designs, they are not found to be effective at reducing sexual violence. Sarah DeGue and her colleagues defined *rigorous evaluation design* as "studies with random assignment to an intervention or control condition . . . or rigorous quasi-experimental designs . . . studies meeting criteria for rigorous evaluation design were required to have at least one follow-up assessment beyond an immediate post-test assessment."[52] In their systematic review, the aforementioned *Men's Program* had no effect on sexual violence perpetration or victimization rates. The *Acquaintance Rape Prevention Program* also had no effect.[53] *The Men's Project* had short term positive effects on self-reported sexual violence perpetration but those effects did not hold at the follow-up measure.[54] *Bringing in the Bystander* was found to have positive effects on knowledge, self-efficacy, and bystander intentions, but mixed effects on attitudes.[55] However, because there was no measure of perpetration or victimization, more research is needed. Only three interventions to date have been found to be effective using rigorous evaluation designs: Safe Dates,[56] Shifting Boundaries,[57] and the Violence against Women Act.[58] However, these three programs have not been implemented and tested at colleges and universities, and they do not involve bystander interventions, so more research is needed to determine best practices for prevention.

It is possible that certain bystander training programs can reduce sexual violence perpetration. A recent study on the effectiveness of the *Green Dot* program found that male students who attended the training had lower rates of violence perpetration than men on two comparison campuses.[59] Similarly, researcher Ann Coker and colleagues examined sexual and interpersonal violence outcomes at the population level instead of among *Green Dot* intervention participants.[60] They found that interpersonal violence victimization and perpetration rates were significantly lower on the intervention campus than on comparison campuses.[61] Rates of unwanted sexual victimization, sexual harassment, stalking, and psychological dating violence were also significantly lower on the intervention campus.[62] These results are promising because they reflect changes in rates of perpetration, which is the ultimate goal of sexual violence prevention.

Self-Defense Programs

Colleges and universities have long offered optional self-defense programs as a way to prevent sexual violence on campus. The first self-defense classes were established at rape crisis centers in the 1970s and rapidly spread throughout the country and to institutions of higher education. Within a matter of years, women started opening their own martial arts studios. Dubbed the "warrior arm" of the anti-sexual violence movement,[63] self-defense programs serve as a model for empowering women to effectively respond to verbal and physical abuse. Peace Over Violence (POV), a rape crisis center founded in Los Angeles, was one of the earliest proponents of girls and women gaining confidence and physical skills to defend against sexual and other forms of violence. In 1986, POV distributed *Self-Defense:*

Women Teaching Women, a video self-defense training program that was widely adopted by rape crisis centers and campuses across the nation.[64]

Self-defense programs multiplied on college campuses in the 1980s. The Rape Aggression Defense (RAD) program is the most popular self-defense program offered on college campuses today. Over 4,000 campuses have used this program to train female students in self-defense. RAD was started by Lawrence Nadeau in 1989. Nadeau is a former Marine, Hapkido black-belt, and law enforcement professional. He started the program while working for the Old Dominion University Police Department in Norfolk, Virginia, in order to improve campus safety for female students. The organization's website touts that is has 11,000 instructors nationwide that have trained 900,000 women.[65] The RAD model is a 12-week course that teaches defensive responses to different types of assaults as well as lessons on defensive decision-making and avoidance of high risk situations in typical college scenarios. For example, it teaches women not to trust others to hold their drinks while they use the restroom, and to be highly skeptical of going to someone's dorm room after a party, even if the person is a friend or acquaintance. RAD has come under fire from some critics for focusing on stranger rape, a type of rape that is rare on college campuses and in society more broadly.[66]

Self-defense classes saw a resurgence on college campuses in the late 2000s with more institutions offering these courses than in the previous decade.[67] In 2014, Nia Sanchez, Miss USA, stirred controversy when she suggested that self-defense training is a good way to reduce sexual violence. Critics were quick to point out that these programs are often based on rape myths and assertions about the risk of assaults by strangers, and are ineffective at best and potentially dangerous, while supporters summoned studies showing that self-defense training reduces an individual's likelihood of experiencing rape or sexual assault.[68]

To date, several studies have found support for empowerment based self-defense training, in that women who participated in comprehensive training were less likely to report sexual assault at follow-up.[69] Some scholars argue that self-defense classes are integral to primary prevention, but only as part of a larger ecological approach to prevention.[70] Empowerment based self-defense focuses on more than physical self-defense tactics. For example, an empowerment based self-defense program is more likely to focus on the various forms of violence against women, including sexual violence committed by someone the student knows. Jocelyn Hollander argues that such a program would provide instruction and education on a range of topics that empower women to choose options that are most useful for them in whatever situations they find themselves facing. Charlene Senn and colleagues designed a self-defense program coupled with lectures, exercises, and discussions about sexual violence prevention.[71] Female students who completed the program reported a significantly lower incidence of completed sexual assaults in the one year time frame studied than female students who did not complete the program.

We find that there is merit to both sides of the argument about self-defense programs. Spending campus resources on training potential victims sends the message that victims bear some responsibility in preventing sexual violence, but academic research confirms that self-defense training reduces sexual violence. Self-defense programs are one of the only campus interventions with adequate research demonstrating their effectiveness, so colleges and universities must find ways to make use of this important tool without sending a victim-blaming message to students.

Survivor Support Programs

Five decades of anti-sexual violence activism on college campuses has also produced various survivor support programs to attend to the trauma and support survivors in ways that enable them to complete their education. The two primary survivor support programs are rape crisis centers and academic support centers. The purpose of these programs is to support survivors.

Rape Crisis Centers

Student activists fought for the first campus rape crisis center at the University of Maryland in 1972, and the University of Pennsylvania established a similar office a year later.[72] Since that time, centers aimed at supporting rape survivors have gone under many different names, but the content of the programs and services have remained remarkably stable. Most offer therapeutic services or referrals for one-on-one counseling, and some offer survivor circles—survivor support groups led by mental health professionals. Today, most campuses either have a center for survivor advocacy and support, or an agreement with one of the 1,300 local rape crisis centers where students can get help after an experience of sexual violence.[73]

In the 1970s and 1980s, women's centers frequently double as campus rape crisis centers. The first women's center opened its doors at the University of Minnesota in 1960 to offer support to mothers who were returning to school to complete their education.[74] The second women's center opened a decade later in 1970 at the University of Massachusetts-Dartmouth as a birth control and abortion referral center. Starting in the mid-1970s, women's centers sprang up on hundreds of campuses in the United States to provide survivor support (and other gender-based) services. The story behind the opening of virtually every rape crisis center or women's center on campus is the story of student and faculty activism. For example, in January of 1985, students at the University of Michigan staged a sit-in in the office of Henry Johnson, the Vice President for Student Services, to demand that he open a rape crisis center on campus.[75] By May of that year, the university allocated

$75,000 to create an anti-sexual assault program, and a year later, the Sexual Assault Awareness and Prevention Program opened its doors.

Today, survivor support services typically fall under campus health centers or programs dedicated to sexual assault prevention. Most campuses have moved away from the rape crisis center and women's center labels to more accurately reflect the range of sexual violence students may encounter and the various identities of survivors, respectively. Survivor activists have also pushed for inclusive service models that take into account the particular needs of students of color and LGBT students.

In recent years, campuses have seen a trend in the hiring of victim advocates, professionals that are akin to social workers with expertise in sexual violence. Victim advocates serve as first responders, shepherding students who have experienced sexual violence through the process of completing a rape examination, obtaining counseling and other forms of therapeutic support, obtaining living and classroom accommodations so they do not encounter their perpetrator on campus, deciding which campus and judicial options to pursue, and going through the adjudication process. Victim advocates accompany survivors to campus hearings, police stations to file a report, and to courtrooms. Survivor advocates provide vital support that improves survivor outcomes and makes both educational and law enforcement institutions more responsive to survivors.[76]

Academic Support

Many colleges and universities have offered academic support services in some form since they first opened their doors, but in recent years, these programs have evolved to offer specialized support for sexual assault survivors. All institutions of higher education were mandated to offer academic accommodations in 1990 with passage of the Clery Act, but it took pressure from the new CARM in 2013 for most schools to do so. Institutions of higher education are still working out how to support survivors in a way that maximizes the likelihood they will stay in school.

Different schools offer survivors different accommodation options. As soon as a student files a claim of sexual violence, the staff member in charge of academic accommodations has the option to rearrange their class schedule to avoid encountering the perpetrator, issue a letter asking the survivor's professors for leniency in completing coursework, and offer direct academic support. They can also restore a student's academic record if it is severely tarnished by trauma symptoms that often result from experience of sexual violence. For example, they can remove a "w" from a student's record if they end up withdrawing from a class late in the semester or erase an entire semester from a student's record if she or he decides they cannot finish their coursework. Schools can also offer a tuition reimbursement if students drop courses due to trauma from sexual violence.

WHAT WORKS TO PREVENT CAMPUS SEXUAL VIOLENCE?

We know that campus sexual assault is the result of a multitude of factors, as discussed in chapter 1. In 2003, a report from the American Psychological Association (APA) concluded that prevention programming must include nine specific strategies to be effective.[77] Prevention programming must be based on the best available theory. Also, these programs must be comprehensive, in that programming cannot focus on a single factor and must address prevention at every sphere of influence. The individuals who are responsible for administering prevention strategies must be well-trained and the material utilized must be socioculturally relevant. Methods/teaching strategies must be varied to reflect varied learning styles and they must build on or support positive relationships. Programs must also include outcome evaluations. The APA also recommends that prevention programs have "sufficient dosage," meaning that they occur with adequate frequency and follow-up, and that they are appropriately timed. The CDC recommends that programs must be focused on decreasing the perpetration of sexual violence to be effective.[78]

However a campus decides to address the epidemic of campus sexual violence, one thing is certain. The program must be multi-pronged and comprehensive. Focusing on only one factor or issue will do nothing to address the overall problem of campus sexual assault. In a report prepared for the White House Task Force to Protect Students from Sexual Assault, DeGue argues for a comprehensive primary prevention strategy moving forward.[79] A comprehensive, ecological model addresses multiple levels of influence, from the individual to the community.[80] Such a model helps to maintain consistent messaging, which is particularly helpful on large campuses where many campus constituencies never come face to face. An ecological approach to prevention addresses individual level primary prevention strategies at its core, but goes much further by addressing relationship, community, and societal level variables related to sexual violence perpetration.

The individual level delineates both personal and biological risk factors for victimization and perpetration. At the individual level, campuses can implement bystander intervention programs like the ones discussed above. These programs can help individuals feel more confident about stepping in when they see something that could be a risky or harmful situation. Other individual level strategies could include programs on healthy relationship boundaries and setting healthy, non-judgmental, and positive norms about gender and sexuality. One dose programs offered during orientation have not been shown to be effective over the longer term.[81] To be effective, these individual level strategies must be based on evidence and provided across multiple sessions. Conversations about prevention must be on-going.

The next level shifts focus to the close relationships that may influence experiences with sexual violence, including peer networks, intimate partners and family members. For example, individuals who surround themselves with peer networks that are supportive of rape myths or who are sexually aggressive may be more likely to adhere to these beliefs and behaviors themselves. The community level expands spheres of influence a step further by accounting for schools, places of employment, neighborhoods, and the characteristics of other institutions that are rape supportive. When an institution shows a lack of understanding or willingness to combat sexual violence, it fosters a rape-supportive campus. Finally, the societal level focuses on the macro-cultural contexts and norms that support sexual violence. These programs require sustained focus on the causes and consequences of sexual violence. Colleges and universities are ideal for societal level interventions because of their educational mission, but shifting cultural norms is difficult, even with a relatively captive audience over four years. Table 6.1 outlines the basic structure of the CDC's socioecological approach to prevention.

Complementing the layers of the socioecological approach, social work professors Erin Casey and Taryn Lindhorst identified six necessary components of multi-level prevention efforts.[82] First and foremost, prevention efforts must be *comprehensive*. At its core, this means that strategies must be implemented across the specific domains of influence, while also involving multiple strategies that target the same outcome.[83] Effective multi-pronged approaches to prevention in other fields provides evidence that a toolkit of strategies that bridge multiple levels and outcomes is necessary.[84] Next, multi-pronged prevention must include *community engagement*.[85] In this re-

Table 6.1. Components of an Effective Sexual Violence Prevention Program

Prevention Level	Variables	Strategies
Individual	Age, income, year in school, substance abuse, prior victimization	Empowerment-based self defense, Bystander intervention
Relationship	Peers, intimate partners, family	Mentoring and/or peer programs, promoting healthy relationships
Community	School, places of employment, neighborhood, dormitory	Programs that shift institutional climate (including processes and policies)
Societal	Social and cultural norms	Programs that shift the broader culture

gard, there must be buy-in from community members both on and off campus. Approaches to sexual violence prevention must include the voices of students, faculty, administrators, and organizations in the community that partner with institutions to address this issue. Sexual assault prevention and response teams that are usually composed of campus administrators must include the individuals for whom these programs and policies are designed for. Further, sexual assault and rape-crisis centers and community mental health offices can partner with universities and share resources. Experts from these organizations can help inform campus level policy and practice.

Importantly, prevention programming must be *contextualized*. Prevention is rooted in both local and campus level norms and larger cultural factors and ideologies. Contextualizing sexual violence prevention necessitates taking account of the historical relationship between sexual violence and any given campus.[86] Consideration should also be given to the ways that various community constituents have framed the problem and their beliefs about how to combat it. As such, nationwide mandates that take a societal approach without regard for local communities are likely not going to be effective. More localized control is particularly important to sexual violence prevention on large campuses or flagship institutions with multiple statewide satellite campuses. Beliefs about sexual violence are contextualized by race, ethnicity, socioeconomic status, and community beliefs.[87] Unfortunately, to date, most prevention programs geared toward colleges and universities have ignored the importance of cultural context. In a large-scale review of college intervention programs, only one program was found to have content aimed at a specific group.[88]

Effective prevention efforts must also be situated in *sound theory*. Much of the focus on CARM activism has focused on legislative action and adjudication of cases of sexual assault. This focus seems logical and based on common sense, but the literature shows that these efforts do not result in decreases in sexual violence. A theoretically sound and theory driven strategy necessitates a change in focus from reaction to prevention. Simultaneously, prevention must shift from simply addressing risk factors for victimization and perpetration to focusing on opportunities for building on the *strengths* that individuals already possess. In other words, prevention should promote positive interactions between members of the community.[89] Promoting social support, individual and community well-being, and social competence may benefit those who are at high risk for victimization, repeat victimization, and perpetration of sexual violence.

An area of promise that has garnered little support on college campuses is the use of restorative justice frameworks to reduce and prevent sexual violence from occurring. In part, this is due to a lack of understanding about what restorative justice entails. The restorative justice approach proposes that when a wrongdoing occurs, the best way to move forward is to heal the harm done to the individual and the community through a mediation process.[90] This process entails facilitated conferences and community circles deciding the best form of reparation. Restorative justice is a sensitive area of research and practice in campus sexual violence. As some critics point out, it entails a facilitated discussion between survivors and their rapist, which can be re-traumatizing, and may not be an appropriate deterrent for violent crimes.[91] Two of the most prominent CARM organizations, End Rape on Campus and Know Your IX, oppose a restorative justice option for campus rape because they believe that shifting away from formal proceedings signals to institutions that they do not have to take sexual violence as seriously.[92]

On the other side, a small but increasing number of researchers, advocates, and survivors are calling for further research on whether restorative justice can reduce campus sexual violence. They argue that restorative justice options would likely increase reporting rates, which can ultimately reduce rates of sexual violence. The use of restorative justice in cases of sexual assault in general, and on college campuses more specifically, has been stymied by the lack of empirical evaluations on the topic. Koss and her colleagues provide a framework for using restorative justice to enhance university compliance with federal law while also providing evidence that such practices enhance justice satisfaction among participants.[93] More research is needed to determine whether restorative justice is an option for addressing campus sexual violence.

A strengths-based approach to prevention encompasses compliance with federal law while also attending to the needs of survivors, potential victims, perpetrators, and potential perpetrators. An important component of campus and community level response and prevention is through the legal and adjudication frameworks in place at a given institution. Indeed, this is where the new CARM has been most effective. In previous chapters, we learned about how activism led to the enactment of legislation aimed at violence on college campuses. The Clery Act requires colleges and universities to publish crime data. It was enacted into law in 1990 and amended in 2008 to include protections against retaliation. Despite the well-intentioned efforts of the original Clery Act and Title IX, there was a clear lack of working knowledge about what these laws required, and few institutions were in compliance. Further, most institutions reported zero instances of sexual violence in any given year. It was attention brought by activists of the new CARM that brought a renewed attention to the issue of campus sexual violence, an amendment to the Clery Act, and the new Campus SaVE Act, which required campuses to include prevention efforts. Dialogue, perhaps promoted through a restorative justice framework, can provide a strengths-based approach that enhances social support and social competence.

Finally, ecological and multi-pronged approaches must address the structural factors that allow sexual violence to occur. Individual beliefs and behaviors are most certainly influenced by structural factors. Violence against women and marginalized groups of people is perpetuated by a lack of political representation, inequities in pay and health care, and norms that promote rape culture. For many decades the analysis of rape and rape norms has been steeped in the structural factors that promote rape culture. Susan Brownmiller was writing about the structural factors related to rape in 1975.[94] The groundwork has already been paved for activists and researchers to continue this path. To continue this work, we must promote a shift in focus.

Shifting Focus and Moving Forward

Traditionally, the focus of sexual violence prevention programs on college campuses has been to stop women from being victimized by men. It is true that the vast majority of survivors of campus sexual assault are women and over 90% of perpetrators are men. However, these facts do not take into account that the highest rates of victimization are for LGBTQ individuals or that the vast majority of men are not perpetrators. These two points become increasingly important for prevention efforts. First, understanding the dynamics of perpetration by and victimization of LGBTQ people and people of color is necessary. Research suggests that LGBT and minority survivors have higher rates of sexual victimization on college campuses, but are less likely to report their experiences.[95] The voices of marginalized individuals play a pivotal role in prevention and response, but the focus of much of the research and activist agenda has remained on white, heterosexual populations. We continue to lack a full understanding of the experiences of survivors and perpetrators that are LGBTQ, black and brown, and/or otherwise underserved and marginalized.

A similar focus must be on men as part of the solution and not part of the problem. The discourse around men as allies has shifted significantly since the second wave of the Feminist Movement. When Brownmiller wrote in 1975 that rape was a sanctioned practice committed by *some men*, but served as tool to keep all women in a state of intimidation, she was tapping into a sentiment that was held and articulated by native and black anti-rape activists for more than 100 years. The sentiment holds true today, but for many, our understanding has evolved. The vast majority of men are not perpetrators, and they have the potential to play an important part in changing the discourse around what behaviors are inappropriate. It is imperative that we strike a balance between engaging men as part of the solution, while recognizing that the vast majority of perpetrators are men, however difficult this may be. The literature on preventing sexual violence suggests that men must engage as allies and model appropriate non-violent behavior, while also holding their peers accountable.[96] Additionally, there is some consensus that the most effective programs to engage men are those that are culturally specific, facilitated by men and for men.[97] Certainly, more research is needed to determine how effective such programs are in the long run, because the most rigorous evaluation studies have not found changes in men's attitudes or behaviors over the long-term.

CONCLUSION

Half a century of campus anti-rape activism has produced an assortment of programs aimed at raising awareness of the problem, preventing sexual violence, and supporting sexual assault survivors. The earliest programs that emerged in the 1970s employed a stranger rape approach that centered on self-defense and support services after the fact. The 1990s brought a new awareness of the prevalence of acquaintance rape, and campus programs evolved to emphasize definitions and understandings of consent, and guidelines for more effective communication. In the 2000s, bystander programs gained traction. These programs train and empower all members of the campus community to step in to prevent sexual violence at various stages of a potentially violent interaction. Today, most campuses offer programs that reflect all three approaches.

This chapter presented a description of the origin, content, and critiques of the programs most frequently employed on college campuses for raising awareness, prevention, and survivor support. In terms of preventing violence, limited academic research lends support to the effectiveness of some bystander programs and self-defense programs.

In terms of best practices, we propose a public health approach that encompasses primary, secondary, and tertiary prevention. As such, researchers who study campus rape must conduct longitudinal studies that include rigorous evaluation designs. These studies must account for the multilevel ecological approach to prevention outlined by the CDC. Research on individual level bystander intervention is important, but the impact of such an intervention cannot be understood without a comprehensive analysis of variables at play at the campus and community level. Similarly, future research should include the voices of those impacted by campus sexual violence to better understand what resources are most essential for those who have already experienced sexual violence and for those who may become victims in the future. Too often, the user voice is left out of conversations about what has been most helpful. Simultaneously, studies that take account of the voices of male allies, community partners, and even perpetrators are crucial to our understanding of prevention programming.

As we will discuss in the next chapter, changes in the U.S. political climate have led to a decrease in focus on and funding for sexual violence response and prevention. The new CARM has focused renewed attention to the issues of sexual violence, which now extends beyond campuses to the broader culture through the #MeToo Movement, but awareness is not enough. Prevention is key, but more research is needed to determine which interventions are the most effective. The most significant impact the CARM could have moving forward is to demand government funding for evidence based preventions.

NOTES

1. Alissa R. Ackerman and Karen J. Terry, "Faulty Sex Offense Policies," In Reddington, Fran & Gene Bonham (Eds). *Flawed Criminal Justice Policy: At the Intersection of the Media, Public Fear and Legislative Response*, Durham, NC: Carolina Academic Press, 2011; Karen J. Terry and Alissa R. Ackerman. "A brief history of major sex Offender laws." *Sex Offender Laws: Failed Policies, New Directions* (2009): 65–98.

2. "Sexual Violence Prevention: Beginning the Dialogue," Centers for Disease Control and Prevention, Atlanta, GA, 2004.

3. Centers for Disease Control and Prevention (2004).

4. "History," *Take Back the Night*, accessed April 30, 2017, https://takebackthenight.org/history/.

5. Megan Gibson, "Take Back the Night," *Time Magazine*, August 12, 2011, accessed January 8, 2014, http://content.time.com/time/specials/packages/article/0,28804, 2088114_2087975_2087967,00.html.

6. "SAAM History," *National Sexual Violence Resource Center*, accessed April 30, 2017, http://www.nsvrc.org/saam/saam-history.

7. "History of the Clothesline Project," *The Clothesline Project,* accessed January 8, 2014, http://www.clotheslineproject.org/History.html.

8. "About the Clothesline Project," *The Clothesline Project*, accessed May 2, 2017, http://clotheslineproject.info/about.html.

9. Ibid.

10. Ibid.

11. Ibid.

12. Eve Ensler, "The Vagina Monologues," accessed January 8, 2014, http://www.eveensler.org/plays/the-vagina-monologues/.

13. Ibid.

14. Caitlin Moscatello, "Here are One Billion Reasons to Get Up and Dance on Valentine's Day," *Glamour*, February 13, 2014, http://www.glamour.com/story/one-billion-rising-for-v-day.

15. Kaitlin Mulhere, "Inclusive Dialogues," *Inside Higher Education*, January 21, 2015, https://www.insidehighered.com/news/2015/01/21/womens-college-cancels-play-saying-it-excludes-transgender-experiences.

16. Scott Jaschik, "The 'Vagina Monologues' Test," *Inside Higher Ed*, April 7, 2006, https://www.insidehighered.com/news/2006/04/07/catholic.

17. Mulhere (2015).

18. Mulhere (2015), Internet page 1.

19. "History," *Denim Day,* accessed January 8, 2014, http://denimdayusa.org/about/history/.

20. "Unified in Denim," *Denim Day*, accessed May 2, 2017, http://denimdayinfo.org/about/#/guess-partnership.

21. "About," *Walk a Mile in Her Shoes,* accessed May 3, 2017, http://www.walkamileinhershoes.org/About/about.html.

22. For example, Samantha Escobar, "Why 'Walk a Mile in Her Shoes' Falls Short (and What You *Can* Do to End Sexual Violence)," *The Gloss*, March 8, 2013, accessed December 30, 2017, http://www.thegloss.com/culture/why-a-mile-in-her-shoes-falls-short-and-what-people-can-do-to-end-sexual-violence/.

23. Peter Vogel, "Walk a Mile UNC Style: A Response to Criticism," *The Siren,* April 10, 2015, accessed December 30, 2017, http://uncsiren.com/walk-mile-unc-style-response-criticism/.

24. Allie Grasgreen, "The Power of SlutWalks," October 5, 2011, accessed May 2, 2017, https://www.insidehighered.com/news/2011/10/05/slutwalks_create_controversy_as_new_approach_fighting_sexual_violence.

25. Kaitlynn Mendes, *Slutwalk: Feminism, Activism and Media*, New York: Palgrave, 2015.

26. Grasgreen (2011).

27. Patricia Coral Hipple, "Hegemonic disguise in resistance to domination: the Clothesline Project's response to male violence against women" (1998); Laura Julier, "Private texts and social activism: Reading the Clothesline Project," *English Education* 26, no. 4 (1994): 249–259; Constance J. Ostrowski, "The clothesline project: women's stories of gender-related violence," *Women and Language* 19, no. 1 (1996): 37.

28. Jill Gregory, April Lewton, Stephanie Schmidt, Diane "Dani" Smith, and Mark Mattern, "Body politics with feeling: The power of the clothesline project," *New Political Science* 24, no. 3 (2002): 433–448.

29. Stephen Cranney, "The Relationship Between Sexual Victimization and Year in School in U.S. Colleges: Investigating the Parameters of the 'Red Zone,'" *Journal of Interpersonal Violence*, 30(17), 2015: 3133–3145.

30. Kimberly Hanson Breitenbecher, "Sexual assault on college campuses: Is an ounce of prevention enough?," *Applied and Preventive Psychology* 9, no. 1 (2000): 23–52.

31. Breitenbecher (2000).

32. Jodi Gold and Susan Villari, *Just Sex: Students Rewrite the Rules on Sex, Violence, Equality, and Activism*, Lanham, MD: Rowman & Littlefield, 1999.

33. Eliza Gray, "Colleges Find New Ways to Tackle Sexual Assault as Students Return," *Time*, August 24, 2015, accessed May 3, 2017, http://time.com/4006145/colleges-new-ways-tackle-sexual-assault/.

34. Gold and Villari (1999).

35. Eilene Zimmerman, "Campuses Struggle with Approaches to Preventing Sexual Assault," *The New York Times*, June 22, 2016, accessed May 5, 2017, https://www.nytimes.com/2016/06/23/education/campuses-struggle-with-approaches-for-preventing-sexual-assault.html?_r=0.

36. Laura Starecheski, "The Power of the Peer Group in Preventing Campus Rape," NPR, August 18, 2014, accessed May 3, 2017, http://www.npr.org/sections/health-shots/2014/08/18/339593542/the-power-of-the-peer-group-in-preventing-campus-rape.

37. "Online Programs," *Culture of Respect*, accessed May 3, 2017, https://cultureofrespect.org/colleges-universities/programs/.

38. L. F. Salazar, A. Vivolo-Kantor, J. Hardin, and A. Berkowitz, "A Web-Based Sexual Violence Bystander Intervention for Male College Students: Randomized Controlled Trial." *Journal of Medical Internet Research* 16, no. 9 (2014): e203.

39. Jennifer Katz, and Jessica Moore, "Bystander education training for campus sexual assault prevention: An initial meta-analysis," *Violence and Victims* 28, no. 6 (2013): 1054–1067.

40. Katz and Moore (2013).

41. Victoria L. Banyard, Elizabeth G. Plante, and Mary M. Moynihan, "Rape prevention through bystander education: Final report to NIJ for grant 2002-WG-BX-0009," Durham: University of New Hampshire (2005); Christine A. Gidycz, Lindsay M. Orchowski, and Alan D. Berkowitz, "Preventing sexual aggression among college men: An evaluation of a social norms and bystander intervention program," *Violence Against Women* 17, no. 6 (2011): 720–742.

42. Jackson Katz, H. Alan Heisterkamp, and Wm. Michael Fleming, "The social justice roots of the mentors in violence prevention model and its application in a high school setting," *Violence Against Women* 17, no. 6 (2011): 684–702.

43. "Living the Green Dot," accessed April 23, 2017, https://www.livethegreendot.com/; "Bringing in the Bystander: Overview," accessed April 23, 2017, http://cola.unh.edu/prevention-innovations/bystander-overview.

44. John D. Foubert, *The men's and women's programs: Ending rape through peer education*. New York: Routledge, 2011.

45. Gidycz, Orchowski, and Berkowitz (2011).

46. Katz and Moore (2013).

47. Courtney E. Ahrens, Marc D. Rich, and Jodie B. Ullman, "Rehearsing for real life: The impact of the InterACT Sexual Assault Prevention Program on self-reported likelihood of engaging in bystander interventions," *Violence Against Women* 17, no. 6 (2011): 760–776; Angela Frederick Amar, Melissa Sutherland, and Erin Kesler, "Evaluation of a bystander education program," *Issues in Mental Health Nursing* 33, no. 12 (2012): 851–857; Victoria L. Banyard, Mary M. Moynihan, and Maria T. Crossman, "Reducing sexual violence on campus: The role of student leaders as empowered bystanders," *Journal of College Student Development* 50, no. 4 (2009): 446–457; Victoria L. Banyard, Mary M. Moynihan, and Elizabethe G. Plante, "Sexual violence prevention through bystander education: An experimental evaluation," *Journal of Community Psychology* 35, no. 4 (2007): 463–481; Ann L. Coker, Bonnie S. Fisher, Heather M. Bush, Suzanne C. Swan, Corrine M. Williams, Emily R. Clear, and Sarah DeGue, "Evaluation of the Green Dot bystander intervention to reduce interpersonal violence among college students across three campuses," *Violence Against Women* 21, no. 12 (2015): 1507–1527; John D. Foubert, and Ryan C. Masin. "Effects of the men's program on US Army soldiers' intentions to commit and willingness to intervene to prevent rape: a pretest posttest study." *Violence and Victims* 27, no. 6 (2012): 911–921; Jennifer Langhinrichsen-Rohling, John D. Foubert, Hope M. Brasfield, Brent Hill, and Shannon Shelley-Tremblay, "The men's program: Does it impact college men's self-reported bystander efficacy and willingness to intervene?" *Violence Against Women* 17, no. 6 (2011): 743–759.

48. Gidycz, Orchowski, and Berkowitz; E. Miller, D. Tancredi, H. McCauley, M. Decker, M. Virata, H. Anderson, et al. "'Coaching boys into men': A cluster-randomized controlled trial of a dating violence prevention program." *Journal of Adolescent Health, 51,* (2012): 431–438; Mary M. Moynihan, Victoria L. Banyard, Julie S. Arnold, Robert P. Eckstein, and Jane G. Stapleton, "Engaging intercollegiate athletes in preventing and intervening in sexual and intimate partner violence," *Journal of American College Health* 59, no. 3 (2010): 197–204.

49. Coker, et al.; Miller, et al.; Sharyn J. Potter and Jane G. Stapleton, "Translating sexual assault prevention from a college campus to a United States military installation: Piloting the know-your-power bystander social marketing campaign," *Journal of Interpersonal Violence* 27, no. 8 (2012): 1593–1621.

50. Banyard, et al.; Gidycz, et al.

51. Sarah McMahon, Judy L. Postmus, Corinne Warrener, and Ruth Anne Koenick, "Utilizing peer education theater for the primary prevention of sexual violence on college campuses," *Journal of College Student Development* 55, no. 1 (2014): 78–85; Sarah McMahon, Jane E. Palmer, Victoria Banyard, Megan Murphy and Christine A. Gidycz, "Measuring Bystander Behavior in the Context of Sexual Violence Prevention Lessons Learned and New Directions," *Journal of Interpersonal Violence* (2015): 0886260515591979.

52. Sarah DeGue, Linda Anne Valle, Melissa K. Holt, Greta M. Massetti, Jennifer L. Matjasko, and Andra Teten Tharp, "A systematic review of primary prevention strategies for sexual violence perpetration," *Aggression and Violent Behavior* 19, no. 4 (2014): 346–362, p. 349.

53. Christine A. Gidycz, Melissa J. Layman, Cindy L. Rich, Marie Crothers, Julius Gylys, Abigail Matorin, and Cecilia Dine Jacobs. "An evaluation of an acquaintance rape prevention program: Impact on attitudes, sexual aggression, and sexual victimization." *Journal of Interpersonal Violence* 16, no. 11 (2001): 1120–1138; Holly A. Pinzone-Glover, Christine A. Gidycz, and Cecilia Dine Jacobs. "An acquaintance rape prevention program: Effects on attitudes toward women, rape-related attitudes, and perceptions of rape scenarios." *Psychology of Women Quarterly* 22, no. 4 (1998): 605–621.

54. Gidycz, Orchowski, and Berkowitz (2011).

55. Banyard, et al. (2007); Mary M. Moynihan, Victoria L. Banyard, Julie S. Arnold, Robert P. Eckstein, and Jane G. Stapleton, "Engaging intercollegiate athletes in preventing and intervening in sexual and intimate partner violence," *Journal of American College Health* 59, no. 3 (2010): 197–204; Sharyn J. Potter and Mary M. Moynihan, "Bringing in the bystander in-

person prevention program to a US military installation: Results from a pilot study," *Military Medicine* 176, no. 8 (2011): 870.

56. Vangie A. Foshee, Karl E. Bauman, Ximena B. Arriaga, Russell W. Helms, Gary G. Koch, and George Fletcher Linder, "An evaluation of Safe Dates, an adolescent dating violence prevention program," *American Journal of Public Health* 88, no. 1 (1998): 45–50; Vangie A. Foshee, Karl E. Bauman, Susan T. Ennett, G. Fletcher Linder, Thad Benefield, and Chirayath Suchindran, "Assessing the long-term effects of the Safe Dates program and a booster in preventing and reducing adolescent dating violence victimization and perpetration," *American Journal of Public Health* 94, no. 4 (2004): 619–624; Vangie A. Foshee, Karl E. Bauman, Wendy F. Greene, Gary G. Koch, George F. Linder, and James E. MacDougall, "The Safe Dates program: 1-year follow-up results," *American Journal of Public Health* 90, no. 10 (2000): 1619.

57. Taylor (2011, 2013).

58. Rachel Boba and David Lilley, "Violence Against Women Act (VAWA) funding: a nationwide assessment of effects on rape and assault," *Violence Against Women* 15, no. 2 (2009): 168–185.

59. Ann L. Coker, Bonnie S. Fisher, Heather M. Bush, Suzanne C. Swan, Corrine M. Williams, Emily R. Clear, and Sarah DeGue, "Evaluation of the Green Dot bystander intervention to reduce interpersonal violence among college students across three campuses," *Violence Against Women* 21, no. 12 (2015): 1507–1527.

60. Ann L. Coker, Heather M. Bush, Bonnie S. Fisher, Suzanne C. Swan, Corrine M. Williams, Emily R. Clear, and Sarah DeGue, "Multi-college bystander intervention evaluation for violence prevention," *American Journal of Preventive Medicine* 50, no. 3 (2016): 295–302.

61. Coker, et al. (2016).

62. Coker, et al. (2016).

63. "Empowerment Through Self-Defense for Women and Girls: A Model for Primary Prevention," *Peace Over Violence,* accessed April 30, 2017, http://www.peaceoverviolence.org/media/downloadables/Empowerment_Through_Self-Defense.pdf.

64. "Pioneers Over Violence," *Peace Over Violence,* accessed April 30, 2017, http://www.peaceoverviolence.org/media/downloadables/Empowerment_Through_Self-Defense.pdf

65. "About R.A.D.," *Rape Aggression Defense Systems,* accessed on April 30, 2017, http://www.rad-systems.com/about_us.html.

66. Susan Schorn, "A Look Inside the Terrible Manual Cops Use to Teach 'Rape Prevention,'" Jezebel, February 25, 2015, accessed April 30, 2017, http://jezebel.com/a-look-inside-the-terrible-manual-cops-use-to-teach-rap-1687694067.

67. Samantha Reid, "College Women Adding Self-Defense Classes to Fall Semester To-Do Lists," *USAToday College,* June 25, 2014, http://college.usatoday.com/2014/06/25/self-defense-classes-gaining-popularity-among-college-women/.

68. Lauren R. Taylor and Lynne Marie Wannamaker, "Actually, Miss USA IS Right: Self-Defense Can Prevent Sexual Assaults," *The Washington Post,* June 16, 2014, https://www.washingtonpost.com/posteverything/wp/2014/06/16/actually-miss-america-is-right-self-defense-can-prevent-sexual-assaults/?utm_term=.2b8da337911f.

69. Jocelyn A. Hollander, "Does self-defense training prevent sexual violence against women?" *Violence Against Women* 20, no. 3 (2014): 252–269; Charlene Y. Senn, Misha Eliasziw, Paula C. Barata, Wilfreda E. Thurston, Ian R. Newby-Clark, H. Lorraine Radtke, and Karen L. Hobden, "Efficacy of a sexual assault resistance program for university women," *New England Journal of Medicine* 372, no. 24 (2015): 2326–2335.

70. Jocelyn A. Hollander, "The importance of self-defense training for sexual violence prevention," *Feminism & Psychology* 26, no. 2 (2016): 207–226; Martha McCaughey and Jill Cermele, "Changing the Hidden Curriculum of Campus Rape Prevention and Education Women's Self-Defense as a Key Protective Factor for a Public Health Model of Prevention," *Trauma, Violence, & Abuse* (2015): 1524838015611674; Martha E. Thompson, "Empowering self-defense training," *Violence Against Women* 20, no. 3 (2014): 351–359.

71. Charlene Y. Senn, Misha Eliasziw, Paula C. Barata, Wilfreda E. Thurston, Ian R. Newby-Clark, H. Lorraine Radtke, and Karen L. Hobden, "Efficacy of a Sexual Assault Resistance Program for University Women," *New England Journal of Medicine*, 372 (2015): 2326–2335.

72. Jodi Gold and Susan Villari, *Just Sex: Students Rewrite the Rules on Sex, Violence, Equality, and Activism*, Lanham, MD: Rowman & Littlefield, 1999.

73. National Alliance to End Sexual Violence, "Campus Sexual Assault," June 2014, accessed May 4, 2017, http://endsexualviolence.org/where-we-stand/campus-sexual-assault.

74. Gwendolyn Beetham, "The Academic Feminist: We Heart Women's Centers," *Feministing*, September 9, 2014, accessed May 4, 2017, http://feministing.com/2014/09/15/the-academic-feminist-we-heart-womens-centers/.

75. "Our History, Sexual Assault Prevention and Awareness Center," *University of Michigan,* accessed April 30, 2017, https://sapac.umich.edu/article/158.

76. Casey Smith, "How Victims Advocates Support Student Sexual Assault Survivors," *USATodayCollege*, April 3, 2017, accessed May 4, 2017, http://college.usatoday.com/2017/04/03/how-victim-advocates-support-student-sexual-assault-survivors.

77. Nation, et al. (2003).

78. Centers for Disease Control and Prevention. (2014) *Preventing sexual violence on college campuses: Lessons from research and practice.* Retrieved January 5, 2017 from https://www.notalone.gov/schools/

79. Centers for Disease Control and Prevention (2014).

80. Sarah DeGue, Melissa K. Holt, Greta M. Massetti, Jennifer L. Matjasko, Andra Teten Tharp, and Linda Anne Valle, "Looking ahead toward community-level strategies to prevent sexual violence," *Journal of Women's Health* 21, no. 1 (2012): 1–3.

81. Centers for Disease Control and Prevention (2014).

82. Erin A. Casey and Taryn P. Lindhorst, "Toward a multi-level, ecological approach to the primary prevention of sexual assault prevention in peer and community contexts," *Trauma, Violence, & Abuse* 10, no. 2 (2009): 91–114.

83. A. Jason Leonard, Carrie J. Curie, Stephanie M. Townsend, Steven B. Pokorny, Richard B. Katz, and Joseph L. Sherk, "Health promotion interventions," *Child & Family Behavior Therapy* 24, no. 1-2 (2002): 67–82; Edison J. Trickett, "Context, culture, and collaboration in AIDS interventions: Ecological ideas for enhancing community impact," *Journal of Primary Prevention* 23, no. 2 (2002): 157–174.

84. Robert D. Felner, Tweety Yates Felner, and Morton M. Silverman, "Prevention in mental health and social intervention," In *Handbook of Community Psychology*, pp. 9–42. Springer US, 2000.

85. Cheryl Merzel and Joanna D'Afflitti, "Reconsidering community-based health promotion: promise, performance, and potential," *American Journal of Public Health* 93, no. 4 (2003): 557–574; Vivian Tseng, Daniel Chesir-Teran, Rachel Becker-Klein, May L. Chan, Valkiria Duran, Ann Roberts, and Nenshad Bardoliwalla, "Promotion of social change: A conceptual framework," *American Journal of Community Psychology* 30, no. 3 (2002): 401–427.

86. Tseng, et al. (2002).

87. Lisa Aronson Fontes, *Sexual abuse in nine North American cultures: Treatment and prevention*. Vol. 11. Sage, 1995.

88. Linda A. Anderson and Susan C. Whiston, "Sexual assault education programs: A meta-analytic examination of their effectiveness," *Psychology of Women Quarterly* 29, no. 4 (2005): 374–388.

89. Nation, et al. (2003).

90. Harry Mika and Howard Zehr, "A Restorative Framework for Community Justice Practice," In Kieran McEvoy and Tim Newburn, Eds., *Criminology, Conflict Resolution and Restorative Justice*. Basingstoke, Hampshire, UK and New York, NY: Palgrave MacMillan, 135–152, 2003.

91. Stacy Teicher Khadaroo, "Campus Sexual Assault: Should Restorative Justice Be An Option?" *NPR*, October 13, 2017, accessed December 31, 2017, https://www.csmonitor.com/EqualEd/2017/1013/Campus-sexual-assault-Should-restorative-justice-be-an-option.

92. Ibid.

93. Mary P. Koss, Jay K. Wilgus, and Kaaren M. Williamsen, "Campus sexual misconduct: Restorative justice approaches to enhance compliance with Title IX guidance," *Trauma, Violence, & Abuse* 15, no. 3 (2014): 242–257; Mary P. Koss, "The RESTORE program of restorative justice for sex crimes: Vision, process, and outcomes," *Journal of Interpersonal Violence* 29, no. 9 (2014): 1623–1660; Jill Levenson and Alissa R. Ackerman, "The Stanford Rape Case: Are We Having the Wrong Conversation?" *Psychology Today Guest Blog,* 2016. https://www.psychologytoday.com/blog/the-guest-room/201607/the-stanford-rape-case.

94. Susan Brownmiller, *Against Our Will,* New York: Simon and Schuster (1975).

95. Christopher P. Krebs, Christine H. Lindquist, Tara D. Warner, Bonnie S. Fisher, and Sandra L. Martin, "The differential risk factors of physically forced and alcohol- or other drug-enabled sexual assault among university women," *Violence and Victims* 24, no. 3 (2009): 302–321; Alan M. Gross, Andrea Winslett, Miguel Roberts, and Carol L. Gohm, "An examination of sexual violence against college women," *Violence Against Women* 12, no. 3 (2006): 288–300.

96. Michael Flood, "Changing men: Best practice in sexual violence education," *Women Against Violence: An Australian Feminist Journal* 18 (2006): 26.

97. Leanne R. Brecklin and David R. Forde, "A meta-analysis of rape education programs," *Violence and Victims* 16, no. 3 (2001): 303–321; Mary J. Heppner, Helen A. Neville, Kendra Smith, Dennis M. Kivlighan Jr, and Beth S. Gershuny, "Examining immediate and long-term efficacy of rape prevention programming with racially diverse college men," *Journal of Counseling Psychology* 46, no. 1 (1999): 16.

Chapter Seven

"Let's Change the Culture"

The Future of the Campus Anti-Rape Movement

"I told the head of your studio that HW [Harvey Weinstein] raped me. Over & over I said it. He said it hadn't been proven. I said I was the proof."

Actor Rose McGowan tweeted these words at Amazon studio head Jeff Bezos after she publicly outed Harvey Weinstein as a serial rapist in October of 2017. The ongoing national conversation on sexual harassment/violence that the new CARM began back in 2013 turned a corner the day the *New York Times* broke the Weinstein allegations. Angelina Jolie, Gwyneth Paltrow, Ashley Judd, and a slew of other celebrity women came forward to report their experiences with Weinstein. The Weinstein revelations produced a snowball effect where hundreds of women (and some men) publicly named high-profile predators. Giants in different industries were fired or stepped down from their positions, including actor Kevin Spacey, director James Toback, comedian Louis C. K., television host Matt Lauer, comedian and Senator Al Franken, actor Jeffrey Tambor, host Charlie Rose, and entertainment mogul Russell Simmons.

The celebrity status of the Weinstein victims/survivors generated the most intense public discussion of sexual harassment/violence we have ever seen in the United States, and it generated a wave of public survivorship in the #MeToo campaign that, like the early CARM movement, was made possible by social media. To date, 1.7 million people in 85 countries have posted about #MeToo on social media, many sharing personal stories of sexual harassment and sexual assault.[1] The #MeToo campaign did not magically appear out of thin air in 2017. Anti-sexual violence activist Tarana Burke created the "Me Too" campaign back in 1997, and actress Alyssa Milano popularized it on Twitter in 2017, but it joined a national dialogue that had already been under way for three years. This dialogue shifted focus from institutions of higher education to the entertainment industry in 2015 when 35 women went public about sexual violence from famed comedian Bill Cosby. (To date, 60 women have gone public with allegations of sexual violence against Cosby.[2]) Cosby survivors appeared on the cover of the *New York Magazine* in July of 2015, causing a national stir.

The national discussion of sexual violence shifted focus from Cosby to the news media in 2016 when cable news host Gretchen Carlson successfully removed Fox News head Roger Ailes for sexual harassment, and in 2017, popular Fox hosts Bill O'Reilly and Eric Bolling were removed from Fox News after multiple allegations of sexual misconduct surfaced.[3] The #MeToo campaign marks a turning point in terms of the number of survivors who have gone public, the swift response from many industries (to fire men with multiple allegations), heightened public support for addressing the crisis, and greater belief that victims/survivors are telling the truth when they come

Figure 7.1.   Cosby Survivors on the Cover of *New York Magazine*, July, 2015.
New York Magazine *cover, used with permission*

forward.[4] The work of a scrappy band of student and faculty activists, armed with laptops and federal complaints, primed the pump for this turning point.

As a relatively new social movement, the CARM has enjoyed many successes, the most notable being the ongoing national dialogue that culminated in the #MeToo campaign. But as of yet, the new CARM has not measurably reduced rates of campus rape, and it faces many challenges endemic to social movements as it moves forward. In this closing chapter, we present an overview of CARM successes, then detail what we see as the biggest challenges to the new CARM moving forward. Sexual violence is a salient issue in the United States right now, but it will take a great deal of time and enormous resources to shift cultural norms so that campuses and other spaces are relatively free from sexual violence. In the time it takes to shift campus culture (which requires a shift in the broader culture), the public will likely become fatigued of hearing stories about sexual assault/rape, and many activists will tire from the protracted struggle. These points were true when top government officials cared about the issue, and with the election of Donald J. Trump, survivors no longer have the empathetic ear of the president. Upon coming into office in January of 2017, the Trump Administration immediately reversed some of the Obama-era campus rape regulations and sent a clear message that it will not advance the interests of sexual assault survivors, on or off campus. The new CARM has enormous barriers to success moving forward, not the least of which is a political climate hostile to survivor interests.

We begin this chapter with an analysis of the successes of the new CARM. We then analyze challenges facing the movement, specifically, the new political environment, an emboldened backlash, a new campus climate, and a likely loss of movement momentum. We close with a look at what lies ahead for the new CARM.

CARM SUCCESS

The biggest success of the new CARM to date has been to launch the second national dialogue about sexual harassment/violence (the first being in the early 1990s in response to Anita Hill's senate testimony during the confirmation process of Justice Clarence Thomas). The nation's leading newspapers and international press have provided extensive on-going coverage of movement efforts, and campus rape has received ample coverage in popular news blogs, the feminist blogosphere, and several documentary films. The new CARM's use of public survivorship via social and mainstream media set the stage for women going public about Cosby, Fox News personalities, Weinstein, and others.

Another major accomplishment of the new CARM is enactment of stronger laws to address campus sexual violence. Anti-sexual violence advocates have written and lobbied for campus rape laws for decades, and CARM activists worked with experts, advocates, and legislators to craft and pass the Campus SaVE Act in 2014. Also, the Obama Administration solicited input from academic experts and survivor activists, many of whom were CARM activists, to create a report on the campus rape crisis. The White House issued its report in April of 2014 that recommends that campuses conduct annual climate surveys, adopt prevention measures, and improve their reporting and investigation processes.[5] CARM activists also strengthened the enforcement of existing laws by filing federal complaints with the Department of Education (ED). The spate of federal complaints filed in 2013 and 2014 led to over 300 ED investigations into potential violations, which sent a clear message to institutions of higher education that the government was stepping up oversight.[6]

The success of passing new laws, and improving enforcement of existing laws, is somewhat tempered by a lack of funding and personnel for the ED. The ED is overwhelmed with the current number of Title IX investigations, and even though funding for these investigations doubled from 2014–2016,[7] cases now take about five years to investigate. As we saw with the Clery Act, passed in 1990 and ignored by most institutions for two decades, laws on the books do not translate into implementation without oversight. This means that new CARM activists must maintain pressure on the ED, elected officials, and institutions of higher education to ensure that Title IX, Clery, and Campus SaVE provisions are enforced.[8]

Another success of the new CARM has been to shift the way colleges and universities address campus sexual violence. In a nutshell, institutions of higher education now make campus sexual violence a high priority. The public nature of the new CARM—online campaigns targeting specific colleges and universities, survivors sharing their experiences in social media—has been a game changer because institutions can no longer rely on the silence of survivors to hide their mishandling of campus rape. While some colleges and universities prioritized the campus rape issue before the new CARM, most did not. Today, institutions run the risk of being targeted by an on-campus student campaign or the national CARM network if this issue is not a priority. The prioritization of campus rape has likely led to less institutional betrayal of survivors after they experience sexual violence, but research is needed to know for sure. Even though CARM has increased the salience of campus rape, prioritizing an issue does not automatically translate into effective violence reduction policies and practices.

The new CARM has not had success in measurably reducing campus violence due to the enormity and complexity of the issue, a lack of research on best practices, and perverse institutional disincentives. Campuses face many challenges in reducing campus rape, namely, that they are working with students who are coming into their community with nearly two decades of rape culture socialization. Additionally, institutions have only limited research on best practices for preventing sexual violence, and establishing a comprehensive program requires intense resources, expertise, and personnel. Colleges and universities are incentivized to provide a safe environment for their students, for reasons of basic humanity and the potential for reputational loss if they are seen as an unsafe place to send young adults. But these incentives are met with opposing reputational and economic disincentives for administrators to minimize the campus rape problem, as we explore later in this chapter. One of the weaknesses of the new CARM is the rather prevalent idea that reducing campus sexual violence is simply a matter of administrator will, so the movement has yet to demand the most basic element of reducing sexual violence: research on how to do so.

To sum up, while the new CARM has been successful in raising public awareness, strengthening legislation, and getting colleges and universities to prioritize campus rape, the movement has yet to make serious headway in reducing rates of sexual violence on campus. The new CARM was working toward coherent goals the first few years of the movement, despite the leaderlessness nature of new network movements, but today, the movement has less direction. This is due in part to social movement bureaucratization that causes activists working with CARM non-profits to focus on more narrow organizational goals; due in part to activist attrition from exhausting emotional work and the backlash; and due in part to the emphasis of titular leaders on garnering media attention in ways that have caused movement divisions. Going forward, even though the #MeToo campaign has momentarily renewed activist energy, the new CARM still faces major hurdles, the most pressing being a newly hostile political environment.

THE POLITICAL CLIMATE

Even though sexual violence could be an issue that everyone cares equally about (since people of all political persuasions experience rape), it is not. Instead, culture war politics that pit some Republicans against "anything feminist" has turned campus rape into a partisan political issue. Furthermore, the election of Trump to the highest office was a game changer for the new CARM. The election of an alleged sexual predator to the White House furthers rape culture, and Trump's political appointments and budget are practical indicators that the federal government is no longer behind the efforts of the new CARM. We examine these aspects of the political climate in turn.

"Predator-in-Chief"

One month before the presidential election in 2016, the *Washington Post* obtained and then released a 2005 recording of Donald Trump making lewd comments about women.[9] On the recording, Trump can be heard saying, "You know I'm automatically attracted to beautiful—I just start kissing them. It's like a magnet. Just kiss. I don't even wait. . . . And when you're a star, they let you do it. . . . You can do anything. . . . Grab them by the pussy. You can do anything."[10]

In his own words, the Republican nominee for president was bragging about sexually assaulting women.

In the wake of the release of this recording, members of the media and politicians from both parties were quick to publicly denounce Trump's comments, but for many Republicans, the Access Hollywood tape did not diminish their support for Trump's candidacy.[11] By the end of October of 2016, twelve women had come forward to report that Trump sexually harassed/assaulted them.[12] The allegations had patterns. They involved Trump twice kissing a Miss USA contestant without her consent; Trump groping a woman in the seat next to him on a plane; Trump kissing a receptionist without her permission; Trump telling the camera "I'll be dating her in 10 years. Can you believe it?" (in reference to a 12-year-old Paris Hilton); Trump telling a gathering of 14-year-olds that he would be dating them in a couple of years; Trump sexually assaulting a reporter from *People Magazine* at Mar-A-Lago; Trump groping a family friend, a business associate, and Miss Washington USA; Trump walking in on multiple beauty contestants over the years while they were changing; Trump raping his ex-wife Ivana (as detailed in her divorce deposition); and Trump raping a 13-year-old at a party at convicted pedophile Jeffrey Epstein's house (as detailed in court documents from the plaintiff and a witness statement from a woman who procured underage girls for Epstein).[13]

Despite a dozen allegations and Trump's own words, he went on to win the presidential election and was labeled "Predator In-Chief"[14] and "Groper in Chief"[15] in the press. In response to Trump's election, legal professor Gillian Chadwick wrote "apparently Trump was right when he told Billy Bush, 'when you're a star, they let you do it. You can do anything.'"[16] Survivors of sexual violence experienced elevated trauma responses in the lead up to election night and in the aftermath of Trump's inauguration.[17] Many survivors faced increased fear and anxiety and felt silenced and unseen. How was it possible that in 2016 a man with many allegations of sexual assault and a released recording of him admitting to this behavior could still win the Electoral College? The short answer for many activists was *rape culture.* Feminists who had been working on the issues of sexual violence for decades, and new CARM activists, had a rude awakening. Even though sexual violence was on the national political agenda and most Americans had become aware of it as a social problem, rape culture is alive and well in the United States.

Once elected, Trump again caused alarm amongst survivor activists when he defended Bill O'Reilly against claims of sexual harassment. On April 5, 2017, in response to questions about several sexual harassment lawsuits settled by Fox News against O'Reilly, Trump told a reporter from the *New York Times*, "I think he's a person I know well—he is a good person. I think he shouldn't have settled; personally I think he shouldn't have settled. Because you should have taken it all the way. I don't think Bill did anything wrong."[18] Within a matter of weeks, additional women came forward alleging that O'Reilly had sexually harassed them, and on April 19, 2017, Fox News fired its most popular host.[19] In similar fashion, in the fall of 2017, Trump backed Alabama senate candidate Roy Moore after multiple allegations surfaced that he had been sexually inappropriate with teenage girls when he was a district attorney.[20] One woman, Leigh Corfman, alleged that Moore had sexual relations with her when she was 14 years old and he was 32 years old. Even though the #MeToo Movement was in full swing, Trump tweeted his support of this alleged child sexual predator. The president of the United States expressing public support for a man who, like Trump, faced numerous complaints of sexual misconduct, was troubling for many survivors and those who work in the anti-violence movement.

Political Appointments

On a practical level, Trump's appointment of Betsy DeVos as the new secretary of education meant that campus violence has been deprioritized. During her confirmation hearing, DeVos would not commit to upholding the guidelines for addressing campus rape established under the Obama Administration that lay out specific standards for how long investigations should take, the appropriate standard of evidence to use, and requirements for processing complaints.[21] When asked about whether she would uphold the guidelines in the 2011 Dear Colleague Letter (DCL), DeVos replied that it would be "premature" to commit to it.[22] In response to DeVos' testimony before the senate, Democratic senators Bob Casey (D-Penn.) and Patty Murray (D-WA) wrote a letter to president-elect Trump expressing their concern about the Administration rescinding the 2011 DCL given that it has been "instrumental in providing these schools with the tools they need to address the scourge of campus sexual assault."[23] In September of 2017, DeVos rescinded the 2011 DCL.[24] At the same time, she also issued new guidelines that allow schools to use a different standard of proof for sexual violence that results in fewer findings of responsibility for rapists, and a new rule that schools can use mediation as an option in campus rape cases.

Beyond changing regulations, as the secretary of education, DeVos has tremendous power in determining college and university accountability for sexual violence. She can slow the work of the Clery and the Office for Civil Rights (OCR) divisions within the Department of Education by simply reallocating personnel and other resources to stymie the work of these already understaffed offices. She can also appoint directors of the Clery division and OCR who do not support survivor-centered approaches to addressing sexual violence. Elections have consequences, and Trump's election has profound consequences for the work of the new CARM.

DeVos' reversal of Obama-era policies is far from over. Her actions so far, and rhetoric on the matter, are taken straight from the playbook of the Foundation for Individual Rights (FIRE), an organization to which she contributed $25,000 from 2010 to 2013.[25] FIRE is ostensibly a campus free-speech organization, and in the campus rape debate, they side exclusively with students accused of rape. FIRE wants to do away with every Obama-era guideline on sexual violence. For example, FIRE wants schools to use the legal "beyond a reasonable doubt" standard that would allow virtually every sexual predator on campus to go unpunished (instead of the 5% of total sexual predators who currently receive some sort of punishment for their actions). FIRE also advocates for law enforcement to process campus rape cases instead of schools, a process that provides victims even less justice than campus adjudications, as discussed in the chapter on shifting legal landscapes. (It is worth noting that getting expelled for raping on campus carries penalties similar to getting expelled for plagiarism: They have about the same expulsion rates, neither is listed on one's transcripts, and the perpetrator of either violation can transfer during the adjudication process or after with relative ease. FIRE's intense focus on procedural issues with campus rape and not other violations, like plagiarism, does not make sense unless viewed through a rape culture lens that privileges the rights of some students over others.) DeVos' support for FIRE is a troubling indication that the work of the Obama Administration to reduce campus rape will perhaps be entirely undone during Trump's time in office.

Budget Cuts

Within the first few months of Trump's presidency, he proposed an 18% cut in funding for Health and Human Services and a 4% cut to the Department of Justice, the two agencies that fund the Violence Against Women Act (VAWA).[26] The location of these cuts would be up to the discretion of the two agency heads, but there is no doubt that funding for sexual violence prevention will be reduced under this budget given its low priority for the Trump Administration. Mona McLaughlin, a representative from the National Network to End Domestic Violence, estimates that Trump's first budget would cut access to shelters and support services for survivors of domestic and sexual violence for 260,000 people.[27] At the time we are writing this, the Trump presidency is still new and it remains to be seen what policies he will prioritize aside from repealing the Affordable Care Act and building a wall on the southern border, but given his lack of concern about sexual violence, as evidenced in his personal behavior, cabinet picks, and budgets, it is safe to assume that he will not champion campus sexual assault prevention. Trump's election has also emboldened new CARM backlash forces, the topic of the next section.

THE EMBOLDENED BACKLASH

The backlash of the early 1990s against the campus anti-rape movement effectively shut down the campus rape debate, but the current backlash—which is far more organized with better reach and funding—has not been effective so far. This ineffectiveness is likely due to the fact that we now have many more studies confirming rates of sexual violence on campus, and because social media enables CARM activists to frame the debate and counter misinformation. But the backlash against the new CARM is substantial, and the election of Trump has emboldened it.

President Obama's open support for eliminating rape on college campuses had the collateral effect of making it a partisan issue. The backlash of the 1990s was led by men's rights groups that oppose any and all feminist efforts to advance gender justice, but the new backlash is being orchestrated by well-positioned conservative commentators and organizations with media platforms. As soon as the CARM moved into the national spotlight, talk show hosts Glenn Beck and Laura Ingraham responded that the campus rape problem was overstated.[28] Conservative columnists George Will,[29] Jay Ambrose,[30] Cathy Young,[31] Naomi Schaefer Riley,[32] Emily Yoffe, and Heather MacDonald[33] entered the fray with editorials dismissing sexual violence as a manufactured problem driven by dishonest women. A collection of nonprofits has worked like a well-oiled machine to discredit the new CARM, including FIRE, the American Enterprise Institute,[34] and the Manhattan Institute for Policy Research.[35] This network of organizations is funded by top conservative donors, including the DeVos family, Charles and David Koch, the Castle Rock Foundation, and the Scaife Family Foundation—conservative families that seek to influence policy through think tanks and advocacy groups that advance right wing reforms in education and other policy domains.[36]

Much like the backlash of the early 1990s, today's rape apologia comes in four distinct forms: denying the problem exists, blaming victims, vilifying whistleblowers, and protecting perpetrators. We describe each of these themes of the backlash in turn to give the reader a sense of the backlash that has already begun.

Denying the Problem

The most popular backlash tactic is to challenge the data. Many backlashers claim that the problem of campus rape has been overstated. They criticize the sample selection and response rate of the 2007 Campus Sexual Assault (CSA) study, the basis for the White House statistic that 1 in 5 college women face attempted or completed sexual assault.[37] While it is easy to poke holes in the methodology of one study, especially if readers are statistical neophytes, this approach fails to acknowledge that the CSA figures are about the same as similar studies conducted by researchers at the Medical University of South Carolina,[38] the Centers for Disease Control and Prevention,[39] and the Harvard School of Public Health.[40]

Some in the backlash challenge the 1 in 5 statistic because they do not think that "incapacitated sexual assault" is "real rape." Conservative columnist Cathy Young writes that "a far better solution would be to draw a clear line between forced sex (by violence, threats or incapacitation) and unwanted sex due to alcohol-impaired judgment, miscommunication or verbal pressure." Naomi Schafer Riley states that "there's been no epidemic of sexual assault but instead a preponderance of sexual encounters fueled by bad judgment and free-flowing alcohol." These ideas sound oddly similar to men's rights activist Warren Farrell's assertion in the 1990s that "date rape" was "buyer's remorse."[41] Today, Men's Rights Activists (MRAs) are part of the backlash— challenging the definition of rape, taking to the streets to plaster posters with "just because you regret a one night stand doesn't mean it wasn't consensual"[42] and flooding the anonymous rape reporting systems at different colleges with fake rape reports.[43]

One of the problems with the "real rape" argument is that it ignores the law. All 50 states have laws that say an incapacitated party cannot consent to sex, with some variations on the definition of "incapacitation." For example, "incapacitation" in Colorado is defined as being "physically helpless," "unconscious, asleep, or otherwise unable to indicate willingness to act," or "substantially impaired from any drug or intoxicant." Florida defines "incapacitation" as "mentally incapacitated" or "temporarily incapable of appraising or controlling a person's own conduct due to the influence of a narcotic, anesthetic, or intoxicating substance administered without his or her consent or due to any other act committed upon that person without his or her consent." But regardless of how the state defines incapacitation, the common thread is that it forecloses the possibility of consent.

Blaming the Victim

There are many outspoken conservatives on the issue of campus rape who place the onus on young women to prevent rape in ways that are both damaging and distracting. For example, Emily Yoffe penned a piece entitled, "The Best Rape Prevention: Tell College Women to Stop Getting Drunk."[44] Beyond blaming survivors, Yoffe inaccurately classifies rape as a drunken miscommunication problem instead of a problem of rape culture in which one-in-ten college men rape, and one-in-three of those who rape do so more than once. Serial campus rapists' principal weapon is alcohol, and they are able to hide in plain sight within a male-dominated party culture where men provide the venues, parties and drinks to women, often with the explicit purpose of hooking up. Perpetuating the misconception that raping an intoxicated woman (or man) isn't "real rape" simply emboldens college rapists to continue to use their weapon of choice—alcohol. Victim blamers also tend to ignore the evidence that rapists target women (and men) who are sober, too.[45]

Vilifying Whistleblowers

Some members of the backlash go after survivors who speak up, or publicly name survivors, in an effort to chill public survivorship. For example, on June 6, 2014, *Washington Post* writer George Will published a column arguing that being a rape survivor is a "coveted status" that "confers privileges," and implied that those who report rape are "delusional."[46] CARM activist Wagatwe Wanjuki responded to Will's claims with the viral hashtag campaign #survivorprivilege in which survivors shared facts about what their rapes cost them. Others backlashers have levied brutal attacks against survivors by encouraging men's rights groups to troll their social media profiles and publishing private documents with revealing personal details. In the spring, A Voice for Men, a website affiliated with 1990s backlasher Warren Farrell, published an illegally obtained copy of a Title IX complaint against Emerson College that includes deeply private details about several sexual assaults/rapes.[47] The website included the names of the survivors but redacted the names of all of the alleged rapists, effectively discouraging future survivors from filing complaints. In a similar vein, FIRE published lawsuit documents filed by a student rapist expelled from Occidental College that included the names of witnesses in the case but not the perpetrator.[48] The witnesses were then subjected to a vile email campaign from MRAs. For example, one witness received an email asking "What kind of a radical fucking man hating dyke are you?"[49] Another witness was told by a stranger to "Please, slice your goddamn wrists, nail your pussy shut and go wait tables before you harm someone else. It's bitches and whores like you who give women a bad name." That same witness pointed out the silencing effect of being publicly named: "Future witnesses might not step forward or tell the whole truth because they do not want their friends and family—let alone the world—to know that they had been drinking or smoking the night of an incident, all important pieces to a testimony."[50]

Protecting Perpetrators

The last major tactic of the backlash is to protect perpetrators—framing them as the real victims because they are seen as "guilty until proven innocent."[51] Backlashers that make this argument fail to acknowledge that campus proceedings have historically allowed most perpetrators to go unpunished, and data show that this is still overwhelmingly the case. Backlashers who protect perpetrators frame college men found responsible for rape as victims of false rape reports.[52] When a person comes forward to report a rape, there is a 92 percent to 98 percent chance they are telling the truth, so false rape reporting is not a common problem,[53] but perpetrators not being held accountable is.

Protection of perpetrators has become a legal tactic due to organizations like FIRE and SAVE Services, a group that fights against what it calls "rape hoaxes." These organizations recruit young men to sue schools after they have been expelled for sexual misconduct.[54] Men found responsible for sexual misconduct have sued Columbia University, Xavier University, Duke University, Vassar College, the University of California San Diego, Indiana University, and many other institutions of higher education in recent years. Since 2011, more than 150 men found responsible for sexual violence have sued their institutions claiming due process violations.[55] The sheer volume of these lawsuits speaks to the organized nature of the litigation efforts. FIRE offers free legal counsel for perpetrators but not victims (who have historically suffered egregious injustice in campus rape adjudications), so their claim to be concerned about due process is dubious. This new wave of due process litigation often ends in settlements as schools wish to keep their names out of the press.[56] Oddly enough, many of these due process claims are filed using Title IX with the argument that colleges are acting with gender bias against men in adjudicating sexual violence on campus.

Backlash tactics of denying a campus rape problem exists, blaming the victim, vilifying whistleblowers, and protecting the perpetrators have yet to effectively undercut the success of the new CARM. The general public is better informed about the causes and consequences of sexual assault, and while rape myths persist, they can now be debunked in real time by experts. For example, Yoffe's victim-blaming piece inspired instant and searing denouncements from *Jezebel*, *Feministing*, *The Huffington Post*, *The Atlantic*, *Salon*, and even *Slate*'s own Amanda Hess. Another example was the rapid response from CNN, *Salon*, *U.S. News & World Report*, and other major outlets condemning George Will's comments about survivor privilege. The editor of the *St. Louis Post-Dispatch* dropped Will's syndicated column and issued an apology stating that the piece was "offensive and inaccurate." Nonetheless, the political environment under Trump probably spells a renewed backlash. Backlash forces now have a kindred spirit in Trump and DeVos.

Backlashers are using the newly hostile political environment to advance their political position through the courts, the executive branch, and the legislative branch. The question is whether the new CARM can sustain its momentum in the face of new political opposition, the emboldened backlash, and educational institutions that face competing incentives and disincentives to truly address campus sexual violence. We explore this third challenge for the movement in the next section.

THE CAMPUS CLIMATE

In the fall of 2016, professor and CARM activist Caroline Heldman met with Jonathan R. Alger, the president of James Madison University, a school that was infamously ridiculed by Jon Stewart on The Daily Show for expelling three students found responsible for rape "after graduation"[57] in 2014. Heldman had been brought to campus by concerned members of the community to give a lecture on the CARM, and the president seemed displeased by the invitation. During their meeting, when talk turned to the success of the new CARM, Alger told Heldman that everything would change with campus rape as soon as there was a change in political leadership, meaning the election of Donald Trump, and he was right. Once Trump was elected to office, some college administrators breathed a sigh of relief that new accountability measures enacted by the ED under Obama would not be enforced with the same rigor. To be fair, many campus presidents and other administrators remain dedicated to continuing the policies and procedures they adopted under the Obama Administration, but lessened accountability from government officials takes the pressure off. Lack of federal enforcement portends a new campus climate, yet another challenge for the new CARM.

Without proper federal oversight, most institutions of higher education ignored Clery Act guidelines (issued in 1990) for over two decades, and failed to follow Title IX guidelines (issued in 2001) for over a decade. The new CARM forced colleges and universities to pay attention by filing a wave of Clery Act and Title IX complaints, which speaks to the power of grassroots activism, but also to the necessity of government oversight. Without government will to enforce these guidelines, campuses have the option of essentially ignoring them. This is an easier path than the expensive and intensive process of figuring out how to effectively reduce campus sexual violence. True reform requires schools to shift rape culture, a herculean undertaking even with the will and resources to do so. Colleges cannot single-handedly shift broader rape culture because this would require multiple societal institutions working together to address deep-seated sexist beliefs upheld by everyone in our society. Rape culture describes a society in which rape is common and normalized by societal attitudes and practices.[58] In U.S. society, rape is tacitly condoned through denial of the rape epidemic, denial of the harms of rape, not considering rape a "real" crime, victim-blaming, trivializing rape, and the normalization of female sexual objectification and rape eroticization in pop culture. But colleges can shift rape culture on their campuses by implementing a multi-tiered socioecological intervention model, as discussed in the last chapter. To date, some institutions of higher education have balked at making even basic changes that would shift rape culture.

It seems like common sense that schools would make sure that their student body understands legal definitions of consent, sexual battery, sexual assault, and rape before stepping a foot on campus, or at least by the end of the first week of classes. But few students understand legal definitions of rape and there is widespread confusion about what constitutes consent. According to a recent national study, over 40 percent of students say that getting undressed or getting a condom constitutes consent to sexual acts (they do not).[59] When it comes to male attitudes about rape, psychologist Sarah Edwards and colleagues find that 31.7 percent of male college students say they would "have intercourse with a woman against her will" if there were no consequences, but that number drops to (a still astonishingly high) 13.6 percent of male students if the word "rape" is used.[60] This drop indicates that approximately one-in-five male college students do not know that having sex against someone's will is rape. Many women are also unaware of what constitutes rape. Seventy-one percent of college women who were raped while intoxicated, and 47 percent of women who were forcibly raped, do not classify what happened to them as rape.[61] Instead, they classify these experiences as an "unpleasant incident" or a lesser crime.[62] Schools benefit from hazy definitions of consent because this keeps reported rape numbers low.[63] If more survivors came forward to report sexual violence, schools would have to provide more staff resources to handle the complaints and, at the same time, a steep increase in rape allegations would threaten the school's reputation and bottom line.

It also seems like common sense that schools would have clear sanctions tied to different types of sexual misconduct and publish them, like many schools do for plagiarism, theft, and other violations of the student code of conduct.[64] But officials are reluctant to develop standard sanctions and advertise them because this would mean they would lose the ability to apply sanctions in an individualized way that takes other factors into account, such as whether the student is a star athlete or how much money the perpetrator's family has contributed to the institution.[65] No institution of higher education in the United States publishes or uses specific punishments for different acts of sexual misconduct. A key element of shifting rape culture is sending the message that this behavior will not be tolerated, and it is impossible to send this message without establishing uniform punishments for different acts of sexual violence.

Why are some campus officials so averse to making even modest changes to address the campus problem? We argue that this is not caused by uncaring or "bad" administrators and staff members. Most campus administrators went into this career because they care deeply about students. Instead, lagging response to campus rape is better explained by institutional disincentives and perverse incentives that work against real reform: cost, lack of expertise, financial loss, and reputational loss. We briefly describe each of these structural issues in turn.

The first disincentive for real reform is cost. As noted above, shifting rape culture means educating students about definitions of consent and sexual violence, but this would lead to an immediate increase in students reporting incidences of sexual violence. More survivors coming forward means more staff members are needed to adjudicate cases and provide support services for survivors. Currently, only one-in-ten campus sexual assault survivors report their experience to campus authorities. If even half of survivors filed a complaint with their school, the cost would go up approximately 400%. Title IX officers are trained professionals with commensurate salaries, and many external investigators are attorneys or law enforcement professionals that command a high hourly wage. In simple economic terms, an informed student body translates into more reporting of sexual assault, which is expensive for colleges and universities.

The second issue driving tepid response from some institutions is lack of trained professionals. The new CARM forced college officials to pay attention to sexual violence on campus, and given previous oversight of this issue, there was little demand in higher education for professionals who are properly trained on this issue. It will take years for graduate programs to train enough people to fill the campus demand for sexual violence experts, and in the meantime, many institutions are hiring expensive experts-for-hire.[66] Campuses flush with resources can afford to hire experts dedicated to preventing and adjudicating sexual violence, while schools that are cash-strapped cannot offer their students the improved safety and support that trained professionals provide. The shortage of experts on sexual violence prevention is further compounded by the lack of research on best practices analyzed in the last chapter. This means that even "experts" with excellent legal training who are up to date on the latest theories and findings from psychology, sociology, social work, and public health still do not have the knowledge they need to create an effective socioecological program on their campus given that so little research on best practices is available.

The third and fourth institutional challenges for reforming rape culture on campus—reputational and financial damage—are connected. Effectively addressing campus rape requires colleges and universities to gather accurate data on their actual numbers (through a campus climate survey) and encouraging survivors to report incidences. The first campuses that tell the truth about their numbers will be labeled "Rape University" in the minds of many because the true numbers are so high on virtually every campus. This reputational loss translates into fewer applicants and a loss of revenue. For example, Dartmouth and Amherst applicants dropped 14 percent and 8 percent, respectively, after each school made national headlines for mishandling sexual assault on campus.[67] One recent study finds that if a school scandal is mentioned in the *New York Times* at least five times, the school will face an average 9 percent drop in applications the following year.[68] Colleges and university officials thus have perverse economic incentives connected to reputational damage to keep their number of sexual assault reports artificially low. The job of a campus administrator tasked with tackling sexual violence is tough. We know of many campus administrators who have doubled-down in their commitment to reducing campus violence now that the political will has diminished, while other administrators see relaxed federal oversight as an opportunity to focus on the many other pressing concerns of running a complex human organization. This new political environment does not mean that all or even most colleges and universities will suddenly stop offering programs they have put in place in the past few years, but it does mean that they will not be compelled by the ED to push forward on finding and implementing best practices. The new CARM has been successful in bringing about reforms in campus policy and procedures because the federal government responded to their concerns. Today, the ED is not capitulating to survivor activists, so the question is whether new CARM activists can find ways to keep institutions on the path to meaningful reform without a powerful government ally.

MOVEMENT MOMENTUM

The new CARM faces many internal challenges that are common to social movements in general: slowing momentum and internal struggles. In this section we analyze why and how the social movement is slowing, and what this means for activism and progress on the issue. As laid out in a previous chapter, social movements typically move through four stages: emergence, coalescence, bureaucratization, and decline.[69] The new CARM is in the bureaucratization stage, as evidenced by the multitude of national organizations that activists have established since 2013 that specifically address sexual violence on campus—End Rape On Campus, Know Your IX, SurvJustice, Survivors Eradicating Rape Culture, Faculty Against Rape, and others. These organizations offer resources on student rights and actions they can take; facilitate the filing of Title IX and Clery complaints; provide referrals for survivor support services; and offer media training. Actions that were ad hoc and grassroots at the start of the movement are now being handled by survivor activists who have become experts; some through attending law school, others through experience in the movement for half a decade. The frenetic energy of the early years of the movement has dissipated, and even though it has been renewed with the #MeToo Movement, this new energy will also soon evaporate as public attention turns to other societal ills. The outrage over survivor mistreatment is renewed with each new class of college students, and many new activists join the new CARM each year, but the movement is no longer in the process of finding its way onto the national agenda. It has arrived, and with it, the mechanization and activist exhaustion that tend to slows movement momentum. The filing of new federal complaints barely registers on the national press radar, and little ado is made about lawsuit settlements or direct action such as a march or an occupation. In short, the momentum that drove the new CARM for five years is slowing, the natural progression of social movements over time.

Another factor slowing the momentum of the movement is compassion fatigue, meaning that some members of the public have grown tired of hearing yet another case of sexual violence.[70] The term compassion fatigue is used in academic literature to refer to first responders and social workers who become immune to the tragedies of the clients they serve. It can also be applied to the public when they are inundated with stories about a pressing societal problem such as AIDS, homelessness, and childhood sexual abuse.[71] No research exists on compassion fatigue with sexual violence, but this fatigue is inevitable given the emotional valence of the issue and the fact that moderate and heavy consumers of media have been exposed to numerous online and print stories, radio segments, news shows, and documentaries on the subject. Kinnick and her colleagues find that about 30 percent of Americans report compassion fatigue for social issues that are on the national agenda and receive a lot of media coverage,[72] so it is possible that the new CARM and the larger #MeToo campaign will maintain momentum with a critical mass of Americans for years to come.

Internal struggles also present a challenge for the new CARM moving forward. Mediation expert Kenneth Cloke writes that "Internal conflicts are endemic and natural to progressive political and social movements, in part because it is difficult to agree on how to define and change highly complex, volatile and evolving social problems."[73] Since the start of the movement, new CARM activists have publicly disagreed on proposed legislation, the use of federal complaints, survivors settling lawsuits instead of going to court, whose names should be in the paper, who started the new CARM, who should get credit for what work, the erasure of long-time anti-sexual violence activists, profiting off of survivor stories, publishing survivor stories without permission, who "owns" the movement, and a multitude of other concerns. We have no doubt that some activists of the new CARM will take exception to the account of the movement in this book because it does not adequately credit their work. Credit and ownership have been major points of contention in the movement since its inception. To date, we find that these internal struggles have curbed the effectiveness of the movement because activists were not able to come together with a shared set of goals and strategies for achieving those goals. Early energy and momentum was squandered on in-fighting. Furthermore, some early activists have left the new CARM because they found the internal strife to be re-traumatizing and emotionally exhausting. These struggles have plagued the new CARM from the start, and they present a major challenge to movement sustainability moving forward.

LOOKING AHEAD

Like the Greek myth of Sisyphus, cursed to forever roll an immense boulder up a hill, the fight against sexual violence in the United States has been long and rarely fruitful. African-American women led the organized charge against sexual violence from Reconstruction into the 20th century, and when white feminists got involved in anti-rape work in the 1970s, the leadership of black women on this issue was virtually erased. Activists have been organized on college campuses for the past half a century, but what is happening now is different. The new movement is networked—decentralized, connected through hidden online networks, and without formal leadership. Its reach is wider than any previous movement against sexual violence, and it has deeply pierced public consciousness. It started a national dialogue that culminated in the #MeToo Movement in 2017, the most high-profile moment of grappling with sexual harassment/violence in U.S. history.

On college campuses, school administrators were able to sidestep necessary reforms to their assault/rape policies and practices for decades because survivors did not realize that their experiences of institutional betrayal were shared. This new networked movement has given survivor activists far more power in holding educational institutions accountable. Our analysis shows that the success of the new CARM is due to promoting public survivorship, garnering mainstream media coverage, controlling the message, and fortuitous political timing. The networked nature of the movement enabled activists to organize and strategize on a national level, and to assist one another in filing federal complaints and filing lawsuits. These networks empowered activists and contributed to survivor healing through resource sharing and online emotional support. The new normal of public survivorship has also empowered survivors to speak about their experiences, and to be named in public spaces. These aspects of the new CARM account for its effectiveness after five decades of previous campus activism that resulted in only minor progress on the issue.

Our case study analysis confirms that online technology facilitates grass-roots activism, which improves democracy by increasing citizen voice and participation. The new CARM has mobilized citizens across the United States to participate in organizing around issues of campus sexual violence, and it provided forums for discussion, resource sharing, and healing that were not possible prior to the advent of online communication technologies. Activists used online networks to organize, and leveraged social media to garner media coverage, which in turn inspired a national conversation about the issue and action from the highest levels of government.

Compared to half a century of previous activism around campus rape, our findings suggest that new networked movements are more effective than classic social movements in putting issues on the national agenda. The national debate about campus rape in the early 1990s was quickly shut down by a backlash that diminished the importance of the issue by labeling it "date rape" and suggesting that women who claimed rape were lying. Today, CARM activists control the terms of the debate through social media and public survivorship in ways that counter a similar backlash. Even though media is more politically partisan today than it was in the early 1990s, and conservative publications have used the same tactics as the backlash that silenced the groundswell of activism two decades ago, the backlash has simply not been effective because of real time response from new CARM activists.

The new CARM has been one of the most effective contemporary social movements when it comes to raising public awareness of the issue, getting on the national policy agenda, and pressuring schools to start the lengthy process of effective reform. It faces many challenges in moving forward—a hostile political terrain that may reverse new laws and guidelines; a return to lax federal enforcement of existing laws; an emboldened backlash; school administrators with perverse incentives against effective reform; the slowing momentum of the movement; internal movement struggles; lack of a common set of goals moving forward; and lack of adequate research on best practices for reducing campus sexual violence.

The challenges of the new CARM are numerous and daunting, but even if the movement disappeared today, it has established a new public awareness of the problem that will not disappear for at least a generation. Campuses have institutionalized meaningful reforms, such as more transparent, fairer adjudication processes and better survivor support services. Many administrators are committed to reducing sexual violence on their campus, and to do away with their new policies and practices would stir opposition from staff, faculty, and students. But perhaps most importantly, the new CARM laid the groundwork for the #MeToo campaign and inspired a new wave of feminist activism, the likes of which we have not seen in half a century. Girls today are growing up in a post-Weinstein culture that offers a heightened feminist consciousness, whether they use that word or not. Rape culture continues to define American culture, but we will never go back to a time when most survivors remained silent because they knew no one would believe them.

NOTES

1. Andrea Park, "#MeToo Reaches 85 Countries with 1.7M Tweets," *CBS News*, October 4, 2017. Accessed December 31, 2017, https://www.cbsnews.com/news/metoo-reaches-85-countries-with-1-7-million-tweets/.

2. Chichi Esteban and Manuel Roig-Franzia, "Bill Cosby's Survivors Now Number 60. Here's Who They Are," *The Washington Post*, August 3, 2016. Accessed December 31, 2017, https://www.washingtonpost.com/graphics/lifestyle/cosby-women-accusers/.

3. Emily Steel and Michael S. Schmidt, "Bill O'Reilly Settled New Harassment Claim, Then Fox Renewed His Contract," *New York Times*, October 21, 2017. Accessed December 31, 2017, https://www.nytimes.com/2017/10/21/business/media/bill-oreilly-sexual-harassment .html?_r=0. The first author made public allegations of gender discrimination and sexual harassment against Bill O'Reilly and Eric Bolling.

4. Danielle Kurtzleben, "Poll: Americans Overwhelmingly Support 'Zero Tolerance' on Sexual Harassment," *National Public Radio*. December 14. Accessed January 1, 2018, https://www.npr.org/2017/12/14/570601136/poll-sexual-harassment-ipsos.

5. The White House, "FACT SHEET: Not Alone—Protecting Students from Sexual Assault," April 29, 2014. Accessed May 1, 2014. http://www.whitehouse.gov/the-press-office/2014/04/29/fact-sheet-not-alone-protecting-students-sexual-assault.

6. "Title IX: Tracking Sexual Assault Investigations," *The Chronicle of Higher Education*. Accessed January 1, 2018, https://projects.chronicle.com/titleix/.

7. Tyler Kingkade, "Federal Campus Rape Investigations Near 200, and Finally Get More Funding," *The Huffington Post*, January 6, 2016. http://www.huffingtonpost.com/entry/federal-funding-campus-rape-investigations_us_568af080e4b014efe0db5f76.

8. W. James Antle III, "How Campus Rape Became a Partisan Issue," *The Week*, December 12, 2014. http://theweek.com/articles/441603/how-rape-became-partisan-issue.

9. David Farenhold, "Trump recorded having extremely lewd conversation about women in 2005," *The Washington Post,* October 8, 2016. Accessed on May 5, 2017, https://www.washingtonpost.com/politics/trump-recorded-having-extremely-lewd-conversation-about-women-in-2005/2016/10/07/3b9ce776-8cb4-11e6-bf8a-3d26847eeed4_story.html?utm_term=.acef568e8444.

10. Farenhold (2016).

11. Kurtis Lee, "Fellow Republicans assail Trump for lewd comments about women in leaked audio," *The Los Angeles Times,* October 7, 2016. Accessed May 6, 2017, http://www.latimes.com/nation/politics/trailguide/la-na-live-updates-trailguide-fellow-republicans-assail-trump-for-1475887136-htmlstory.html.

12. Gabrielle Olya, "Twelfth Woman Comes Forward to Accuse Donald Trump of Sexual Assault," *People,* October 31, 2016. Accessed on May 6, 2017, http://people.com/bodies/twelfth-woman-accuses-donald-trump-sexual-assault/.

13. "An Exhaustive List of the Allegations Women Have Made against Trump," *The Cut*, October 27, 2016, http://nymag.com/thecut/2016/10/all-the-women-accusing-trump-of-rape-sexual-assault.html.

14. Gillian Chadwick, "Predator In Chief: President Trump and the Glorification of Sexual Violence," *HuffPo,* November 30, 2016. Accessed May 6, 2017, http://www.huffingtonpost.com/entry/predator-in-chief-president-trump-and-the-glorification_us_583efc56e4b08347769c060f.

15. Nicholas Kristoff, "Donald Trump, Groper in Chief," *New York Times Sunday Review,* October 7, 2016. Accessed May 6, 2017, https://www.nytimes.com/2016/10/09/opinion/sunday/donald-trump-groper-in-chief.html.

16. Chadwick (2016).

17. Ashley Welch, "Sexual assault survivors struggle to cope with Trump election," *CBS News,* November 17, 2016. Accessed May 6, 2017, http://www.cbsnews.com/news/sexual-assault-survivors-cope-with-donald-trump-election/.

18. Michael M. Grynbaum and Jim Rutenberg, "Trump, Asked About Accusations Against Bill O'Reilly, Calls Him a 'Good Person,'" *The New York Times,* April 5, 2017, https://www.nytimes.com/2017/04/05/business/media/trump-oreilly-fox-murdochs.html.

19. For full disclosure, the first author was one of the women who came forward to publicly report that O'Reilly had engaged in sexual harassment and gender discrimination against her.

20. Billy Perrigo, "'We Need Roy Moore.' President Trump Endorses Moore Despite Sexual Misconduct Allegations," *Time Magazine,* December 4, 2017. Accessed December 31, 2017, http://time.com/5047360/donald-trump-we-need-roy-moore-sexual-misconduct-allegations/.

21. Tyler Kingkade, "Trump's Education Secretary Nominee Won't Commit to Keeping Campus Rape Rules," *Buzzfeed,* January 17, 2017, https://www.buzzfeed.com/tylerkingkade/betsy-devos-title-ix?utm_term=.atNKyNqd3G#.aj0ZDOKp3w.

22. Quoted in Ibid.

23. Bob Casey and Patty Murray, Letter to President Elect Donald J. Trump, January 5, 2017, https://www.documentcloud.org/documents/3253529-Casey-Murray-to-Trump-Re-2011-Dear-Colleague.html.

24. Kimberly Hefling and Caitlin Emma, "Obama-Era School Sexual Assault Policy Rescinded," *Politico,* September 22, 2017. Accessed January 1, 2018, https://www.politico.com/story/2017/09/22/obama-era-school-sexual-assault-policy-rescinded-243016.

25. Anna Orso, "Trumps Education Pick Donated to Philly Group with Controversial Campus Rape Stance," *Politifact,* January 19, 2017. http://www.politifact.com/pennsylvania/statements/2017/jan/19/bob-casey/trumps-education-pick-donated-philly-group-controv/.

26. Jessica Lahitou, "All the Ways Rape Culture Was Encouraged in Trump's First 100 Days," Bustle, May 5, 2017, https://www.bustle.com/p/all-the-ways-rape-culture-was-encouraged-in-trumps-first-100-days-54286.

27. Ibid.

28. Alexandra Boguhn, "Conservative Media Jump on Sexual Assault Truther Bandwagon, Cry Foul on White House Report," Media Matters for America, April 30, 2014, https://www.mediamatters.org/research/2014/04/30/conservative-media-jump-on-sexual-assault-truth/199098.

29. George Will, "George Will: Colleges Become a Victim of Progressivism," *The Washington Post,* June 6, 2014, https://www.washingtonpost.com/opinions/george-will-college-become-the-victims-of-progressivism/2014/06/06/e90e73b4-eb50-11e3-9f5c-9075d5508f0a_story.html?utm_term=.1791715995e0.

30. Jay Ambrose, "Jay Ambrose Commentary: Campus Rape Is a Problem, But It's Been Exaggerated," *The Columbus Dispatch,* August 8, 2014, http://www.dispatch.com/content/stories/editorials/2014/08/08/campus-rape-is-a-problem-but-its-been-exaggerated.html.

31. Cathy Young, "Guilty Until Proven Innocent: The Skewed White House Crusade on Sexual Assault," *Time,* May 5, 2014, http://www.dispatch.com/content/stories/editorials/2014/08/08/campus-rape-is-a-problem-but-its-been-exaggerated.html.

32. Naomi Schaefer Riley, "The Real Rx for Campus- Give up on Liberal 'Answers,'" *The New York Post,* May 6, 2014, http://nypost.com/2014/05/06/the-real-rx-for-campus-rape-give-up-on-liberal-answers/.

33. Heather MacDonald, "The Phony Campus Rape Crisis," *The Weekly Standard,* November 2, 2015, http://www.weeklystandard.com/an-assault-on-common-sense/article/1051200.

34. Mark J. Perry, "How About a 'Renewed Call' for the White House to Stop Spreading False Information about Campus Sexual Assault?" *American Enterprise Institute*, April 29, 2014, http://www.aei.org/publication/how-about-a-renewed-call-for-the-white-house-to-stop-spreading-false-information-about-campus-sexual-assault/.

35. Heather MacDonald, "Campus Rape Dogma in the Age of Promiscuity," February 11, 2016, https://www.manhattan-institute.org/html/campus-rape-dogma-age-promiscuity-8513.html.

36. Pam Vogel, "Here are the Corporations and Right-Wing Funders Backing the Education Reform Movement," Media Matters for America, April 27, 2016, https://www.mediamatters.org/research/2016/04/27/here-are-corporations-and-right-wing-funders-backing-education-reform-movement/210054.

37. Christopher P. Krebs, Christine H. Lindquist, Tara D. Warner, Bonnie S. Fisher, and Sandra L. Martin, "The Campus Sexual Assault Survey," U.S. Department of Justice, December, 2007, https://www.ncjrs.gov/pdffiles1/nij/grants/221153.pdf.

38. Dean G. Kilpatrick, Heidi S. Resnick, Kenneth J. Ruggiero, Lauren M. Conoscenti, and Jenna McCauley, "Drug-facilitated, Incapacitated, and Forcible Rape: A National Study," U.S. Department of Justice, July, 2007, https://www.ncjrs.gov/pdffiles1/nij/grants/219181.pdf.

39. Roni Caryn Rabin, "Nearly 1-in-5 Women in U.S. Survey Say They Have Been Raped or Sexually Assaulted," *The New York Times*, December 14, 2011, http://www.nytimes.com/2011/12/15/health/nearly-1-in-5-women-in-us-survey-report-sexual-assault.html?_r=0&mtrref=undefined&gwh=80B3B1105B5463FE16E4F445CFC17240&gwt=pay.

40. Meichun Mohler-Kuo, George W. Dowdall, Mary P. Koss, and Henry Wechsler, "Correlates of Rape While Intoxicated in a National Sample of College Women," Harvard School of Public Health, September 2, 2003, http://archive.sph.harvard.edu/cas/Documents/rapeintox/037-Mohler-Kuo.sep1.pdf.

41. As quoted in Monica Hesse, "Men's Rights Activists, Gathering to Discuss All the Ways Society Has Done Them Wrong," *Washington Post*, June 30, 2014, https://www.washingtonpost.com/lifestyle/style/mens-rights-activists-gathering-to-discuss-all-the-ways-society-has-done-them-wrong/2014/06/30/a9310d96-005f-11e4-8fd0-3a663dfa68ac_story.html.

42. "'Men's Rights' Group Behind Sexual Assault Posters," *CBC News,* July 10, 2013, http://www.cbc.ca/news/canada/edmonton/men-s-rights-group-behind-sexual-assault-posters-1.1353362.

43. Emily Matchar, "'Men's Rights' Activists Are Trying the Redefine the Meaning of Rape," *New Republic*, February 26, 2014, https://newrepublic.com/article/116768/latest-target-mens-rights-movement-definition-rape.

44. Emily Yoffe, "The Best Rape Prevention: Tell College Women to Stop Getting Drunk," *Slate*, October 15, 2013, http://www.slate.com/articles/double_x/doublex/2013/10/sexual_assault_and_drinking_teach_women_the_connection.html.

45. Bonnie S. Fisher, Leah E. Daigle, and Francis T. Cullen, *Unsafe in the Ivory Tower: The Sexual Victimization of College Women*, 2010, New York: Sage Publications.

46. George Will, "Colleges Become the Victims of Progressivism," *The Washington Post.* June 6, 2014, http://www.washingtonpost.com/opinions/george-will-college-become-the-victims-of-progressivism/2014/06/06/e90e73b4-eb50-11e3-9f5c-9075d5508f0a_story.html.

47. Robert O'Hara, "A VFM Exclusive: Documentation of Title IX complaint against Emerson College Surfaces, Questionable Accusations Abound," *A Voice for Men*, June 19, 2014, http://www.avoiceformen.com/mens-rights/false-rape-culture/avfm-exclusive-documentation-of-title-ix-complaint-against-emerson-college-surfaces-questionable-accusations-abound-2/.

48. Tyler Kingkade, "Sexual Assault Witnesses at Occidental College Subject to Vile Harassment Emails," *The Huffington Post*, July 22, 2014, http://www.huffingtonpost.com/2014/07/22/occidental-harassment-sexual-assault-report_n_5609909.html.

49. Quoted in Ibid.

50. Quoted in Ibid.

51. For an example of this backlash theme, see Ashe Schow, "Backlash: College Men Challenge 'Guilty Until Proven Innocent' Standard for Sex Assault Cases," *The Washington*

Examiner, August 11, 2014, http://www.washingtonexaminer.com/backlash-college-men-challenge-guilty-until-proven-innocent-standard-for-sex-assault-cases/article/2551863.

52. John Lauerman, "College Men Accused of Sexual Assault Say Their Rights Violated," *Bloomberg News,* December 16, 2013, https://www.bloomberg.com/news/articles/2013-12-16/college-men-accused-of-sexual-assault-say-their-rights-violated.

53. National Sexual Violence Resource Center, "False Reporting: Overview," Department of Justice, Office on Violence Against Women, 2012, http://www.nsvrc.org/sites/default/files/Publications_NSVRC_Overview_False-Reporting.pdf.

54. Emily Shugerman, "Men Sue in Sexual Assault Cases," Ms. Blog, June 18, 2014, http://msmagazine.com/blog/2014/06/18/men-sue-in-campus-sexual-assault-cases/.

55. T. Rees Shapiro, "Expelled for Sex Assault, Young Men are Filing More Lawsuits to Clear Their Names," *The Washington Post*, April 28, 2017, https://www.washingtonpost.com/local/education/expelled-for-sex-assault-young-men-are-filing-more-lawsuits-to-clear-their-names/2017/04/27/c2cfb1d2-0d89-11e7-9b0d-d27c98455440_story.html?utm_term=.4279dd1d6a21.

56. Ibid.

57. Tyler Kingkade, "James Madison University Punished Sexual Assault with 'Expulsion After Graduation,'" June 18, 2014, http://www.huffingtonpost.com/2014/06/18/james-madison-university-sexual-assault_n_5509163.html.

58. Alexandra Rutherford, "Sexual Violence Against Women: Putting Rape Research in Context." *Psychology of Women Quarterly* 35, no. 2 (2011): 342–347.

59. Nick Anderson and Peyton M. Craighill, "College Students Remain Deeply Divided Over What Consent Actually Means," *Washington Post*, June 14, 2015, https://www.washingtonpost.com/local/education/americas-students-are-deeply-divided-on-the-meaning-of-consent-during-sex/2015/06/11/bbd303e0-04ba-11e5-a428-c984eb077d4e_story.html?utm_term=.f16577e302b6.

60. Sarah R. Edwards, Kathryn A. Bradshaw, and   Verlin B. Hinsz, " Denying Rape but Endorsing Forceful Intercourse: Exploring Differences Among Responders," *Violence and Gender*, December 2014, 1(4) : 188–193.

61. Dean G. Kilpatrick, Heidi S. Resnick, Kenneth J. Ruggiero, Lauren M. Conoscenti, and Jenna McCauley, "Drug-Facilitated, Incapacitated, and Forcible Rape: A National Study, U.S. Department of Justice," 2007, https://www.ncjrs.gov/pdffiles1/nij/grants/219181.pdf.

62. Ibid.

63. Kristen Lombardi, "A Lack of Consequences for Sexual Assault," The Center for Public Integrity, February 24, 2010, https://www.publicintegrity.org/2010/02/24/4360/lack-consequences-sexual-assault.

64. *The Columbus Dispatch*, "Reports on College Crime Are Deceptively Inaccurate," September 30, 2014, http://www.dispatch.com/content/stories/local/2014/09/30/campus-insecurity.html.

65. Kate Murphy, "Stanford Sexual Assault Victim Demands Tough Sanctions for Offenders*," Washington Post*, June 7, 2014, https://www.washingtonpost.com/politics/stanford-sexual-assault-victim-demands-tougher-sanctions-for-offenders/2014/06/07/43580f2c-ee7d-11e3-b84b-3393a45b80f1_story.html?utm_term=.b6cd92781bd7.

66. Tovia Smith, "To Tackle Sexual Assault, Colleges Enlist Investigators—For-Hire," NPR, October 29, 2014, http://www.npr.org/2014/10/29/359875452/to-tackle-sexual-assault-cases-colleges-enlist-investigators-for-hire.

67. Stephanie Haven, "Will Campus Sexual-Assault Probes Affect Enrollment ?" McClachty, July 16, 2014, http://www.mcclatchydc.com/news/crime/article24770584.html.

68. Tyler Kingkade, "How Media Coverage of Campus Scandals Impacts College Applications," *The Huffington Post*, July 8, 2016, http://www.huffingtonpost.com/entry/college-scandals-applications_us_577e6ac1e4b0344d514e1bf9.

69. Jonathan Christiansen, "Four Stages of Social Movements," EBSCO Research Starters, 2009. Accessed June 10, 2014, http://www.ebscohost.com/uploads/imported/thisTopic-dbTopic-1248.pdf.

70. Lauren Nelson, "So You're Tired of Hearing about 'Rape Culture?'" The Good Men Project, March 20, 2013, https://goodmenproject.com/ethics-values/so-youre-tired-of-hearing-about-rape-culture/.

71. Katherine N. Kinnick, Dean M. Krugman, and Glen T. Cameron, "Compassion Fatigue: Communication and Burnout Toward Social Problems," *Journal of Mass Communication Quarterly*, August, 1996, 73(3): 687–707.

72. Ibid.

73. Kenneth Cloke, "Conflict and Movements for Social Change: The Politics of Mediation and the Mediation of Politics," Mediate, July, 2013, https://www.mediate.com/articles/ClokeK16.cfm.

Bibliography

Abbey, Antonia, and Pam McAuslan. "A longitudinal examination of male college students' perpetration of sexual assault." *Journal of Consulting and Clinical Psychology* 72, no. 5 (2004): 747.

Abbey, Antonia, A. Monique Clinton-Sherrod, Pam McAuslan, Tina Zawacki, and Philip O. Buck. "The relationship between the quantity of alcohol consumed and the severity of sexual assaults committed by college men." *Journal of Interpersonal Violence* 18, no. 7 (2003): 813–833.

Abbey, Antonia. "Lessons learned and unanswered questions about sexual assault perpetration." *Journal of Interpersonal Violence* 20, no. 1 (2005): 39–42.

Abbey, Antonia, Tina Zawacki, Philip O. Buck, A. Monique Clinton, and Pam McAuslan. "Sexual assault and alcohol consumption: What do we know about their relationship and what types of research are still needed?" *Aggression and Violent Behavior* 9, no. 3 (2004): 271–303.

Ackerman, Alissa R. and Karen J. Terry. "Faulty Sex Offense Policies." In Reddington, Fran & Gene Bonham (Eds). "Flawed Criminal Justice Policy: At the Intersection of the Media, Public Fear and Legislative Response." Durham, NC: Carolina Academic Press, 2011.

Ahrens, Courtney E., Marc D. Rich, and Jodie B. Ullman. "Rehearsing for real life: The impact of the InterACT Sexual Assault Prevention Program on self-reported likelihood of engaging in bystander interventions." *Violence Against Women* 17, no. 6 (2011): 760–776.

Altbach, P.G. "Student Political Activism." In *International Higher Education: An Encyclopedia*, edited by P. G. Altbach, New York and London: Garland, (1991): 247–260.

Amar, Angela Frederick, Melissa Sutherland, and Erin Kesler. "Evaluation of a bystander education program." *Issues in Mental Health Nursing* 33, no. 12 (2012): 851–857.

Ambrose, Jay. "Jay Ambrose Commentary: Campus Rape Is a Problem, But It's Been Exaggerated." *The Columbus Dispatch*, August 8, 2014, http://www.dispatch.com/content/stories/editorials/2014/08/08/campus-rape-is-a-problem-but-its-been-exaggerated.html.

American Council on Education. "New Campus Obligations Under Violence Against Women Act." March 20, 2013. http://www.acenet.edu/news-room/Pages/MEMO-New-Campus-Sexual-Assault-Policies-and-Procedures-Under-Violence-Against-Women-Act.aspx.

Anderson, Linda A., and Susan C. Whiston. "Sexual assault education programs: A meta-analytic examination of their effectiveness." *Psychology of Women Quarterly* 29, no. 4 (2005): 374–388.

Anderson, Nick and Peyton M. Craighill. "College Students Remain Deeply Divided Over What Consent Actually Means." *Washington Post*, June 14, 2015, https://www.washingtonpost.com/local/education/americas-students-are-deeply-divided-on-the-meaning-of-consent-during-sex/2015/06/11/bbd303e0-04ba-11e5-a428-c984eb077d4e_ story.html?utm_term=.f16577e302b6.

Andersen, Travis. "Harvard Faces Title IX Inquiry." *The Boston Globe*, April 25, 2011. http://
www.boston.com/news/education/higher/articles/2011/04/25/harvard_law_faces_
title_ix_inquiry/.

Antle III, W. James. "How Campus Rape Became a Partisan Issue." *The Week*, December 12,
2014. http://theweek.com/articles/441603/how-rape-became-partisan-issue.

Apollon, Dominique. "Millennials, Activism, and Race." *Applied Research Center*, 2012. Accessed June 20, 2014, http://www.arc.org/millenials.

"'Ask First' at Antioch," *New York Times*, October 11, 1993. Accessed April 30, 2017, http://
www.nytimes.com/1993/10/11/opinion/ask-first-at-antioch.html.

Bailey, Jennifer. "Voicing Oppositional Conformity: Sarah Winnemucca and the Politics of
Rape, Colonialism, and 'Citizenship': 1870-1890," PhD Diss., (2012).

Baker, Katie. "College Sexual Assault Guru Stands Up for Accused Rapists." *Buzzfeed*, May 1,
2014. http://www.buzzfeed.com/katiejmbaker/college-sexual-assault-guru-stands-up-for-ac-
cused-rapists.

Baker, Katie. "Rape Victims Don't Trust the Fixers Colleges Hire to Help Them." *Buzzfeed*,
April 25, 2014. http://www.buzzfeed.com/katiejmbaker/rape-victims-dont-trust-the-fixers-
colleges-hire-to-help-the.

Banyard, Victoria L., Mary M. Moynihan, and Maria T. Crossman. "Reducing sexual violence
on campus: The role of student leaders as empowered bystanders." *Journal of College
Student Development* 50, no. 4 (2009): 446–457.

Banyard, Victoria L., Mary M. Moynihan, and Elizabethe G. Plante. "Sexual violence prevention through bystander education: An experimental evaluation." *Journal of Community
Psychology* 35, no. 4 (2007): 463–481.

Banyard, Victoria L., Elizabeth G. Plante, and Mary M. Moynihan. "Rape prevention through
bystander education: Final report to NIJ for grant 2002-WG-BX-0009." Durham: University of New Hampshire (2005).

Baptiste, Edward E. "'Cuffy,' 'Fancy Maids,' and 'One-Eyed Men': Rape, Commodification,
and the Domestic Slave Trade in the United States." *The American Historical Review* 106,
(2001): 1619–1650.

Barber, Benjamin. *Jihad vs. McWorld: How globalism and tribalism are Reshaping the World*.
New York, NY: Ballantine Books, 1996.

Baumeister, Roy F., Kathleen R. Catanese, and Harry M. Wallace. "Conquest by force: A
narcissistic reactance theory of rape and sexual coercion." *Review of General Psychology*
6, no. 1 (2002): 92.

Beetham, Gwendolyn. "The Academic Feminist: We Heart Women's Centers." *Feministing*,
September 9, 2014. Accessed May 4, 2017, http://feministing.com/2014/09/15/the-academ-
ic-feminist-we-heart-womens-centers/.

Bennett, Melanie. "Sexual Misconduct Adjudication: The Single Investigator Model." *Edu-
Risk*, April, 2016, https://www.edurisksolutions.org/blogs/?Id=2801.

Beusman, Callie. "Colleges Fire and Silence Faculty Who Speak Out About Rape." Jezebel,
June 13, 2014. http://jezebel.com/colleges-silence-and-fire-faculty-who-speak-out-about-r-
1586169489.

Bidwell, Allie. "Bipartisan Bill Would Boost College Accountability on Sexual Assault." *U.S.
News and World Report*, June 4, 2015. Accessed December 30, 2017, https://
www.usnews.com/news/articles/2015/06/04/bipartisan-house-bill-would-boost-funding-for-
campus-sexual-assault-investigations.

Bidwell, Allie. "College Sexual Violence Complaints Up 1,000 in 5 Years." *U.S. News and
World Report*, May 5, 2015. https://www.usnews.com/news/blogs/data-mine/2015/05/05/
college-title-ix-sexual-violence-complaints-increase-more-than-1-000-percent-in-5-years.

Black, Michele C., Kathleen C. Basile, Matthew J. Breiding, and George W. Ryan. "Prevalence
of sexual violence against women in 23 states and two US territories, BRFSS 2005."
Violence Against Women 20, no. 5 (2014): 485–499.

Boba, Rachel, and David Lilley. "Violence Against Women Act (VAWA) funding: a nationwide assessment of effects on rape and assault." *Violence Against Women* 15, no. 2 (2009):
168–185.

Boeringer, Scot B. "Associations of rape-supportive attitudes with fraternal and athletic participation." *Violence Against Women* 5, no. 1 (1999): 81–90.

Boeringer, Scot B. "Influences of fraternity membership, athletics, and male living arrangements on sexual aggression." *Violence Against Women* 2, no. 2 (1996): 134–147.

Bolger, Dana. "When Schools Put their Brands Before Assaulted Students," *Al Jazeera America*, June 10, 2014. http://america.aljazeera.com/opinions/2014/6/college-sexual-violencera-peeducationtitleixbranding.html.

Bombardieri, Marcella. "Harvard Professor Challenges Denial of Tenure." *The Boston Globe*, June 13, 2014. http://www.bostonglobe.com/metro/2014/06/12/harvard-professor-chal-lenges-tenure-denial/E64ruokHoD1WpokjwsbR3M/story.html.

Boguhn, Alexandra. "Conservative Media Jump on Sexual Assault Truther Bandwagon, Cry Foul on White House Report." Media Matters for America, April 30, 2014, https://www.mediamatters.org/research/2014/04/30/conservative-media-jump-on-sexual-assault-truth/199098.

Bowcott, Bowen. "Rape Myths Not Behind Low Conviction Rate, Says Leading Family Lawyer." *The Guardian*, March 25, 2013. http://www.theguardian.com/society/2013/mar/25/rape-myths-low-conviction-rate.

Brecklin, Leanne R., and David R. Forde. "A meta-analysis of rape education programs." *Violence and Victims* 16, no. 3 (2001): 303–321.

Breitenbecher, Kimberly Hanson. "Sexual assault on college campuses: Is an ounce of prevention enough?" *Applied and Preventive Psychology* 9, no. 1 (2000): 23–52.

"Bringing in the Bystander: Overview." Accessed April 23, 2017, http://cola.unh.edu/prevention-innovations/bystander-overview.

Brownmiller, Susan. *Against Our Will.* New York: Simon and Schuster, 1975.

Bublick, Ellen. "Tort Suits Filed by Rape and Sexual Assault Victims in Civil Courts: Lessons for Courts, Classrooms and Constituencies." Arizona Legal Studies Discussion Paper 6, no. 16 (2006).

Calmes, Jackie. "Obama Seeks to Raise Awarness of Rape on Campus." *New York Times*, January 22, 2014. Accessed December 30, 2017, https://www.nytimes.com/2014/01/23/us/politics/obama-to-create-task-force-on-campus-sexual-assaults.html?_r=0.

Campbell, Rebecca. "Rape Survivors' Experiences With the Legal and Medical Systems: Do Rape Victim Advocates Make a Difference?." *Violence Against Women* 12, no. 1 (2006): 30–45.

Campbell, Rebecca. "The neurobiology of sexual assault." *National Institute of Justice* (2012).

Campbell, Rebecca. "The psychological impact of rape victims." *American Psychologist* 63, no. 8 (2008): 702.

Campus Safety. "Clery Act Fine Increases to 35K Per Violation." *Campus Safety Magazine*, 2012. http://www.campussafetymagazine.com/Channel/University-Security/News/2012/10/02/Clery-Act-Fines-Increased-to-35-000-Per-Violation.aspx.

Campus Safety. "Clery Act Needs Whistleblower Protection." *Campus Safety Magazine*. 2007. http://www.campussafetymagazine.com/article/clery-act-needs-whistleblower-protection/Clery_Act,_Director_of_the_Year,_Officers,_Podcast,_Title_IX0.

Cantor, David, Bonnie Fisher, Susan Chibnall, Reanne Townsend, Hyunshik Lee, Carol Bruce, and Gail Thomas. "Report on the AAU campus climate survey on sexual assault and sexual misconduct." *Association of American Universities* 21 (2015).

Caplan-Bricker, Nora. "How Title IX Became Our Best Tool Against Harassment." *New Republic*, June 1, 2012. Accessed December 30, 2017, https://newrepublic.com/article/104237/how-title-ix-became-our-best-tool-against-sexual-harassment.

Carroll, Cody. "New Campus Regulations under Campus SaVE Address Sexual Violence." April 29, 2014, http://www.tcu360.com/campus/2014/04/32272.new-regulations-under-campus-SaVE-act-address-sexual-violence.

Carty, Victoria and Jake Onyett. "Protest, Cyberactivism and New Social Movements: The Reemergence of the Peace Movement Post 9/11." *Social Movements Studies* 5 no. 3, (2007): 229–249.

Casey, Bob and Patty Murray. "Letter to President Elect Donald J. Trump." January 5, 2017, https://www.documentcloud.org/documents/3253529-Casey-Murray-to-Trump-Re-2011-Dear-Colleague.html.

Casey, Erin A., and Taryn P. Lindhorst. "Toward a multi-level, ecological approach to the primary prevention of sexual assault prevention in peer and community contexts." *Trauma, Violence, & Abuse* 10, no. 2 (2009): 91–114.

Cass, Amy I. "Routine activities and sexual assault: An analysis of individual-and school-level factors." *Violence and Victims* 22, no. 3 (2007): 350–366; Stotzer, Rebecca L., and Danielle MacCartney. "The role of institutional factors on on-campus reported rape prevalence." *Journal of Interpersonal Violence* 31, no. 16 (2016): 2687–2707.

Castells, Manuel. *Networks of Outrage and Hope: Social Movements in the Internet Age.* Cambridge, UK: Polity Press (2012).

CBC News. "'Men's Rights' Group Behind Sexual Assault Posters." July 10, 2013, http://www.cbc.ca/news/canada/edmonton/men-s-rights-group-behind-sexual-assault-posters-1.1353362.

CBS Philly. "Complaints Filed Against 4 Colleges Over Rapes, Including Swarthmore." *CBSPhilly.com.* May 22, 2013. http://philadelphia.cbslocal.com/2013/05/22/complaints-filed-against-4-colleges-over-rapes-including-swarthmore-college/.

Celis, William. "Date Rape and a List at Brown." *New York Times*, November 18, 1990. Accessed April 15, 2017, http://www.nytimes.com/1990/11/18/us/date-rape-and-a-list-at-brown.html.

Center for Public Integrity. "Campus Sexual Assault Statistics Don't Add Up." December 2, 2009. http://www.publicintegrity.org/2009/12/02/9045/campus-sexual-assault-statistics-don-t-add.

Centers for Disease Control and Prevention. "The social-ecological model: A framework for prevention." Injury Center: Violence Prevention (2009).

Centers for Disease Control and Prevention. "Sexual Violence Prevention: Beginning the Dialogue." Atlanta, GA, 2004.

Centers for Disease Control and Prevention. *Preventing sexual violence on college campuses: Lessons from research and practice.* Accessed January 5, 2017 from https://www.notalone.gov/schools/.

Chadwick, Gillian. "Predator in Chief: President Trump and the Glorification of Sexual Violence." *HuffPo,* November 30, 2016. Accessed May 6, 2017, http://www.huffingtonpost.com/entry/predator-in-chief-president-trump-and-the-glorification_us_583efc56e4b08347769c060f.

Change.org. "Remove Judge Persky from the Bench for Decision in Brock Turner Rape Case." Accessed May 10, 2017. https://www.change.org/p/california-state-house-impeach-judge-aaron-persky.

Chemaly, Soraya. "UConn Student Receives Rape Threats After Suggesting School Address 'Frightening' Atmosphere for Women." RH Reality Check, May 1, 2013. http://rhrealitycheck.org/article/2013/05/01/uconns-mascot/.

Christiansen, Jonathan. "Four Stages of Social Movements." EBSCO Research Starters, 2009. Accessed June 10, 2014, http://www.ebscohost.com/uploads/imported/thisTopic-dbTopic-1248.pdf.

Clery Center for Security on Campus. "Our History." 2014. http://clerycenter.org/our-history.

Clery Center for Security on Campus. "The Campus Sexual Violence Elimination (SaVE) Act." 2014. http://clerycenter.org/campus-sexual-violence-elimination-SaVE-act.

Cloke, Kenneth. "Conflict and Movements for Social Change: The Politics of Mediation and the Mediation of Politics." Mediate, July, 2013, https://www.mediate.com/articles/ClokeK16.cfm.

Clymer, Charles. "Men are 32X More Likely to be Killed by Lightning than Falsely Accused of Rape." *Blogspot,* January 5, 2014, http://charlesclymer.blogspot.com/2014/01/men-are-32x-more-likely-to-be-killed-by.html.

Coker, Ann L., Heather M. Bush, Bonnie S. Fisher, Suzanne C. Swan, Corrine M. Williams, Emily R. Clear, and Sarah DeGue. "Multi-college bystander intervention evaluation for violence prevention." *American Journal of Preventive Medicine* 50, no. 3 (2016): 295–302.

Coker, Ann L., Bonnie S. Fisher, Heather M. Bush, Suzanne C. Swan, Corrine M. Williams, Emily R. Clear, and Sarah DeGue. "Evaluation of the Green Dot bystander intervention to reduce interpersonal violence among college students across three campuses." *Violence Against Women* 21, no. 12 (2015): 1507–1527.

Colorado College. "Sexual Misconduct Response & Resources." Accessed June 10, 2014, http://www.coloradocollege.edu/other/studentguide/pathfinder/college-policies/sexual-misconduct-resources.dot.

Constanza-Chock, Sasha. "Youth and Social Movements: Key Lessons for Allies." *The Kinder & Braver World Project*, December 17, 2012. Accessed June 10, 2014, http://cyber.law.harvard.edu/sites/cyber.law.harvard.edu/files/KBWYouthandSocialMovements2012_0.pdf.

Conway, Madeline and Steven Lee. "Undergraduates Challenge College's Sexual Assault Policy Under Title IX." *The Harvard Crimson*, April 3, 2014. http://www.thecrimson.com/article/2014/4/3/title-ix-complaint-college/.

Cooney, Samantha and Emma Bogler. "Q&A With Administrators: Recent Changes to Sexual Assault Adjudication Processes." *The Columbia Daily Spectator*, March 3, 2014, http://columbiaspectator.com/news/2014/03/03/qa-administrators-recent-changes-sexual-assault-adjudication-processes.

Cosentino, Dom. "This is What Happens When You Accuse a Notre Dame Football Player of Sexually Assaulting You." Deadspin, April 6, 2012. Accessed December 20, 2017, https://deadspin.com/5897809/this-is-what-happens-when-you-accuse-a-notre-dame-football-player-of-sexually-assaulting-you.

Cranney, Stephen. "The Relationship Between Sexual Victimization and Year in School in U.S. Colleges: Investigating the Parameters of the 'Red Zone.'" *Journal of Interpersonal Violence*, 30(17), 2015: 3133–3145.

Crosset, Todd W., Jeffrey R. Benedict, and Mark A. McDonald. "Male student-athletes reported for sexual assault: A survey of campus police departments and judicial affairs offices." *Journal of Sport & Social Issues* 19, no. 2 (1995): 126–140.

Crosset, Todd W., James Ptacek, Mark A. McDonald, and Jeffrey R. Benedict. "Male student-athletes and violence against women: A survey of campus judicial affairs offices." *Violence Against Women* 2, no. 2 (1996): 163–179.

Culture of Respect. "Online Programs." Accessed May 3, 2017, https://cultureofrespect.org/colleges-universities/programs/.

Cupp-Ressler, Tara. "Profit and peril in the anti-rape industry." Accessed December 3, 2016. https://thinkprogress.org/profit-and-peril-in-the-anti-rape-industry-e497c017b0ec#.g3cfe8xyo.

Dartmouth. "Proposed Sexual Assault Policy Q&As." Accessed June 12, 2014, http://www.dartmouth.edu/~president/sap/sapqa.html.

DeGue, Sarah, Melissa K. Holt, Greta M. Massetti, Jennifer L. Matjasko, Andra Teten Tharp, and Linda Anne Valle. "Looking ahead toward community-level strategies to prevent sexual violence." *Journal of Women's Health* 21, no. 1 (2012): 1–3.

DeGue, Sarah, Linda Anne Valle, Melissa K. Holt, Greta M. Massetti, Jennifer L. Matjasko, and Andra Teten Tharp. "A systematic review of primary prevention strategies for sexual violence perpetration." *Aggression and Violent Behavior* 19, no. 4 (2014): 346–362.

DeLeon Peter and Linda DeLeon. "What Ever Happened to Policy Implementation? An Alternative Approach." *Journal of Public Administration Research and Theory* 12, no. 4, (2002): 467–492.

Denim Day. "History." Accessed January 8, 2014, http://denimdayusa.org/about/history/.

Denim Day. "Unified in Denim." Accessed May 2, 2017, http://denimdayinfo.org/about/#/guess-partnership.

Department of Education. "The Evergreen State College." Office for Civil Rights, April 4, 1995, https://www2.ed.gov/policy/gen/leg/foia/misc-docs/ed_ehd_1995.pdf.

Department of Justice, Office of Justice Programs, Bureau of Justice Statistics, "National Crime Victimization Survey," 2010–2014 (2015).

Department of Justice, Office of Justice Programs, Bureau of Justice Statistics, "Rape and Sexual Victimization Among College-Aged Females," 1995–2013 (2014).

Dockterman, Eliana. "Students File Title IX Assault Complaint Against Columbia University." *Time*, April 24, 2014. http://time.com/76762/students-file-title-ix-sexual-assault-complaint-against-columbia-university/.

Donovan, Roxanne A. "Tough or Tender: (Dis)Similarities in White College Students' Perceptions of Black and White Women." *Psychology of Women Quarterly* 35, no. 3, (2011): 458–468.

Dowd Hall, Jacquelyn. "The Mind That Burns in Each Body:Women, Rape, and Racial Violence," in *Desire: The Politics of Sexuality*, edited by Ann Snitow, Christine Stansell, and Sharon Thompson, 339–360. London: Virago, 1983.

Dries, Kate. "University of Chicago Gets Its Own 'Rapist List.'" Jezebel, September 22, 2014. http://jezebel.com/university-of-chicago-gets-its-own-rapist-list-1637594348.

Duhaime-Ross, Arielle. "Rolling Stone Just Wrecked an Incredible Year of Progress for Rape Victims." *The Verge*, December 5, 2014. https://www.theverge.com/2014/12/5/7342317/rolling-stone-retraction-rape-blame-consent.

ED Act Now. "Department of Education: Hold Colleges Accountable That Break the Law by Refusing to Protect Students from Sexual Assault." *Change.org.* Accessed June 15, 2014, http://www.change.org/petitions/department-of-education-hold-colleges-accountable-that-break-the-law-by-refusing-to-protect-students-from-sexual-assault.

Edwards, Sarah R., Kathryn A. Bradshaw, and Verlin B. Hinsz. " Denying Rape but Endorsing Forceful Intercourse: Exploring Differences Among Responders." *Violence and Gender*, December 2014, 1(4) : 188–193.

Ehrhart, J. and B. Sandler. *Campus gang rape: Party games.* Unpublished manuscript, Association of American Colleges, Project on the Status and Education of Women, Washington, DC, 1985.

Eilperin, Juliet. "Biden and Obama Rewrite the Rulebook on Campus Sexual Assault." *Washington Post*, July 3, 2016, https://www.washingtonpost.com/politics/biden-and-obama-rewrite-the-rulebook-on-college-sexual-assaults/2016/07/03/0773302e-3654-11e6-a254-2b336e293a3c_story.html?utm_term=.bab85f9fc80c.

End Rape on Campus, "Our Team." 2013. Accessed June 18, 2014, http://endrapeoncampus.org/our-team/.

Ensler, Eve. "The Vagina Monologues." Accessed January 8, 2014, http://www.eveensler.org/plays/the-vagina-monologues/.

Epifano, Angie. "An Account of Sexual Assault at Amherst College." *The Amherst Student*, 2011. http://bit.ly/1laUKnL.

Escobar, Samantha. "Why 'Walk a Mile in her Shoes' Falls Short (And What You *Can* Do To End Sexual Violence)." The Gloss, March 8, 2013. Accessed December 30, 2017, http://www.thegloss.com/culture/why-a-mile-in-her-shoes-falls-short-and-what-people-can-do-to-end-sexual-violence/.

Eskenazi, Gerald. "Athletic aggression and sexual assault." *The New York Times,* p. A27. (June 3, 1990).

Esteban, Chichi and Manuel Roig-Franzia. "Bill Cosby's Survivors Now Number 60. Here's Who They Are." *The Washington Post*, August 3, 2016. Accessed December 31, 2017, https://www.washingtonpost.com/graphics/lifestyle/cosby-women-accusers/.

Everett, Gwen. "List Alleging Names of Sexual Assaulters Appears in Campus Bathrooms." *The Brown Daily Herald*, April 27, 2017. http://www.browndailyherald.com/2017/04/27/list-alleging-names-sexual-assaulters-appears-campus-bathrooms/.

Farenhold, David. "Trump recorded having extremely lewd conversation about women in 2005." *The Washington Post,* October 8, 2016. Accessed on May 5, 2017, https://www.washingtonpost.com/politics/trump-recorded-having-extremely-lewd-conversation-about-women-in-2005/2016/10/07/3b9ce776-8cb4-11e6-bf8a-3d26847eeed4_story.html?utm_term=.acef568e8444.

Feagin, Joe. "The Rape of Black Women by White Men: Systemic Racism Again," *Racism Review*, October 11 2009. Accessed March 23, 2017. http://www.racismreview.com/blog/2009/10/11/the-rape-of-black-women-by-white-men-systemic-racism-again/.

Feagin, Joe R. *Racist America: Roots, Current Realities, and Future Reparations.* New York: Routledge, 2001.

Feimster, Crystal N. "Rape and Justice in the Civil War." *The New York Times*. April 25, 2013. Accessed February 11, 2015. http://opinionator.blogs.nytimes.com/2013/04/25/rape-and-justice-in-the-civil-war/?_php=true&_type=blogs&_r=0.

Feimster, Crystal N. *Southern Horrors: Women and the Politics of Rape and Lynching*. Cambridge: Harvard University Press, 2011.

Felch, Jason and Jason Song. "Occidental College Chief Asks for Reconciliation After Accusations." *The Los Angeles Times*, September 20, 2014. http://articles.latimes.com/2013/sep/20/local/la-me-0921-occidental-sexual-assaults-20130921.

Felch, Jason and Jason Song. "UC Berkeley Students File Federal Complaints over Sexual Assault." *The Los Angeles Times*, February 26, 2013. http://articles.latimes.com/2014/feb/26/local/la-me-ln-berkeley-students-complaint-20140226.

Felner, Robert D., Tweety Yates Felner, and Morton M. Silverman. "Prevention in mental health and social intervention." In *Handbook of Community Psychology*, pp. 9–42. New York: Springer US, 2000.

Feminist Majority Foundation. "The Triumphs of Title IX." Accessed January 13, 2016, http://www.feminist.org/education/TriumphsOfTitleIX.pdf.

Fischer, Gloria J. "Deceptive, verbally coercive college males: Attitudinal predictors and lies told." *Archives of Sexual Behavior* 25, no. 5 (1996): 527–533.

Fisher, Bonnie S., Francis T. Cullen, and Michael G. Turner. "The Sexual Victimization of College Women. Research Report." (2000).

Fisher, Bonnie S., Leah E. Daigle, and Francis T. Cullen, *Unsafe in the Ivory Tower: The Sexual Victimization of College Women*, 2010, New York: Sage Publications.

Fisher, Bonnie S., John J. Sloan, Francis T. Cullen, and Chunmeng Lu. "Crime in the ivory tower: The level and sources of student victimization." *Criminology* 36, no. 3 (1998): 671–710.

Flaherty, Colleen. "Endangering a Trust." *Inside Higher Ed*, February 4, 2015. Accessed December 30, 2017, https://www.insidehighered.com/news/2015/02/04/faculty-members-object-new-policies-making-all-professors-mandatory-reporters-sexual.

Flood, Michael. "Changing men: Best practice in sexual violence education." *Women Against Violence: An Australian Feminist Journal* 18 (2006): 26.

Foley, Linda A., Christine Evancic, Karnik Karnik, Janet King, and Angela Parks. "Date Rape: Effects of Race of Assailant and Victim and Gender of Subjects on Perceptions." *The Journal of Black Psychology* 21, no. 1. (1995): 6–18.

Fontes, Lisa Aronson. *Sexual abuse in nine North American cultures: Treatment and prevention*. Vol. 11. Sage, 1995.

Ford, Jessie, and José G. Soto-Marquez. "Sexual Assault Victimization Among Straight, Gay/Lesbian, and Bisexual College Students." *Violence and Gender* 3, no. 2 (2016): 107–115.

Foshee, Vangie A., Karl E. Bauman, Ximena B. Arriaga, Russell W. Helms, Gary G. Koch, and George Fletcher Linder. "An evaluation of Safe Dates, an adolescent dating violence prevention program." *American Journal of Public Health* 88, no. 1 (1998): 45–50.

Foshee, Vangie A., Karl E. Bauman, Susan T. Ennett, G. Fletcher Linder, Thad Benefield, and Chirayath Suchindran. "Assessing the long-term effects of the Safe Dates program and a booster in preventing and reducing adolescent dating violence victimization and perpetration." *American Journal of Public Health* 94, no. 4 (2004): 619–624.

Foshee, Vangie A., Karl E. Bauman, Wendy F. Greene, Gary G. Koch, George F. Linder, and James E. MacDougall. "The Safe Dates program: 1-year follow-up results." *American Journal of Public Health* 90, no. 10 (2000): 1619.

Foubert, John D., and Ryan C. Masin. "Effects of the men's program on US Army soldiers' intentions to commit and willingness to intervene to prevent rape: a pretest posttest study." *Violence and Victims* 27, no. 6 (2012): 911–921.

Foubert, John D. *The Men's and Women's Programs: Ending Rape through Peer Education*. New York: Routledge, 2011.

Freedman, Estelle B. *Redefining Rape*. Boston: Harvard University Press, 2013.

Garrett-Gooding, Joy, and Richard Senter. "Attitudes and acts of sexual aggression on a university campus." *Sociological Inquiry* 57, no. 4 (1987).

Gibson, Megan. "Take Back the Night." *Time Magazine*, August 12, 2011. Accessed January 8, 2014, http://content.time.com/time/specials/packages/article/0,28804,2088114_2087975_2087967,00.html.

Gidycz, Christine A., Melissa J. Layman, Cindy L. Rich, Marie Crothers, Julius Gylys, Abigail Matorin, and Cecilia Dine Jacobs. "An evaluation of an acquaintance rape prevention program: Impact on attitudes, sexual aggression, and sexual victimization." *Journal of Interpersonal Violence* 16, no. 11 (2001): 1120–1138.

Gidycz, Christine A., Lindsay M. Orchowski, and Alan D. Berkowitz. "Preventing sexual aggression among college men: An evaluation of a social norms and bystander intervention program." *Violence Against Women* 17, no. 6 (2011): 720–742.

Gilbert Ryan, James. "The Memphis Riots of 1866: Terror in a Black Community During Reconstruction." *The Journal of Negro History* 62 (1977).

Gloria Ryan, Erin. "Here's the 'Rapist List.'" Flyer Being Anonymously Handed Out at Columbia," Jezebel, May 13, 2014, http://jezebel.com/rapist-list-mysteriously-appearing-in-columbia-universi-1575660992/1575819470.

Gold, Jodi and Susan Villari. *Just Sex: Students Rewrite the Rules on Sex, Violence, Equality, and Activism.* New York: Rowman & Littlefield, 1999.

Goldman, Russell. "School Accused of Covering Up Student's Murder." *ABCNews.com*, June 20, 2007. http://abcnews.go.com/US/story?id=3296170.

Gordon, Claire. "Title IX Complaint Against Yale Has a Case." *The Huffington Post.* April 1, 2011. http://www.huffingtonpost.com/claire-gordon/yale-sexual-harassment-title-ix_b_843273.html.

Gordon, Claire. "Why College Rape Victims Don't Go to the Police." *Al Jazeera America,* May 14, 2014. http://america.aljazeera.com/watch/shows/america-tonight/articles/2014/5/19/why-college-rapevictimsdonatgotothepolice.html.

Gordy, Cynthia. "Recy Taylor: A Symbol of Jim Crow's Forgotten Horror." *The Root*, February 9, 2011. Accessed January 25, 2013. http://www.theroot.com/articles/culture/2011/02/recy_taylor_a_symbol_of_jim_crows_forgotten_horror.html.

Gorman, Ryan. "Outrage at Football Fan with Sign 'Taunting' Girl Who Killed Herself after Alleged Sexual Assault . . .But He Claims He Was Trying to 'Raise Awareness.'" *Daily Mail*, September 8, 2013. Accessed December 30, 2017. http://www.dailymail.co.uk/news/article-2415625/Lizzy-Seeberg-Outrage-football-fan-sign-taunting-girl-killed-herself.html.

Gottschall, Jonathan. "Explaining Wartime Rape." *Journal of Sex Research* 41 (2004): 129–136.

Grasgreen, Allie. "The Power of SlutWalks." October 5, 2011. Accessed May 2, 2017, https://www.insidehighered.com/news/2011/10/05/slutwalks_create_controversy_as_new_approach_fighting_sexual_violence.

Gray, Eliza. "Colleges Find New Ways to Tackle Sexual Assault as Students Return." *Time*, August 24, 2015. Accessed May 3, 2017, http://time.com/4006145/colleges-new-ways-tackle-sexual-assault/.

Greenberg, Benjamin. "Alabama Senate Apologizes to Recy Taylor for 1944 Rape Case," *Colorlines*, April 22, 2011. Accessed March 23, 2017. http://www.colorlines.com/articles/alabama-senate-apologizes-recy-taylor-1944-rape-case.

Greensite, Gillian. "History of the Rape Crisis Movement." *California Coalition Against Sexual Assault.* November 1, 2009. Accessed January 25, 2014. http://www.calcasa.org/2009/11/history-of-the-rape-crisis-movement.

Gregory, Jill, April Lewton, Stephanie Schmidt, Diane "Dani" Smith, and Mark Mattern. "Body politics with feeling: The power of the clothesline project." *New Political Science* 24, no. 3 (2002): 433–448.

Gross, Alan M., Andrea Winslett, Miguel Roberts, and Carol L. Gohm. "An examination of sexual violence against college women." *Violence Against Women* 12, no. 3 (2006): 288–300.

Gross, Ken and Andrea Fine. "After Their Daughter Is Murdered at College, Her Grieving Parents Mount a Campaign for Student Safety." *People Magazine*, February 19, 1990. http://www.people.com/people/archive/article/0,,20116872,00.html.

Grynbaum, Michael M. and Jim Rutenberg. "Trump, Asked About Accusations Against Bill O'Reilly, Calls Him a 'Good Person.'" *The New York Times*, April 5, 2017, https://www.nytimes.com/2017/04/05/business/media/trump-oreilly-fox-murdochs.html.

Gutstein, Donald. *How the Internet Undermines Democracy*. Toronto, Canada, 1999.

Haag, Matthew. "Rolling Stone Settles Lawsuit Over Debunked Campus Rape Article." *The New York Times*, April 22, 2017. https://www.nytimes.com/2017/04/11/business/media/rolling-stone-university-virginia-rape-story-settlement.html?_r=0.

Hague, Brian and Brian Loader, *Digital democracy: Discourse and Decision Making in the Information Age*. London, England: Routledge, 1999.

Hahn, Jennifer. "Schoolgirl Dreams." Accessed January 14, 2016, http://www.feminist.org/education/TriumphsOfTitleIX.pdf, p.47.

Hanson, Hayley E. "The Department of Education Announces the Largest Clery Fine in History—$2.4 Million." *Higher Education Legal Insights*, November 4, 2016. http://www.highereducationlegalinsights.com/2016/11/the-department-of-education-announces-the-largest-clery-fine-in-history-2-4-million/.

Harris, Grant T., and N. Zoe Hilton. "Theoretical note: Interpreting moderate effects in interpersonal violence." *Journal of Interpersonal Violence* 16, no. 10 (2001): 1094–1098.

Harvey, Taylor. "Victim into Advocate: One Sexual Assault Survivor's Fight for Justice." *The Daily Cardinal*. April 11, 2013. Accessed June 19, 2014, http://host.madison.com/daily-cardinal/news/campus/victim-into-advocate-one-sexual-assault-survivor-s-fight-for/article_fddc55ea-a277-11e2-8f72-001a4bcf887a.html.

Hattersley Gray, Robin. "Sexual Assault Statistics." *Campus Safety Magazine*, March 5, 2012, http://www.campussafetymagazine.com/article/Sexual-Assault-Statistics-and-Myths.

Haven, Stephanie. "Will Campus Sexual-Assault Probes Affect Enrollment?" McClachty, July 16, 2014, http://www.mcclatchydc.com/news/crime/article24770584.html.

Heath, Nicole M., Shannon M. Lynch, April M. Fritch, and Maria M. Wong. "Rape Myth Acceptance Impacts the Reporting of Rape to the Police: A Study of Incarcerated Women." *Violence Against Women* 19, no. 9 (2013): 1065–1078.

Hefling, Kimberly and Caitlin Emma. "Obama-Era School Sexual Assault Policy Rescinded." *Politico*, September 22, 2017. Accessed January 1, 2018, https://www.politico.com/story/2017/09/22/obama-era-school-sexual-assault-policy-rescinded-243016.

Heppner, Mary J., Helen A. Neville, Kendra Smith, Dennis M. Kivlighan Jr, and Beth S. Gershuny. "Examining immediate and long-term efficacy of rape prevention programming with racially diverse college men." *Journal of Counseling Psychology* 46, no. 1 (1999): 16.

Hess, Amanda. "How the Internet Revolutionized Campus Anti-Rape Activism." *Slate.com*, 2013. http://www.slate.com/blogs/xx_factor/2013/03/20/occidental_college_sexual_assault_case_how_the_internet_revolutionized_campus.html.

Hesse, Monica. "Men's Rights Activists, Gathering to Discuss All the Ways Society Has Done Them Wrong." *Washington Post*, June 30, 2014. https://www.washingtonpost.com/lifestyle/style/mens-rights-activists-gathering-to-discuss-all-the-ways-society-has-done-them-wrong/2014/06/30/a9310d96-005f-11e4-8fd0-3a663dfa68ac_story.html.

Hipolit, Melissa. "Feds. Investigate U.Va., W&M Over Sexual Assault Complaints." *CBS 6 News,* May 2, 2014. http://wtvr.com/2014/05/02/feds-investigating-uva-wm-for-handling-of-sexual-assault-complaints-1/.

Hipple, Patricia Coral. "Hegemonic disguise in resistance to domination: the Clothesline Project's response to male violence against women." (1998).

Hirschorn, M. "Behavior of students in fraternities worsens on many campuses as membership soars." *Chronicle of Higher Education,* pp. A34–A36. (March 16, 1988).

Hollander, Jocelyn A. "Does self-defense training prevent sexual violence against women?" *Violence Against Women* 20, no. 3 (2014): 252–269.

Hollander, Jocelyn A. "The importance of self-defense training for sexual violence prevention." *Feminism & Psychology* 26, no. 2 (2016): 207–226.

Huffstutter, P. J. "3 Lose School Jobs in Slaying Cover-up." *The Los Angeles Times*, July 17, 2007. http://articles.latimes.com/2007/jul/17/nation/na-dickinson17.

James, Joy. *Resisting State Violence: Radicalism, Gender, and Race in U.S. Culture*. Minneapolis: University of Minnesota Press, 1996.

Jaschik, Scott. "The 'Vagina Monologues' Test," *Inside Higher Ed*, April 7, 2006. https://www.insidehighered.com/news/2006/04/07/catholic.

Jenkins, Henry, Sangita Shresthova, Liana Gamber-Thompson, and Arely Zimmerman. *By Any Media Necessary: The New Youth Activism*. New York, NY: NYU Press, 2016.

Jones, Charisse. "Nicole Simpson, in Death, Lifting Domestic Violence to the Forefront as National Issue." New York Times, October 13, 1995. Accessed December 20, 2017. http://www.nytimes.com/1995/10/13/us/nicole-simpson-death-lifting-domestic-violence-fore-front-national-issue.html?pagewanted=all.

Julier, Laura. "Private texts and social activism: Reading the Clothesline Project." *English Education* 26, no. 4 (1994): 249–259.

Juris, Jeffrey. "Networked Social Movements: Global Movements for Global Justice" in *The Network Society: a Cross-Cultural Perspective*, Manuel Castells, Ed., Northamton, MA: Edward Elgar Publishers, (2004): 341–362.

Juris, Jeffrey S. "The New Digital Media and Activist Networking within Anti–Corporate Globalization Movements." *The Annals of the American Academy of Political and Social Science* 597 no. 1 (2005): 189–208.

Kaiser, Christopher. "Celebrating Title IX and Its Relevance to Our Work." *Speaking Out*. Accessed June 13, 2014, http://taasa.org/blog/category/sexual-assault-laws/Speaking.

Kanin, Eugene J. "Male aggression in dating-courtship relations." *American Journal of Sociology* 63, no. 2 (1957): 197–204.

Kann, L., E. O. Olsen, T. McManus, S. Kinchen, D. Chyen, W. A. Harris, and H. Wechsler. "Centers for Disease Control and Prevention (CDC) Sexual identity, sex of sexual contacts, and health-risk behaviors among students in grades 9–12—youth risk behavior surveillance, selected sites, United States, 2001-2009." *Morbidity and Mortality Weekly Report. Surveillance Summaries* (Washington, DC: 2002) 60, no. 7 (2011): 1–133.

Katz, Jackson, H. Alan Heisterkamp, and Wm. Michael Fleming. "The social justice roots of the mentors in violence prevention model and its application in a high school setting." *Violence Against Women* 17, no. 6 (2011): 684–702.

Katz, Jennifer and Jessica Moore. "Bystander education training for campus sexual assault prevention: An initial meta-analysis." *Violence and Victims* 28, no. 6 (2013): 1054–1067.

Kaukinen, Catherine, Michelle Miller, and Rachael A. Powers. *Addressing Violence Against Women on Campus*. Philadelphia, Temple University Press, 2017.

Kelderman, Eric. "Risk Managers Extend Their Turf to Every Corner of Campus." *The Chronicle of Higher Education*, November 22, 2009. http://chronicle.com/article/Campus-Risk-Managers-Extend/49226/.

Kidd, Dorothy. "Which would you rather: Seattle or Porto Alegre?" Paper presented at the "Our media" pre-conference of the International Association for Media and Communication Research, Barcelona, 2002.

Kilpatrick, Dean G., Heidi S. Resnick, Kenneth J. Ruggiero, Lauren M. Conoscenti, and Jenna McCauley. "Drug-Facilitated, Incapacitated, and Forcible Rape: A National Study," U.S. Department of Justice, 2007, https://www.ncjrs.gov/pdffiles1/nij/grants/219181.pdf.

Kingkade, Tyler. "A supergroup of academics is trying to stop people who profit from campus rape." *Huffington Post*. Accessed December 3, 2016. http://www.huffingtonpost.com/entry/professor-group-fighting-campus-rape_us_55e5120de4b0aec9f35459d9.

Kingkade, Tyler. "Amherst, Vanderbilt Accused of Botching Sexual Assault Complaints." *The Huffington Post*, November 14, 2013. http://www.huffingtonpost.com/2013/11/14/amherst-vanderbilt-sexual-assault_n_4271138.html.

Kingkade, Tyler. "Dartmouth Under Investigation for Handling of Sexual Harassment Complaints." *The Huffington Post*, July 23, 2013. http://www.huffingtonpost.com/2013/07/23/dartmouth-investigation-sexual-harassment_n_3639096.html.

Kingkade, Tyler. "College Sexual Assault Policies Get Mediocre Grade from Students in Survey." *The Huffington Post*, May 10, 2013. http://www.huffingtonpost.com/2013/05/10/college-sexual-assault-policies-survey_n_3211272.html.

Kingkade, Tyler. "College Sexual Assault Victim Advocates Hail VAWA," *The Huffington Post*, March 1, 2013, http://www.huffingtonpost.com/2013/03/01/college-sexual-assault-vawa_n_2786838.html.

Kingkade, Tyler. "Federal Campus Rape Investigations Near 200, and Finally Get More Funding." *The Huffington Post*, January 6, 2016. http://www.huffingtonpost.com/entry/federal-funding-campus-rape-investigations_us_568af080e4b014efe0db5f76.

Kingkade, Tyler. "How a Title IX Harassment Case at Yale in 1980 Set the Stage for Today's Sexual Assault Activism." *The Huffington Post*, June 10, 2014. Accessed December 30, 2017, https://www.huffingtonpost.com/2014/06/10/title-ix-yale-catherine-mackinnon_n_54 62140.html.

Kingkade, Tyler. "How Media Coverage of Campus Scandals Impacts College Applications." *The Huffington Post*, July 8, 2016, http://www.huffingtonpost.com/entry/college-scandals-applications_us_577e6ac1e4b0344d514e1bf9.

Kingkade, Tyler. "James Madison University Punished Sexual Assault with 'Expulsion After Graduation.'" June 18, 2014, http://www.huffingtonpost.com/2014/06/18/james-madison-university-sexual-assault_n_5509163.html.

Kingkade, Tyler. "Occidental College Subject of Federal Investigation Over Sexual Assault Response." *The Huffington Post*, May 8, 2013. http://www.huffingtonpost.com/2013/05/08/occidental-federal-investigation-sexual-assault_n_3240402.html.

Kingkade, Tyler. "Occidental Faculty 'No Confidence' Vote Rebukes Administrators for Handling of Sexual Assault." *The Huffington Post*, May 6, 2013. http://www.huffingtonpost.com/2013/05/06/occidental-faculty-sexual-assault-no-confidence_n_3220863.html.

Kingkade, Tyler. "Professors Are Being Forced to Reveal Sexual Assault Confidences, Like It or Not." *The Huffington Post*, May 11, 2016. Accessed December 30, 2017, https://www.huffingtonpost.com/entry/mandatory-reporting-college-sexual-assault_us_573 25797e4b016f37897792c.

Kingkade, Tyler. "Prosecutors Rarely Bring Charges in College Rape Cases." *The Huffington Post*, June 17, 2014. http://www.huffingtonpost.com/2014/06/17/college-rape-prosecutors-press-charges_n_5500432.html.

Kingkade, Tyler. "Senators Fight for a Vote on Campus Rape Rules." *The Huffington Post*, April 26, 2016. Accessed December 30, 2017, https://www.huffingtonpost.com/entry/senators-campus-rape-bill_us_571f8a2ae4b01a5ebde359f7.

Kingkade, Tyler. "Senators Push for More Staff at Agency to Investigate Sexual Abuse at Colleges." *The Huffington Post*. April 4, 2014, http://www.huffingtonpost.com/2014/04/04/agency-sexual-assault-investigations-mccaskill-gillibrand_n_5092748.html.

Kingkade, Tyler. "There are Far More Title IX Investigations of Colleges Than Most People Know." *The Huffington Post*, June 16, 2016. http://www.huffingtonpost.com/entry/title-ix-investigations-sexual-harassment_us_575f4b0ee4b053d433061b3d.

Kingkade, Tyler. "Trump's Education Secretary Nominee Won't Commit to Keeping Campus Rape Rules." *Buzzfeed*, January 17, 2017, https://www.buzzfeed.com/tylerkingkade/betsy-devos-title-ix?utm_term=.atNKyNqd3G#.aj0ZDOKp3w.

Kingkade, Tyler. "UConn Failed to Investigate Sexual Assault Reports and Protect Victims, Complaint Claims," *The Huffington Post*, October 21, 2013. http://www.huffingtonpost.com/2013/10/21/uconn-sexual-assault-complaint_n_4133713.html.

Kingkade, Tyler. "UNC 'Courage Project' Vandalized by Person without Courage." *The Huffington Post*, August 28, 2013. http://www.huffingtonpost.com/2013/08/28/unc-courage-project-vandalized_n_3831667.html.

Kingkade, Tyler. "UNC Faces Federal Investigation into Retaliation Complaint by Sexual Assault Survivor." *The Huffington Post*, July 7, 2013, http://www.huffingtonpost.com/2013/07/07/unc-investigation-retaliation_n_3555886.html.

Kingkade, Tyler. "University of Colorado-Boulder Faces New Claim of Mishandling Sexual Assaults." *The Huffington Post*, August 28, 2013. http://www.huffingtonpost.com/2013/08/28/cu-boulder-federal-complaint-sexual-assult_n_3826702.html?utm_hp_ref=college.

Kingkade, Tyler. "University of Oregon Facing Federal Complaint for Hiding Gang Rape Report." *The Huffington Post*, May 15, 2014, http://www.huffingtonpost.com/2014/05/15/university-of-oregon-complaint-rape_n_5331120.html.

Kingkade, Tyler. "USC, Occidental Admit Underreporting Campus Sex Offenses." *The Huffington Post,* October 10, 2013. http://www.huffingtonpost.com/2013/10/10/usc-occidental-sex offenses_n_4073117.html?utm_hp_ref=college.

Kingkade, Tyler. "University of North Carolina Routinely Violates Sexual Assault Survivor Rights, Students Claim." *The Huffington Post,* June 20, 2013. http://huff.to/1laVFEK.

Kingkade, Tyler. "Yale Faces $165,000 Clery Act Fine for Failing to Report Sex Offenses on Campus," *The Huffington Post,* May 15, 2013. http://www.huffingtonpost.com/2013/05/15/yale-clery-act_n_3280195.html.

Kingkade, Tyler. "Sexual Assault Witnesses at Occidental College Subject to Vile Harassment Emails." *The Huffington Post,* July 22, 2014. http://www.huffingtonpost.com/2014/07/22/occidental-harassment-sexual-assault-report_n_5609909.html.

Kinnick, Katherine N., Dean M. Krugman, and Glen T. Cameron. "Compassion Fatigue: Communication and Burnout Toward Social Problems." *Journal of Mass Communication Quarterly,* August, 1996, 73(3): 687–707.

Kirkpatrick, Clifford, and Eugene Kanin. "Male sex aggression on a university campus." *American Sociological Review* 22, no. 1 (1957): 52–58.

Know Your IX, "Petition: Department of Education: Hold colleges accountable that break the law by refusing to protect students from sexual assault." 2013. Change.org, https://www.change.org/p/department-of-education-hold-colleges-accountable-that-break-the-law-by-refusing-to-protect-students-from-sexual-assault.

Koren, Marina. "Telling the Story of the Stanford Rape Case." *The Atlantic,* June 6, 2016. https://www.theatlantic.com/news/archive/2016/06/stanford-sexual-assault-letters/485837/.

Koss, Mary P. "Hidden rape: Incidence, prevalence, and descriptive characteristics of sexual aggression and victimization in a national sample of college students." *Sexual Assault* 2 (1988): 3–25.

Koss, Mary P. "The hidden rape victim: Personality, attitudinal, and situational characteristics." *Psychology of Women Quarterly* 9, no. 2 (1985): 193–212.

Koss, Mary P. "The RESTORE program of restorative justice for sex crimes: Vision, process, and outcomes." *Journal of Interpersonal Violence* 29, no. 9 (2014): 1623–1660.

Koss, Mary P. and John A. Gaines. "The prediction of sexual aggression by alcohol use, athletic participation, and fraternity affiliation." *Journal of Interpersonal Violence,* 8 (1993): 94–108.

Koss, Mary P., Christine A. Gidycz, and Nadine Wisniewski. "The scope of rape: incidence and prevalence of sexual aggression and victimization in a national sample of higher education students." *Journal of Consulting and Clinical Psychology* 55, no. 2 (1987): 162.

Koss, Mary P., Kenneth E. Leonard, Dana A. Beezley, and Cheryl J. Oros. "Nonstranger sexual aggression: A discriminant analysis of the psychological characteristics of undetected offenders." *Sex Roles* 12, no. 9-10 (1985): 981–992.

Koss, Mary P., and Cheryl J. Oros. "Sexual Experiences Survey: a research instrument investigating sexual aggression and victimization." *Journal of Consulting and Clinical Psychology* 50, no. 3 (1982): 455.

Koss, Mary P., Jay K. Wilgus, and Kaaren M. Williamsen. "Campus sexual misconduct: Restorative justice approaches to enhance compliance with Title IX guidance." *Trauma, Violence, & Abuse* 15, no. 3 (2014): 242–257.

Krakauer, Jon. *Missoula: Rape and the justice system in a college town.* Anchor, 2016.

Krebs, Christopher, Christine Lindquist, Marcus Berzofsky, Bonnie Shook-Sa, Kimberly Peterson, Michael Planty, Lynn Langton, and Jessica Stroop. "Campus climate survey validation study final technical report." *Bureau of Justice Statistics Research and Development Series* (2016): 1–193.

Krebs, Christopher P., Christine H. Lindquist, Tara D. Warner, Bonnie S. Fisher, and Sandra L. Martin. "The Campus Sexual Assault Survey," U.S. Department of Justice, December, 2007, https://www.ncjrs.gov/pdffiles1/nij/grants/221153.pdf.

Krebs, Christopher P., Christine H. Lindquist, Tara D. Warner, Bonnie S. Fisher, and Sandra L. Martin. "The campus sexual assault (CSA) study: Final report." Washington, DC: National Institute of Justice, US Department of Justice (2007). https://www.ncjrs.gov/pdffiles1/nij/grants/219181.pdf.

Krebs, Christopher P., Christine H. Lindquist, Tara D. Warner, Bonnie S. Fisher, and Sandra L. Martin. "College women's experiences with physically forced, alcohol- or other drug-enabled, and drug-facilitated sexual assault before and since entering college." *Journal of American College Health* 57, no. 6 (2009): 639–649.

Krebs, Christopher P., Christine H. Lindquist, Tara D. Warner, Bonnie S. Fisher, and Sandra L. Martin. "The differential risk factors of physically forced and alcohol- or other drug-enabled sexual assault among university women." *Violence and Victims* 24, no. 3 (2009): 302–321.

Kristoff, Nicholas. "Donald Trump, Groper in Chief." *New York Times Sunday Review*, October 7, 2016. Accessed May 6, 2017, https://www.nytimes.com/2016/10/09/opinion/sunday/donald-trump-groper-in-chief.html.

Kurtzleben, Danielle. "Poll: Americans Overwhelmingly Support 'Zero Tolerance' on Sexual Harassment." *National Public Radio*. December 14. Accessed January 1, 2018, https://www.npr.org/2017/12/14/570601136/poll-sexual-harassment-ipsos.

Lacher, Rebecca and Pedro A. Ramos. "U.S. Department of Education Levies More Fines for Clery Act Violations." *Mondaq*, January 30, 2014, http://www.mondaq.com/unitedstates/x/289764/Education/US+Department+Of+Education+Levies+More+Fines+For+Clery+Act+Violations.

Lahitou. Jessica. "All the Ways Rape Culture was Encouraged in Trump's First 100 Days." *Bustle*, May 5, 2017, https://www.bustle.com/p/all-the-ways-rape-culture-was-encouraged-in-trumps-first-100-days-54286.

Langhinrichsen-Rohling, Jennifer, John D. Foubert, Hope M. Brasfield, Brent Hill, and Shannon Shelley-Tremblay. "The men's program: Does it impact college men's self-reported bystander efficacy and willingness to intervene?" *Violence Against Women* 17, no. 6 (2011): 743–759.

Laub, Arielle. "Gina Smith and Leslie Gomez to Take on Occidental's Sexual Assault Policy." *Occidental Weekly*, April 9, 2013. http://occidentalweekly.com/news/2013/04/09/gina-smith-and-leslie-gomez-to-take-on-occidentals-sexual-assault-policy/.

Lauerman, John. "College Men Accused of Sexual Assault Say Their Rights Violated." *Bloomberg News*, December 16, 2013, https://www.bloomberg.com/news/articles/2013-12-16/college-men-accused-of-sexual-assault-say-their-rights-violated.

Lee, Kurtis. "Fellow Republicans assail Trump for lewd comments about women in leaked audio." *The Los Angeles Times*, October 7, 2016. Accessed May 6, 2017, http://www.latimes.com/nation/politics/trailguide/la-na-live-updates-trailguide-fellow-republicans-assail-trump-for-1475887136-htmlstory.html.

Leonard, A. Jason, Carrie J. Curie, Stephanie M. Townsend, Steven B. Pokorny, Richard B. Katz, and Joseph L. Sherk. "Health promotion interventions." *Child & Family Behavior Therapy* 24, no. 1–2 (2002): 67–82.

Lerner, Gerda. *Black Women in White America: A Documentary History*. New York: Vintage, 1992.

Levenson, Jill and Alissa R. Ackerman. "The Stanford Rape Case: Are We Having the Wrong Conversation?" *Psychology Today Guest Blog*, 2016. https://www.psychologytoday.com/blog/the-guest-room/201607/the-stanford-rape-case.

Lievrouw, Leah A. *Alternative and Activist New Media*. Cambridge, UK: Polity Press, (2011): 5.

Lighty, Todd and Rich Campbell. "Ex-Notre Dame Player's Remarks Reopen Wound." *Chicago Tribune*, February 24, 2014. Accessed December 20, 2017. http://articles.chicagotribune.com/2014-02-26/news/ct-seeberg-interview-met-20140226_1_lizzy-seeberg-tom-seeberg-seeberg-case.

Lighty, Todd, Stacy St. Clair, and Jodi S. Cohen. "Few Arrests, Convictions in Campus Sex Assault Cases." *Chicago Tribune*, June 16, 2011. http://articles.chicagotribune.com/2011-06-16/news/ct-met-campus-sexual-assaults-0617-20110616_1_convictions-arrests-assault-cases.

Lim, Merlyna. "Clicks, Cabs, and Coffee Houses: Social Media and Oppositional Movements in Egypt, 2001-2011." *Journal of Communication*, 62 (2012): 231–248.

Lipka, Sara. "Ignorance and Low Priority of Clery Act Violations May Extend Beyond Penn State." *The Chronicle of Higher Education*. July 1, 2012. http://chronicle.com/article/Ignorance-Low-Priority-of/132839/.

Lipka, Sara. "Lincoln U. of Missouri faces $275,000 Fine for Clery Act Violations." *The Chronicle of Higher Education*, November 11, 2013, http://chronicle.com/article/Lincoln-U-of-Missouri-Faces/142929/.

Lisak, David and Paul M. Miller. "Repeat Rape and Multiple Offending Among Undetected Rapists." *Violence and Victims* 17, no. 1 (2001): 73–84.

"Living the Green Dot." Accessed April 23, 2017, https://www.livethegreendot.com/.

Logan Greene, Patricia, and Kelly Cue Davis. "Latent profiles of risk among a community sample of men: Implications for sexual aggression." *Journal of Interpersonal Violence* 26, no. 7 (2011): 1463–1477.

Lombardi, Kristen. "A Lack of Consequences for Sexual Assault." The Center for Public Integrity, February 24, 2010, http://www.publicintegrity.org/2010/02/24/4360/lack-consequences-sexual-assault.

Longsway, Kimberly A. and Louise F. Fitzgerald. "Rape Myths: In Review." *Psychology of Women Quarterly* 18, no. 2, (2012): 133–164.

Lu, Jenny. "Students Announce Second Federal Complaint Against Swarthmore." *Daily Gazette*, April 26, 2013, http://daily.swarthmore.edu/2013/04/26/19921/.

MacDonald, Heather. "Campus Rape Dogma in the Age of Promiscuity." February 11, 2016, https://www.manhattan-institute.org/html/campus-rape-dogma-age-promiscuity-8513.html.

MacDonald, Heather. "The Phony Campus Rape Crisis," *The Weekly Standard*, November 2, 2015, http://www.weeklystandard.com/an-assault-on-common-sense/article/1051200.

Malamuth, Neil M., Daniel Linz, Christopher L. Heavey, Gordon Barnes, and Michele Acker. "Using the confluence model of sexual aggression to predict men's conflict with women: a 10-year follow-up study." *Journal of Personality and Social Psychology* 69, no. 2 (1995): 353.

Malamuth, Neil M., and Nancy Wilmsen Thornhill. "Hostile masculinity, sexual aggression, and gender-biased domineeringness in conversations." *Aggressive Behavior* 20, no. 3 (1994): 185–193.

Malamuth, Neil M., Robert J. Sockloskie, Mary P. Koss, and Jeffrey S. Tanaka. "Characteristics of aggressors against women: Testing a model using a national sample of college students." *Journal of Consulting and Clinical Psychology* 59, no. 5 (1991): 670.

Malone, Trey. Suicide note reprinted by The Good Men Project, November 5, 2012, https://goodmenproject.com/ethics-values/lead-a-good-life-everyone-trey-malones-suicide-note/#ICFM7hoUxep8iatH.99.

Maloy, C., J. Sheril, C. Bausell, D. Siegle, and C. Raymond. (n.d.) Unpublished manuscript, Towson State University Center for the Study and Prevention of Campus Violence. Towson, MD.

Martin, Patricia Yancey. "The rape prone culture of academic contexts fraternities and athletics." *Gender & Society* 30, no. 1 (2016): 30–43.

Matchar, Emily. "'Men's Rights' Activists Are Trying the Redefine the Meaning of Rape." *New Republic*, February 26, 2014. https://newrepublic.com/article/116768/latest-target-mens-rights-movement-definition-rape.

Mattews, Dylan. "Student Activists Push Obama to Act on Sexual Assault. This is Where They Want to Go From Here." *Vox*, May 7, 2014. Accessed January 1, 2018, https://www.vox.com/2014/5/7/5690682/student-activists-pushed-obama-to-act-on-sexual-assault-this-is-where.

Matthews, Nancy A. *Confronting Rape: The Feminist Anti-Rape Movement and the State*. New York: Routledge, 1994.

McCaughey, Martha, and Jill Cermele. "Changing the Hidden Curriculum of Campus Rape Prevention and Education Women's Self-Defense as a Key Protective Factor for a Public Health Model of Prevention." *Trauma, Violence, & Abuse* (2015): 1524838015611674.

McDonough, Katie. "UNC Faces Federal Charges Over Complaint by Sexual Assault Whistle Blower." *Salon*, July 8, 2013. http://www.salon.com/2013/07/08/unc_faces_federal_charges_over_complaint_by_sexual_assault_whistle_blower/.

McGuire, Danielle L. *At the Dark End of the Street: Black Women, Rape, and Resistance—a New History of the Civil Rights Movement from Rosa Parks to the Rise of Black Power.* New York: Random House, 2011.

McGuire, Danielle L. "It Was Like All of Us Had Been Raped: Sexual Violence, Community Mobilization, and the African American Freedom Struggle." *The Journal of American History* 91, (2004): 906–931.

McMahon, Sarah, Jane E. Palmer, Victoria Banyard, Megan Murphy, and Christine A. Gidycz. "Measuring Bystander Behavior in the Context of Sexual Violence Prevention: Lessons Learned and New Directions." *Journal of Interpersonal Violence* (2015): 0886260515591979.

McMahon, Sarah, Judy L. Postmus, Corinne Warrener, and Ruth Anne Koenick. "Utilizing peer education theater for the primary prevention of sexual violence on college campuses." *Journal of College Student Development* 55, no. 1 (2014) 78–85.

Mendes, Kaitlynn. *Slutwalk: Feminism, Activism and Media.* New York: Palgrave, 2015.

Medina, Jennifer. "Sex Ed Lesson: 'Yes Means Yes,' But It's Tricky," *The New York Times*, October 14, 2015. https://www.nytimes.com/2015/10/15/us/california-high-schools-sexual-consent-classes.html?_r=0.

Megan, Kathleen. "Herbst Calls Allegation That UConn Is Indifferent to Reports of Sexual Assault 'Astonishingly Misguided.'" *The Courant*, October 23, 2013. http://articles.courant.com/2013-10-23/news/hc-uconn-herbst-title-ix-complaint-trustees-1024-20131022_1_uconn-president-susan-herbst-sexual-assault-sexual-violence.

Mervosh, Sara. "New Baylor Lawsuit Alleges 52 Rapes by Football Players in 4 Years, 'Show 'em a Good Time' Culture." *The Dallas Morning News*, January 27, 2017, https://www.dallasnews.com/news/baylor/2017/01/27/new-baylor-lawsuit-describes-show-em-good-time-culture-cites-52-rapes-football-players-4-years.

Merzel, Cheryl, and Joanna D'Afflitti. "Reconsidering community-based health promotion: promise, performance, and potential." *American Journal of Public Health* 93, no. 4 (2003): 557–574.

Mika, Harry and Howard Zehr. "A Restorative Framework for Community Justice Practice" In, Kieran McEvoy and Tim Newburn, Eds., *Criminology, Conflict Resolution and Restorative Justice.* Basingstoke, Hampshire, UK and New York, NY: Palgrave MacMillan, 135–152, 2003.

Miller, E., D. Tancredi, H. McCauley, M. Decker, M. Virata, H. Anderson, et al. "'Coaching boys into men': A cluster-randomized controlled trial of a dating violence prevention program." *Journal of Adolescent Health, 51,* (2012): 431–438.

Mills, Nicolaus. "How Antioch College Got Rape Right 20 Years Ago." *The Daily Beast*, December 10, 2014. Accessed April 30, 2017, http://www.thedailybeast.com/articles/2014/12/10/how-antioch-solved-campus-sexual-offenses-two-decades-ago.

Mimms, Sarah. "Lobbyists Warn Colleges That Participating in Sexual-Assault Survey Could Make Them Look Bad," *National Journal*, June 5, 2014. http://www.nationaljournal.com/congress/lobbyists-warn-colleges-that-participating-in-sexual-assault-survey-could-make-them-look-bad-20140605.

Mogul, Joey, Andrea Ritchie, and Kay Whitlock. *Queer (In)Justice: The Criminalization of LGBT People in the United States.* Boston: Beacon Press, 2012.

Mohler-Kuo, Meichun, George W. Dowdall, Mary P. Koss, and Henry Wechsler, "Correlates of rape while intoxicated in a national sample of college women." *Journal of Studies on Alcohol, 65* no. 1, (2004): 37–45.

Morozov, Evgeny. *The Net Delusion: The Dark Side of Internet Freedom*, New York, NY: PublicAffairs, 2011.

Morse, Robert. "Students Say Rankings Aren't Most Important Factor in College Decision." *U.S. News and World Report*, January 27, 2011. http://www.usnews.com/education/blogs/college-rankings-blog/2011/01/27/students-say-rankings-arent-most-important-factor-in-college-decision.

Moscatello, Caitlin. "Here Are One Billion Reasons to Get Up and Dance on Valentine's Day." *Glamour*, February 13, 2014, http://www.glamour.com/story/one-billion-rising-for-v-day.

Moskovitz, Diana. "Why Title IX Has Failed Everyone on Campus Rape." *Deadspin*, July 7, 2016. http://deadspin.com/why-title-ix-has-failed-everyone-on-campus-rape-1765565925.

Mouilso, Emily R., and Karen S. Calhoun. "Narcissism, psychopathy and five-factor model in sexual assault perpetration." *Personality and Mental Health* 6, no. 3 (2012): 228–241.

Mouilso, Emily R., and Karen S. Calhoun. "Personality and perpetration: narcissism among college sexual assault perpetrators." *Violence Against Women* 22, no. 10 (2016): 1228–1242.

Moynihan, Mary M., Victoria L. Banyard, Julie S. Arnold, Robert P. Eckstein, and Jane G. Stapleton. "Engaging intercollegiate athletes in preventing and intervening in sexual and intimate partner violence." *Journal of American College Health* 59, no. 3 (2010): 197–204.

Mulhere, Kaitlin. "Inclusive Dialogues." *Inside Higher Education*, January 21, 2015. https://www.insidehighered.com/news/2015/01/21/womens-college-cancels-play-saying-it-excludes-transgender-experiences.

Murnen, Sarah K., and Marla H. Kohlman. "Athletic participation, fraternity membership, and sexual aggression among college men: A meta-analytic review." *Sex Roles* 57, no. 1-2 (2007): 145–157.

Murphy, Kate. "Stanford Sexual Assault Victim Demands Tough Sanctions for Offenders." *Washington Post*, June 7, 2014. https://www.washingtonpost.com/politics/stanford-sexual-assault-victim-demands-tougher-sanctions-for-offenders/2014/06/07/43580f2c-ee7d-11e3-b84b-3393a45b80f1_story.html?utm_term=.b6cd92781bd7.

Murphy, Kim. *I Had Rather Die: Rape in the Civil War.* New York: Coachlight Press, 2014.

Murphy, Wendy. "About Wendy Murphy." February 27, 2013. Accessed May 8, 2017, http://www.wendymurphylaw.com/about/#more-11.

Murphy, Wendy. "The Harsh Truth about Campus Sexual Assault." *wendymurphylaw.com*, February 13, 2013. http://bit.ly/1laLrEd.

Murphy, Wendy. "Using Title IX's 'Prompt and Equitable' Hearing Requirements to Force Schools to Provide Fair Judicial Proceedings to Redress Sexual Assault on Campus." *New England Law Review* 40, no. 4 (2006): 1007–1022.

Musil Mctighe, Caryn. "Scaling the Ivory Towers: Title IX has Launched Women into the Studies, Professions, and Administrative Jobs of Their Dreams." Accessed January 14, 2016, http://www.feminist.org/education/TriumphsOfTitleIX.pdf.

National Alliance to End Sexual Violence. "Campus Sexual Assault." June, 2014. Accessed May 4, 2017, http://endsexualviolence.org/where-we-stand/campus-sexual-assault.

National Center for Education Statistics. "Digest of Education Statistics." Accessed April 15, 2017, https://nces.ed.gov/programs/digest/d99/d99t187.asp.

National Center for Education Statistics. "Fast Facts: Title IX." Institute of Education Sciences, 2014, http://nces.ed.gov/fastfacts/display.asp?id=93.

National Institute of Justice. "Sexual Assault on Campuses: What Colleges and Universities Are Doing About It." 2005. https://www.ncjrs.gov/pdffiles1/nij/205521.pdf.

National Sexual Violence Resource Center. "False Reporting: Overview." Department of Justice, Office on Violence Against Women, 2012. http://www.nsvrc.org/sites/default/files/Publications_NSVRC_Overview_False-Reporting.pdf.

National Sexual Violence Resource Center. "SAAM History." Accessed April 30, 2017, http://www.nsvrc.org/saam/saam-history.

Neame, Alexandra. "Revisiting America's 'Date Rape' Controversy." *Family Matters* 68 (2004): 55.

Nelson, Lauren. "So You're Tired of Hearing about 'Rape Culture?'" The Good Men Project, March 20, 2013, https://goodmenproject.com/ethics-values/so-youre-tired-of-hearing-about-rape-culture/.

New, Jake. "Justice Delayed." *Inside Higher Ed*, May 6, 2015. https://www.insidehighered.com/news/2015/05/06/ocr-letter-says-completed-title-ix-investigations-2014-lasted-more-4-years.

North, Anna. "Students Stage Sit-In to Protest College Sexual Assault Policy." *Jezebel*, March 4, 2011, http://jezebel.com/5776436/students-stage-sit-in-to-protest-college-sexual-assault-policy.

O'Hara, Robert. "AVFM Exclusive: Documentation of Title IX Complaint against Emerson College Surfaces, Questionable Accusations Abound." *A Voice for Men*, June 19, 2014. http://www.avoiceformen.com/mens-rights/false-rape-culture/avfm-exclusive-documentation-of-title-ix-complaint-against-emerson-college-surfaces-questionable-accusations-abound-2/.

Ohio State University. "Reporting Sexual Assault." Accessed June 10, 2014, http://dps.osu.edu/police/campus_safety/reporting_sexual_assault.php.

Ogilvie, Jessica. "Rape at Occidental College: Official Hush-Up Shatters Trust." *The LA Weekly*, June 27, 2013. http://www.laweekly.com/2013-06-27/news/rape-occidental-college/.

Ollwerther, Raymond W. "University Subject of Federal Title IX Probe." *Princeton Alumni Weekly*. June 1, 2011. http://paw.princeton.edu/issues/2011/06/01/pages/6913/index.xml.

Olya, Gabrielle. "Twelfth Woman Comes Forward to Accuse Donald Trump of Sexual Assault." *People,* October 31, 2016. Accessed on May 6, 2017, http://people.com/bodies/twelfth-woman-accuses-donald-trump-sexual-assault/.

Orso, Anna. "Trumps Education Pick Donated to Philly Group with Controversial Campus Rape Stance." *Politifact*, January 19, 2017. http://www.politifact.com/pennsylvania/statements/2017/jan/19/bob-casey/trumps-education-pick-donated-philly-group-controv/.

Ostrowski, Constance J. "The clothesline project: women's stories of gender-related violence." *Women and Language* 19, no. 1 (1996): 37.

Oxy Sexual Assault Coalition. "OSAC's 7-Year Timeline." 2013. Accessed June 3, 2014, http://oxysexualassaultcoalition.wordpress.com/timeline/.

Oxy Sexual Assault Coalition. "OSAC's Efforts." 2013. Accessed June 13, 2014, http://oxysexualassaultcoalition.wordpress.com/timeline/.

Park, Andrea. "#MeToo Reaches 85 Countries with 1.7M Tweets." *CBS News*, October 4, 2017. Accessed December 31, 2017, https://www.cbsnews.com/news/metoo-reaches-85-countries-with-1-7-million-tweets/.

Parker, Ashley. "House Renews Violence Against Women Measure." *The New York Times*, February 28, 2013. Accessed June 11, 2015. http://www.nytimes.com/2013/03/01/us/politics/congress-passes-reauthorization-of-violence-against-women-act.html?pagewanted=all.

Parkhill, Michele R., and Antonia Abbey. "Does alcohol contribute to the confluence model of sexual assault perpetration?" *Journal of Social and Clinical Psychology* 27, no. 6 (2008): 529–554.

Parnitzke Smith, Carly and Jennifer J. Freyd. "Dangerous safe havens: Institutional betrayal exacerbates sexual trauma." *Journal of Traumatic Stress* 26, no. 1 (2013): 119–124.

Parnitzke Smith, Carly and Jennifer J. Freyd. "Institutional betrayal." *American Psychologist* 69, no. 6 (2014): 575.

Peace Over Violence. "Empowerment Through Self-Defense for Women and Girls: A Model for Primary Prevention." Accessed April 30, 2017, http://www.peaceoverviolence.org/media/downloadables/Empowerment_Through_Self-Defense.pdf.

Peace Over Violence. "Pioneers Over Violence." Accessed April 30, 2017, http://www.peaceoverviolence.org/media/downloadables/Empowerment_Through_Self-Defense.pdf.

Perrigo, Billy. "'We Need Roy Moore.' President Trump Endorses Moore Despite Sexual Misconduct Allegations." *Time Magazine*, December 4, 2017. Accessed December 31, 2017, http://time.com/5047360/donald-trump-we-need-roy-moore-sexual-misconduct-allegations/.

Perry, Mark J. "How About a 'Renewed Call' for the White House to Stop Spreading False Information about Campus Sexual Assault?" American Enterprise Institute, April 29, 2014, http://www.aei.org/publication/how-about-a-renewed-call-for-the-white-house-to-stop-spreading-false-information-about-campus-sexual-assault/.

Peters, B. *Analysis of college campus rape and sexual assault reports, 2000-2011: Using medical provider data to describe the nature and context of college campus rape and sexual assault reports in Massachusetts.* Boston, Executive Office of Public Safety and Security, 2012.

Peterson, Christine L. "The Clery Act: Costs of Noncompliance." North Carolina Bar Association, November 14, 2013, http://educationlaw.ncbar.org/newsletters/educationlawnov2013/clery.

Pinzone-Glover, Holly A., Christine A. Gidycz, and Cecilia Dine Jacobs. "An acquaintance rape prevention program: Effects on attitudes toward women, rape-related attitudes, and perceptions of rape scenarios." *Psychology of Women Quarterly* 22, no. 4 (1998): 605–621.

Piven, Frances Fox and Richard A. Cloward. *Poor People's Movements: Why They Succeed, How They Fail.* New York: Vintage Books, 1978.

Pokorak, Jeffrey J. "Rape as Badge of Slavery: The Legal History Of, and Remedies For, Prosecutorial Race-Of-Victim Charging Disparities." *Nevada Law Journal* 7 (2006): 1–53.

Potter, Sharyn J., and Mary M. Moynihan. "Bringing in the bystander in-person prevention program to a US military installation: Results from a pilot study." *Military Medicine* 176, no. 8 (2011): 870.

Potter, Sharyn J., and Jane G. Stapleton. "Translating sexual assault prevention from a college campus to a United States military installation: Piloting the know-your-power bystander social marketing campaign." *Journal of Interpersonal Violence* 27, no. 8 (2012): 1593–1621.

Rabe Thomas, Jacqueline. "UConn Prof Says Her Support of Outspoken Student May Cost Her Her Job." *The Connecticut Mirror*, November 13, 2013. http://ctmirror.org/uconn-prof-says-her-support-outspoken-student-may-cost-her-her-job/.

Rabin, Roni Caryn. "Nearly 1-in-5 Women in U.S. Survey Say They Have Been Raped or Sexually Assaulted." *The New York Times*, December 14, 2011, http://www.nytimes.com/2011/12/15/health/nearly-1-in-5-women-in-us-survey-report-sexual-assault.html?_r=0&mtrref=undefined&gwh=80B3B1105B5463FE16E4F445CFC17240&gwt=pay.

Rapaport, Karen, and Barry R. Burkhart. "Personality and attitudinal characteristics of sexually coercive college males." *Journal of Abnormal Psychology* 93, no. 2 (1984): 216–221.

Rape, Abuse & Incest National Network. "Why Will Only 3 Out of Every 100 Rapists Serve Time?" Accessed July 16, 2014, https://rainn.org/get-information/statistics/reporting-rates.

Rape Aggression Defense Systems. "About R.A.D." Accessed April 30, 2017, http://www.rad-systems.com/about_us.html.

Reid, Samantha. "College Women Adding Self-Defense Classes to Fall Semester To-Do Lists," *USAToday College,* June 25, 2014. http://college.usatoday.com/2014/06/25/self-defense-classes-gaining-popularity-among-college-women/.

Roiphe, Katie. *The Morning After: Fear, Feminism, and Sex.* New York: Back Bay Books, 1994.

Rosen, Hannah. *Terror in the Heart of Freedom: Citizenship, Sexual Violence, and the Meaning of Race in the Postemancipation South.* Chapel Hill: University of North Carolina Press, 2009.

Ruiz, Maria. "Petition: Remove Judge Aaron Persky from the Bench for Decision in Brock Turner Rape Case." Change.org, 2017. https://www.change.org/p/california-state-house-impeach-judge-aaron-persky.

Ruiz, Rebecca. "Why Cops Don't Believe Rape Victims?" *Slate*, June 19, 2013. http://www.slate.com/articles/news_and_politics/jurisprudence/2013/06/why_cops_don_t_believe_rape_victims_and_how_brain_science_can_solve_the.html.

Rutherford, Alexandra. "Sexual Violence Against Women: Putting Rape Research in Context." *Psychology of Women Quarterly* 35, no. 2 (2011): 342–347.

Saad, Nardine. "Lady Gaga's Family Learns of Her Sexual Abuse after Emotional Oscars Performance." *Los Angeles Times*, March 2, 2016. http://www.latimes.com/entertainment/gossip/la-et-mg-lady-gaga-family-sexual-abuse-revelation-oscars-20160302-htmlstory.html.

Salazar, L. F., A. Vivolo-Kantor, J. Hardin, & A. Berkowitz. "A Web-Based Sexual Violence Bystander Intervention for Male College Students: Randomized Controlled Trial." *Journal of Medical Internet Research* 16 no. 9, (2014): e203.

Sanday, Peggy Reeves. *Fraternity gang rape: Sex, brotherhood, and privilege on campus.* NYU Press, 2007.

Sanday, Peggy Reeves. "Rape-prone versus rape-free campus cultures." *Violence Against Women* 2, no. 2 (1996): 191–208.

Sander, Libby. "Federal Negotiators Agree to Allow Lawyers in Campus Sex-Assault Hearings." *The Chronicle of Higher Education*, April 2, 2014, http://chronicle.com/article/Federal-Negotiators-Agree-to/145665/.

Sander, Libby. "White House Raises the Bar for Colleges' Handling of Sexual Assault." *The Chronicle of Higher Education*, April 29, 2014. Accessed April 30, 2014 http://chronicle.com/article/White-House-Raises-the-Bar-for/146255/.

Sawyer, Robin G., Estina E. Thompson, and Anne Marie Chicorelli. "Rape myth acceptance among intercollegiate student athletes: A preliminary examination." *American Journal of Health Studies* 18, no. 1 (2002): 19.

Schaefer Riley, Naomi. "The Real Rx for Campus- Give up on Liberal 'Answers.'" *The New York Post*, May 6, 2014, http://nypost.com/2014/05/06/the-real-rx-for-campus-rape-give-up-on-liberal-answers/.

Schorn, Susan. "A Look Inside the Terrible Manual Cops Use to Teach 'Rape Prevention.'" Jezebel, February 25, 2015. Accessed April 30, 2017, http://jezebel.com/a-look-inside-the-terrible-manual-cops-use-to-teach-rap-1687694067.

Schow, Ashe. "Backlash: College Men Challenge 'Guilty Until Proven Innocent' Standard for Sex Assault Cases." *The Washington Examiner*, August 11, 2014. http://www.washingtonexaminer.com/backlash-college-men-challenge-guilty-until-proven-innocent-standard-for-sex-assault-cases/article/2551863.

Schwartz, Martin D., and Carol A. Nogrady. "Fraternity membership, rape myths, and sexual aggression on a college campus." *Violence Against Women* 2, no. 2 (1996): 148–162.

Security on Campus. "Campus Sexual Assault Victims' Bill of Rights." Accessed May 12, 2017, https://rsvp.missouri.edu/wp-content/uploads/sites/5/2014/02/Campus-Sexual-Assault-Victim-Bill-of-Rights.pdf.

Securro, Liz. *Crash Into Me*. Bloomsbury USA, 2011.

Selig, Christine E. "Transforming Our World: U.S. Grassroots Organizations and the Global Justice Movement." Grassroots Global Justice Publications, 2010. http://ggjalliance.org/system/files/TransformingOurWorld_Final_hiRes.pdf.

Senn, Charlene Y., Misha Eliasziw, Paula C. Barata, Wilfreda E. Thurston, Ian R. Newby-Clark, H. Lorraine Radtke, and Karen L. Hobden. "Efficacy of a sexual assault resistance program for university women." *New England Journal of Medicine* 372, no. 24 (2015): 2326–2335.

Shapiro, Joseph. "Campus Rape Victims: A Struggle for Justice." NPR Morning Edition, February 24, 2010. http://www.npr.org/templates/story/story.php?storyId=124001493.

Shapiro, T. Rees. "Expelled for Sex Assault, Young Men Are Filing More Lawsuits to Clear Their Names." *The Washington Post*, April 28, 2017. https://www.washingtonpost.com/local/education/expelled-for-sex-assault-young-men-are-filing-more-lawsuits-to-clear-their-names/2017/04/27/c2cfb1d2-0d89-11e7-9b0d-d27c98455440_story.html?utm_term=.4279dd1d6a21.

Shapiro, T. Rees. "Hear U-Va.'s 'Jackie' Testify About Rolling Stone Rape Story." *The Washington Post*, October 26, 2016. https://www.washingtonpost.com/news/grade-point/wp/2016/10/26/hear-u-va-s-jackie-testify-about-rolling-stones-gang-rape-story/?utm_term=.fc11d5fa48ff.

Shirky, Clay. "The Political Power of Social Media: Technology, the Public Sphere, and Political Change." *Foreign Affairs* 90, no. 1 (2011): 28–41.

Shugerman, Emily. "Men Sue in Sexual Assault Cases." Ms. Blog, June 18, 2014, http://msmagazine.com/blog/2014/06/18/men-sue-in-campus-sexual-assault-cases/.

Shwayder, Maya. "The Same-Sex Domestic Violence Epidemic Is Silent." *The Atlantic*, November 5, 2013. Accessed June 10, 2014, http://www.theatlantic.com/health/archive/2013/11/a-same-sex-domestic-violence-epidemic-is-silent/281131/.

Sinozich, Sofi, and Lynn Langton. "Rape and sexual assault victimization among college-age females, 1995–2013." Report NCJ248471. Washington, DC: US Department of Justice. Bureau of Justice Statistics (2014).

Sloan, John J. "Campus crime and campus communities: An analysis of crimes known to campus police and security." *Journal of Security Administration* 15, no. 2 (1992): 31–47.

Smith, Andrea. *Sexual Violence and American Indian Genocide*. New York: McGraw Hill, 1999: 274.

Smith, Casey. "How Victims Advocates Support Student Sexual Assault Survivors." *USAToday College*, April 3, 2017, Accessed May 4, 2017, http://college.usatoday.com/2017/04/03/how-victim-advocates-support-student-sexual-assault-survivors.

Smith, Roberta. "In a Mattress, a Lever for Art and Protest." *The New York Times*, September 21, 2014. https://www.nytimes.com/2014/09/22/arts/design/in-a-mattress-a-fulcrum-of-art-and-political-protest.html?_r=0.

Smith, Tovia. "To Tackle Sexual Assault, Colleges Enlist Investigators—For-Hire." *NPR*, October 29, 2014. http://www.npr.org/2014/10/29/359875452/to-tackle-sexual-assault-cases-colleges-enlist-investigators-for-hire.

Song, Jason. "Occidental College Reaches Agreement with Students Who Claimed Harassment." *The Los Angeles Times*, April 4, 2014. http://www.latimes.com/local/la-me-oxy-settlement-20140405-story.html.

Spohn, Cassia and David Holleran. "Prosecuting Sexual Assault: A Comparison of Charging Decisions in Sexual Assault Cases Involving Strangers, Acquaintances, and Intimate Partners." National Institute of Justice, 2004. https://www.ncjrs.gov/pdffiles1/nij/199720.pdf.

Steel, Emily and Michael S. Schmidt. "Bill O'Reilly Settled New Harassment Claim, Then Fox Renewed His Contract." *New York Times*, October 21, 2017. Accessed December 31, 2017, https://www.nytimes.com/2017/10/21/business/media/bill-oreilly-sexual-harassment.html?_r=0.

Starecheski, Laura. "The Power of the Peer Group in Preventing Campus Rape," *NPR*, August 18, 2014. Accessed May 3, 2017, http://www.npr.org/sections/health-shots/2014/08/18/339593542/the-power-of-the-peer-group-in-preventing-campus-rape.

Stotzer, R. L. and MacCartney, D. "The role of institutional factors on on-campus reported rape prevalence." *Journal of Interpersonal Violence*, 31(16) (2016): 2687–2707.

Stremlau, Rose. "Rape Narratives on the Northern Paiute Frontier: Sarah Winnemucca, Sexual Sovereignty, and Economic Autonomy, 1844–1891." In *Portraits of Women in the American West*, ed. Dee Garceau, 37-60. New York: Routledge, 2005.

Strong, Melissa. "Educating for Power: How Higher Education Contributes to the Stratification of Social Class." *The Vermont Connection* 28, (2007): 51–59. Accessed March 2, 2014, http://www.uvm.edu/~vtconn/v28/Strong.pdf.

Student Coalition Against Rape (SCAR). "News and Updates." Accessed June 13, 2014. http://studentcoalitionagainstrape.wordpress.com/about-us.

Sue, Valerie M. and Lois A. Ritter. *Conducting Online Surveys*. Thousand Oaks, CA: Sage, 2012.

Suh, Doowon. "Institutionalizing Social Movements: The Dual Strategy of the Korean Women's Movement." *The Sociological Quarterly* 52, no. 3, (2011): 442–471.

SurvJustice. "About Us." 2013. Accessed June 18, 2014. http://survjustice.org/about-us.

Swartout, Kevin M., Mary P. Koss, Jacqueline W. White, Martie P. Thompson, Antonia Abbey, and Alexandra L. Bellis. "Trajectory Analysis of the Campus Serial Rapist Assumption." *JAMA Pediatrics* 169 no. 12, (2015): 1148–1164.

Take Back The Night. "History." Accessed April 30, 2017, https://takebackthenight.org/history/.

Tan, Caroline. "Up Close: Title IX, One Year Later." *Yale Daily News*, April 9, 2012. http://yaledailynews.com/blog/2012/04/09/up-close-title-ix-one-year-later/.

Taylor, Lauren R. and Lynne Marie Wannamaker. "Actually, Miss USA IS Right: Self-Defense Can Prevent Sexual Assaults." *The Washington Post,* June 16, 2014, https://www.washingtonpost.com/posteverything/wp/2014/06/16/actually-miss-america-is-right-self-defense-can-prevent-sexual-assaults/?utm_term=.2b8da337911f.

Teicher Khadaroo, Stacy. "Campus Sexual Assault: Should Restorative Justice Be An Option?" *NPR*, October 13, 2017. Accessed December 31, 2017, https://www.csmonitor.com/EqualEd/2017/1013/Campus-sexual-assault-Should-restorative-justice-be-an-option.

Teicher Khadaroo, Stacy. "Feds Warn Colleges: Handle Sexual Assault Reports Properly." *The Christian Science Monitor*, September 2, 2011. http://www.csmonitor.com/USA/Education/2011/0902/Feds-warn-colleges-handle-sexual-assault-reports-properly.

Terry, Karen J., and Alissa R. Ackerman. "A brief history of major sex offender laws." *Sex Offender Laws: Failed Policies, New Directions* (2009): 65–98.

Testa, Jessica. "Tufts University and Federal Government in Standoff over Sexual Assault Policies." *Buzzfeed*, April 2, 2014. http://www.buzzfeed.com/jtes/tufts-university-and-federal-government-in-stand-off-over-se.

Testa, Maria. "The impact of men's alcohol consumption on perpetration of sexual aggression." *Clinical Psychology Review* 22, no. 8 (2002): 1239–1263.

Testa, Maria, and Michael J. Cleveland. "Does alcohol contribute to college men's sexual assault perpetration? Between- and within-person effects over five semesters." *Journal of Studies on Alcohol and Drugs* 78, no. 1 (2016): 5–13.

The American Lawyer. "Safety Monitor." Accessed June 15, 2014, http://www.americanlawyer-digital.com/americanlawyer-ipauth/201309ip?pg=15#pg15.

The Center for Public Integrity. "A Lack of Consequences for Sexual Assault." 2010. http://www.publicintegrity.org/2010/02/24/4360/lack-consequences-sexual-assault-0.

The Chronicle of Higher Education. "Title IX: Tracking Sexual Assault Investigations." Accessed January 1, 2018, https://projects.chronicle.com/titleix/.

The Clery Center. "Non-Retaliation," *Jean Clery Act Information*. Accessed May 12, 2017, http://www.cleryact.info/non-retaliation.html.

The Clothesline Project. "About the Clothesline Project." Accessed May 2, 2017, http://clotheslineproject.info/about.html.

The Clothesline Project. "History of the Clothesline Project." Accessed January 8, 2014, http://www.clotheslineproject.org/History.html.

The Columbus Dispatch. "Reports on College Crime Are Deceptively Inaccurate." September 30, 2014, http://www.dispatch.com/content/stories/local/2014/09/30/campus-insecurity.html.

The Cut. "An Exhaustive List of the Allegations Women Have Made Against Trump." October 27, 2016, http://nymag.com/thecut/2016/10/all-the-women-accusing-trump-of-rape-sexual-assault.html.

The Feminist Alliance Against Rape. "Initial Invitation Letter (Untitled)." July 30, 1974. Accessed April 12, 2015. http://www.faar-aegis.org/Intro_74/intro_74.html.

The White House. "FACT SHEET: Not Alone—Protecting Students from Sexual Assault." April 29, 2014. Accessed May 1, 2014, http://www.whitehouse.gov/the-press-office/2014/04/29/fact-sheet-not-alone-protecting-students-sexual-assault.

The White House. "The President and the Vice President Speak on Preventing Sexual Assault." January 22, 2014. Accessed January 22, 2014. http://www.whitehouse.gov/photos-and-video/video/2014/01/22/president-and-vice-president-speak-preventing-sexual-assault#transcript.

The White House. "The Second Report of the White House Task Force to Protect Students from Sexual Assault." January 5, 2017. https://www.whitehouse.gov/sites/whitehouse.gov/files/images/Documents/1.4.17.VAW%20Event.TF%20Report.PDF.

Thompson, Martha E. "Empowering self-defense training." *Violence Against Women* 20, no. 3 (2014): 351–359.

Thompson, Martie P., Kevin M. Swartout, and Mary P. Koss. "Trajectories and predictors of sexually aggressive behaviors during emerging adulthood." *Psychology of Violence* 3, no. 3 (2013): 247.

Trickett, Edison J. "Context, culture, and collaboration in AIDS interventions: Ecological ideas for enhancing community impact." *Journal of Primary Prevention* 23, no. 2 (2002): 157–174.

Tseng, Vivian, Daniel Chesir-Teran, Rachel Becker-Klein, May L. Chan, Valkiria Duran, Ann Roberts, and Nenshad Bardoliwalla. "Promotion of social change: A conceptual framework." *American Journal of Community Psychology* 30, no. 3 (2002): 401–427.

Tufekci, Zeynep. *Twitter and Tear Gas: The Power and Fragility of Networked Protest*. New Haven, CT: Yale University Press, 2017.

Tufts University, Public Health & Professional Degree Programs. "Sexual Misconduct Adjudication Process." Accessed on July 3, 2014, http://publichealth.tufts.edu/Student-Services/~/media/PHPD/PDFs-A/Student%20Services/PHPD_SexualMisconductAdjudication Process.pdf.

Tufts University, The Fletcher School. "Sexual Misconduct Adjudication Process." Accessed July 3, 2014, http://fletcher.tufts.edu/Students/StudentHandbook/Appendices/~/media/Fletcher/Student%20Handbook/SMAP.pdf.

Tyler, Kimberly A., Danny R. Hoyt, and Les B. Whitbeck. "Coercive sexual strategies." *Violence and Victims* 13, no. 1 (1998): 47.

University of Michigan. "Our History, Sexual Assault Prevention and Awareness Center." Accessed April 30, 2017, https://sapac.umich.edu/article/158.

U.S. Department of Education. "Dear Colleague Letter." Office for Civil Rights. April 24, 2013, https://www2.ed.gov/about/offices/list/ocr/letters/colleague-201304.html.

U.S. Department of Education, "Dear Colleague Letter: Retaliation."

U.S. Department of Education. "Dear Colleague Letter: Sexual Violence." Office for Civil Rights, April 4, 2011, http://www2.ed.gov/about/offices/list/ocr/letters/colleague-201104.pdf.

U.S. Department of Education. "Title IX and Sex Discrimination." Office for Civil Rights. Accessed May 11, 2017, https://www2.ed.gov/about/offices/list/ocr/docs/tix_dis.html.

U.S. Department of Education. "The Handbook for Campus Safety and Security Reporting." 2011. http://www2.ed.gov/admins/lead/safety/handbook.pdf, p. 77.

U.S. Department of Education. "U.S. Department of Education Releases List of Higher Education Institutions with Open Title IX Sexual Violence Investigations." May 1, 2014. http://www.ed.gov/news/press-releases/us-department-education-releases-list-higher-education-institutions-open-title-i.

Vogel, Pam. "Here are the Corporations and Right-Wing Funders Backing the Education Reform Movement." *Media Matters for America,* April 27, 2016. https://www.mediamatters.org/research/2016/04/27/here-are-corporations-and-right-wing-funders-backing-education-reform-movement/210054.

Vogel, Peter. "Walk a Mile UNC Style: A Response to Criticism." *The Siren,* April 10, 2015. Accessed December 30, 2017, http://uncsiren.com/walk-mile-unc-style-response-criticism/.

Walk a Mile in Her Shoes. "About." Accessed May 3, 2017, http://www.walkamileinhershoes.org/About/about.html.

Walters, Mikel L., Jieru Chen, and Matthew J. Breiding. "The National Intimate Partner and Sexual Violence Survey (NISVS): 2010 findings on victimization by sexual orientation." Atlanta, GA: National Center for Injury Prevention and Control, Centers for Disease Control and Prevention 648, no. 73 (2013): 6.

Wanjuki, Wagatwe. "Raped at Tufts University." Blog, 2014. http://www.rapedattufts.info/.

Warshaw, Robin, *I Never Called It Rape,* New York: Harper Collins, 1994.

Webber, Stephanie. "Brock Turner's Stanford Rape Case: Everything You Need to Know." *US Weekly,* June 7, 2016. http://www.usmagazine.com/celebrity-news/news/brock-turners-stanford-rape-case-everything-you-need-to-know-w209237.

Welch, Ashley. "Sexual assault survivors struggle to cope with Trump election." *CBS News,* November 17, 2016. Accessed May 6, 2017, http://www.cbsnews.com/news/sexual-assault-survivors-cope-with-donald-trump-election/.

Wells, Carrie, Erica L. Green, and Justin Fenton. "Johns Hopkins University Under Fire for Not Disclosing Alleged Rape." *The Washington Post,* May 3, 2014. http://www.washingtonpost.com/pb/local/johns-hopkins-university-under-fire-over-not-disclosing-alleged-rape/2014/05/03/c86582b4-d305-11e3-8a78-8fe50322a72c_story.html.

Wiener, John. "Rape Settlement at Occidental College: Victims Barred from Campus Activism." *The Nation,* September 19, 2013. http://www.thenation.com/blog/176270/rape-settlement-occidental-college-victims-barred-campus-activism#.

Wilson, Robin. "Opening New Front in Campus-Rape Debate, Brown Student Tells Education Department His Side." *The Chronicle of Higher Education,* June 12, 2014. https://chronicle.com/article/Opening-New-Front-in/147047/.

Wheeler, Jennifer G., William H. George, and Barbara J. Dahl. "Sexually aggressive college males: Empathy as a moderator in the "Confluence Model" of sexual aggression." *Personality and Individual Differences* 33, no. 5 (2002): 759–775.

White House Task Force (2014). *Not Alone: The First Report of the White House Task Force to Protect Students from Sexual Assault.* Accessed December 3, 2016. https://www.whitehouse.gov/sites/default/files/docs/report_0.pdf.

Will, George. "George Will: Colleges Become a Victim of Progressivism." *The Washington Post*, June 6, 2014, https://www.washingtonpost.com/opinions/george-will-college-become-the-victims-of-progressivism/2014/06/06/e90e73b4-eb50-11e3-9f5c-9075d5508f0a_story.html?utm_term=.1791715995e0.

Wilhelm, Anthony G. "Virtual Sounding Boards: How Deliberative Is On-line Political Discussion." *Information, Communication and Society* 1, no. 3, (1998): 313–338.

Woolington, Josephine. "Scholar's Sexual Violence Study Rejected." *The Register-Guard*, June 11, 2014. http://registerguard.com/rg/news/local/31703535-75/sexual-survey-freyd-violence-university.html.csp.

Yoffe, Emily. "The Best Rape Prevention: Tell College Women to Stop Getting Drunk." *Slate*, October 15, 2013. http://www.slate.com/articles/double_x/doublex/2013/10/sexual_assault_and_drinking_teach_women_the_connection.html.

Young, Belinda-Rose, Sarah L. Desmarais, Julie A. Baldwin, and Rasheeta Chandler. "Sexual coercion practices among undergraduate male recreational athletes, intercollegiate athletes, and non-athletes." *Violence Against Women* (2016): 1077801216651339.

Young, Cathy. "Guilty Until Proven Innocent: The Skewed White House Crusade on Sexual Assault." *Time*, May 5, 2014, http://www.dispatch.com/content/stories/editorials/2014/08/08/campus-rape-is-a-problem-but-its-been-exaggerated.html.

Zimmerman, Eilene. "Campuses Struggle with Approaches to Preventing Sexual Assault." *The New York Times*, June 22, 2016. Accessed May 5, 2017, https://www.nytimes.com/2016/06/23/education/campuses-struggle-with-approaches-for-preventing-sexual-assault.html?_r=0.

Zorza, Joan. *Violence Against Women, Volume III.* Civic Research Institute, 2006. Accessed March 8, 2016, http://www.civicresearchinstitute.com/toc/VAWA_VOL3_frontmatter.pdf.

Index

About the Authors

Alissa R. Ackerman is an assistant professor in the Division of Politics, Administration, and Justice at California State University, Fullerton. She received her PhD in Criminal Justice from the City University of New York and has held previous faculty posts at the University of Washington, Tacoma, and the University of California, Merced. Dr. Ackerman specializes in sex crimes management policies, the consequences of sexual violence and restorative justice. She is the author of *Introduction to Criminal Justice: A Personal Narrative Approach* (2016) and a coeditor of *Sex Crimes: Transnational Problems and Global Perspectives* (2015), and *The Criminalization of Immigration: Contexts and Consequences* (2014). Dr. Ackerman has also published over twenty peer-reviewed journal articles on issues related to sexual violence.

Dr. Ackerman describes herself as a "survivor scholar" and an artist. She is an outspoken advocate in ending the shame and stigma around sexual violence, and gives lectures on the subject in countries around the world. Dr. Ackerman is one of the nation's leading experts on the effectiveness of public registries for individuals who have committed sexual violence, and her work is frequently featured in radio, television, and other press. Dr. Ackerman also works with survivors as a volunteer member of the outreach team for *Brave Miss World*, a documentary film about sexual violence. She was one of the early members of Faculty against Rape and has been active in the Campus Anti-Rape Movement since its start. Dr. Ackerman is an accomplished painter who uses her artwork to raise money for sexual violence prevention.

Ian Breckenridge-Jackson is a lecturer in the Sociology Department at California State University, Los Angeles. He earned his PhD in sociology from the University of California, Riverside, where he was a National Science Foundation Graduate Research Fellow. He specializes in gender, race, and class inequalities with an emphasis on social movements. Dr. Breckenridge-Jackson was awarded the ASA Community Action Research Initiative Award to engage in community-based research in New Orleans' Lower Ninth Ward and also received a research grant from the UC Center for New Racial Studies to examine volunteerism in post-Katrina New Orleans. His work is featured in leading peer-reviewed journals such as *Politics, Groups, and Identities* and *Policy Matters*, edited volumes including *The Oxford Handbook of U.S. Women's Social Movement Activism* and *The Routledge International Handbook of World Systems Analysis*, and popular outlets including *Time Magazine* and *U.S. News & World Report*. Dr. Breckenridge-Jackson cofounded the Lower Ninth Ward Living Museum, an entirely free and volunteer-run museum and oral history project. His TEDx talk, "Getting More Than We Give: Realities of Volunteerism," has been viewed over 35,000 times and is used for volunteer trainings at nonprofit and educational institutions across the country.

Caroline Heldman is an associate professor of politics at Occidental College in Los Angeles and the research director for the Geena Davis Institute for Gender in Media. Her research specializes in media, the presidency, and systems of power (race, class, gender). Dr. Heldman coedited *Rethinking Madame President: Are We Ready for a Woman in the White House?* (2007) and authored *Protest Politics in the Marketplace: Consumer Activism in the Corporate Age* (2017), *Women, Power, and Politics: The Fight for Gender Equality in the United States* (2017), and *Sex and Gender in the 2016 Presidential Election* (2018).

Dr. Heldman has been active in "real world" politics as a professional pollster and campaign manager. She has made over 500 media appearances as a political commentator for CNN, MSNBC, Fox News, and CNBC. She has also been featured in popular documentaries, including *Missrepresentation*, *The Mask You Live In*, *The Hunting Ground*, *Informant*, *An Open Secret*, *Equal Means Equal*, and *Liberated*. Dr. Heldman was one of many women who went public with allegations of gender discrimination against Bill O'Reilly that led to his firing from Fox News. She splits her time between Los Angeles and New Orleans, where she cofounded the New Orleans Women's Shelter and the Lower Ninth Ward Living Museum. Dr. Heldman also cofounded End Rape on Campus (EROC), Faculty Against Rape (FAR), and the End the Rape Statute of Limitations (ERSOL) campaign.